T0298646

Deep Learning in Medical Image Analysis

This book is designed as a reference text and provides a comprehensive overview of conceptual and practical knowledge about deep learning in medical image processing techniques. The post-pandemic situation teaches us the importance of doctors, medical analysis, and diagnosis of diseases in a rapid manner. This book provides a snapshot of the state of current research between deep learning, medical image processing, and health care with special emphasis on saving human life. The chapters cover a range of advanced technologies related to patient health monitoring, predicting diseases from genomic data, detecting artefactual events in vital signs monitoring data, and managing chronic diseases. This book

- Delivers an ideal introduction to image processing in medicine, emphasizing the clinical relevance and special requirements of the field
- Presents key principles by implementing algorithms from scratch and using simple MATLAB®/Octave scripts with image data
- Provides an overview of the physics of medical image processing alongside discussing image formats and data storage, intensity transforms, filtering of images and applications of the Fourier transform, three-dimensional spatial transforms, volume rendering, image registration, and tomographic reconstruction
- Highlights the new potential applications of machine learning techniques to the solution of important problems in biomedical image applications

This book is for students, scholars, and professionals of biomedical technology and healthcare data analytics.

Artificial Intelligence in Smart Healthcare Systems

Series Editors: Vishal Jain and Jyotir Moy Chatterjee

The progress of the healthcare sector is incremental as it learns from associations between data over time through the application of suitable big data and IoT frameworks and patterns. Many healthcare service providers are employing IoT-enabled devices for monitoring patient health care, but their diagnosis and prescriptions are instance-specific only. However, these IoT-enabled healthcare devices are generating volumes of data (Big-IoT Data), that can be analyzed for more accurate diagnosis and prescriptions. A major challenge in the above realm is the effective and accurate learning of unstructured clinical data through the application of precise algorithms. Incorrect input data leading to erroneous outputs with false positives shall be intolerable in healthcare as patient's lives are at stake. This new book series addresses various aspects of how smart healthcare can be used to detect and analyze diseases, the underlying methodologies, and related security concerns. Healthcare is a multidisciplinary field that involves a range of factors like the financial system, social factors, health technologies, and organizational structures that affect the healthcare provided to individuals, families, institutions, organizations, and populations. The goals of healthcare services include patient safety, timeliness, effectiveness, efficiency, and equity. Smart healthcare consists of m-health, e-health, electronic resource management, smart and intelligent home services, and medical devices. The Internet of Things (IoT) is a system comprising real-world things that interact and communicate with each other via networking technologies. The wide range of potential applications of IoT includes healthcare services. IoT-enabled healthcare technologies are suitable for remote health monitoring, including rehabilitation, assisted ambient living, etc. In turn, healthcare analytics can be applied to the data gathered from different areas to improve healthcare at a minimum expense.

This new book series is designed to be a first-choice reference at university libraries, academic institutions, research and development centres, information technology centres, and any institutions interested in using, design, modelling, and analysing intelligent healthcare services. Successful application of deep learning frameworks to enable meaningful, cost-effective personalized healthcare services is the primary aim of the healthcare industry in the present scenario. However, realizing this goal requires effective understanding, application, and amalgamation of IoT, Big Data and several other computing technologies to deploy such systems in an effective manner. This series shall help clarify the understanding of certain key mechanisms and technologies helpful in realizing such systems.

Deep Learning in Medical Image Analysis:
Recent Advances and Future Trends
Edited by R. Indrakumari, T. Ganesh Kumar, D. Murugan, and Sherimon P.C.

For more information about this series, please visit www.routledge.com/Artificial-Intelligence-in-Smart-Healthcare-Systems/book-series/CRCAISHS

Deep Learning in Medical Image Analysis
Recent Advances and Future Trends

Edited by R. Indrakumari, T. Ganesh Kumar,
D. Murugan, and Sherimon P.C.

CRC Press
Taylor & Francis Group
Boca Raton London New York

CRC Press is an imprint of the
Taylor & Francis Group, an **informa** business

A CHAPMAN & HALL BOOK

Designed cover image: ShutterStock

First edition published 2025
by CRC Press
2385 NW Executive Center Drive, Suite 320, Boca Raton FL 33431

and by CRC Press
4 Park Square, Milton Park, Abingdon, Oxon, OX14 4RN

CRC Press is an imprint of Taylor & Francis Group, LLC

© 2025 selection and editorial matter, R. Indrakumari, T. Ganesh Kumar,
D. Murugan, and Sherimon P.C.; individual chapters, the contributors

ISBN: 978-1-032-37992-0 (hbk)
ISBN: 978-1-032-38036-0 (pbk)
ISBN: 978-1-003-34317-2 (ebk)

DOI: 10.1201/9781003343172

Typeset in Times
by Apex CoVantage, LLC

Contents

Editor Biographies

R. Indrakumari is working as an assistant professor, School of Computing Science and Engineering, Galgotias University, NCR Delhi, India. She has completed an M.Tech in computer and information technology from Manonmaniam Sundaranar University, Tirunelveli. Her main thrust areas are big data, Internet of Things, data mining, dataware housing, and its visualization tools like Tableau, QlikView. She has several top-notch conferences in her resume and has published over 50 quality journal, conference, and book chapters combined.

T. Ganesh Kumar works as an associate professor at the School of Computing Science and Engineering at Galgotias University, Greater Noida, Delhi NCR. He received an ME degree in computer science and engineering from Manonmaniam Sundaranar University, Tamil Nadu, India. He completed his full time PhD degree in computer science and engineering at Manonmaniam Sundaranar University. He received the JRF and SRF during the full time PhD period. He was a co-investigator for two government of India-sponsored funded projects. He has published many reputed international SCI and Scopus-indexed journals and conferences. He is a reviewer of many reputed journals. He has published 16 patents and one granted design patent in India. He is an academic editor in the PLOS One SCIE-indexed journal. He has done the NAAC and NBA accreditation process as a criteria coordinator for Galgotias University.

D. Murugan works as a professor in the Department of Computer Science and Engineering, at Manonmaniam Sundaranar University, Tirunelveli, Tamil Nadu. He has more than 25 years of experience in teaching and research. He was a principal investigator for two Government of India-sponsored funded projects. He has published more than 100 reputed international SCI and Scopus-indexed journals and conferences. He has produced more than 20 doctorates under his PhD guidance. He is an editor and reviewer of many reputed journals. He was a Syndicate member, Interview Committee member, and Inspection Committee for the affiliated colleges of Manonmaniam Sundaranar University. He visited Singapore, Malaysia, and Dubai for academic contributions.

 **Sherimon P.C.** is currently working at the faculty of computer studies, Arab Open University (AOU), Oman. He has 21 years of teaching experience in different institutions. He started his career as a software engineer and later joined Mahatma Gandhi University, India. In 2004, he joined the Higher College of Technology and worked as the head of section in the IT department. He joined AOU in 2010. He holds two master's degrees, in computer science and information technology, and a PhD in computer science. He won the first National Research award from TRC, Oman, in the information and communication technology sector. He has published around 42 research papers in Springer, ACM, etc. He has presented papers at various international conferences in the United States, the United Kingdom, Russia, China, Malaysia, India, Kuwait, Jordan, Ajman, and Oman. He worked as chairman and scientific committee member in various conferences. He has also delivered keynote addresses at various conferences. He serves as the reviewer of TRC and other international journals.

Contributors

Anitha Julian
Saveetha Engineering College
Chennai, India

V. Anusuya Devi
CSE Department
School of Computing
Kalasalingam Academy of Research
    and Education,
Krishnankoil, India

A. R. Arunachalam
Dr. MGR Educational and Research
    Institute
Chennai, India

B. Bharathi Kannan
Hindusthan College of Engineering and
    Technology
Coimbatore, India

L. Dharani
Dr. MGR Educational and Research Institute
Chennai, India

P. Ganesh
Annamalai University
Chidambaram, India

T. Ganesh Kumar
Galgotias University
Noida, India

Ilavendhan Anandraj
Vellore Institute of Technology
Chennai, India

R. Kavitha
Dr. MGR Educational and Research Institute
Chennai, India

S. T. Lenin
Mahendra Engineering College
Namakkal, TamilNadu, India

R. Lotus
Vel Tech Rangarajan Dr. Sagunthala
    R&D Institute of Science and
    Technology
Chennai, India

M. Manohar
Sadakathullah Appa College
Tirunelveli, India

M. Mohan
Mahendra Engineering College
Namakkal, Tamilnadu, India

R. Mothi
Mahendra Engineering College
Namakkal, Tamilnadu, India

M. Muthuvinayagam
Mahendra Engineering College
Namakkal, Tamilnadu, India

Priti Rishi
SRM Institute of Science and
    Technology
Chennai, India

P. Radha Jayalakshmi
Dr. MGR Educational and
    Research Institute
Chennai, India

P. S. Rajakumar
Dr. MGR Educational and Research
    Institute
Chennai, India

R. Rajeswari
Dr. MGR Educational and Research
  Institute
Chennai, India

C. Ramesh Kumar
Galgotias University
Noida, India

R. Ramyadevi
Saveetha Engineering College
Chennai, India

G. Sakthi
Galgotias University
Noida, India

T. Sam Pradeepraj
CSE Department
School of Computing
Kalasalingam Academy of Research
  and Education,
Krishnankoil, India

Seema Dev Aksatha
Sri Krishna Arts and Science College
Coimbatore, India

V. Sheeja Kumari
Saveetha Institute of Medical and
  Technical Sciences
Chennai, India

P. G. Sivagaminathan
Koneru Lakshmaiah Education
  Foundation
Andhra Pradesh, India

Thirumurugan Shanmugam
College of Applied Sciences Suhar
Oman

K. Uma
VIT University
Vellore, India

G. Vennira Selvi
Presidency University
Bangalore, India

G. Victo Sudha George
Dr. MGR Educational and Research
  Institute
Chennai, India

C. Vigneshwaran
Mahendra Engineering College
Chennai, India

Vijayaprabakaran K
Vellore Institute of Technology
Chennai, India

1 Journey into the Digital Frontier

Demystifying Neural Networks and Deep Learning

Anitha Julian and R. Ramyadevi

1.1 INTRODUCTION

Section 1.2 gives an overview on the basic concepts of neural networks and deep learning. It also explains the types of neurons namely, perceptron and sigmoid neuron.

Section 1.3 elaborately discusses the real-life applications of neural networks. The thrust is on its implications to medical applications. An overview of the varied medical applications wherein artificial intelligence (AI) plays a major role are detailed.

Section 1.4 covers the working of the neural network namely the backpropagation algorithm. This algorithm is a fundamental algorithm in deep learning and has enabled the development of a wide range of neural network architectures that can solve complex problems.

Section 1.5 shows how neural networks can be improved to perform any sort of function while solving problems. This calls for picking the cross-entropy cost function, a better cost function. Four regularization techniques, namely, L1 and L2 regularization, dropout, and artificial extension of the training data, as well as more effective methods for setting the network's weights, are provided. These techniques also improve the networks' ability to generalize beyond the training data.

Section 1.6 discusses the role of deep learning as an advancement over neural networks. Deep learning's capacity to automatically discover valuable characteristics from raw data, as opposed to requiring human experts to manually extract pertinent features, is one of its primary advantages. This has eliminated the need for considerable feature engineering and allowed the development of very precise systems in a variety of applications.

1.2 OVERVIEW ON NEURAL NETWORKS AND DEEP LEARNING

Neural networks are machine learning algorithms that are modelled after the functionality and organization of the human brain. Neurons, which are interconnected nodes that communicate with one another to process and analyze input, make up

DOI: 10.1201/9781003343172-1

1

these systems. A neural network's neurons are arranged into layers, each layer handling a particular component of data processing. While the output layer creates the network's ultimate output, the input layer receives the raw data. In between, there can be one or more hidden layers that perform complex computations on the data.

For tasks like audio and image identification, natural language processing, and decision-making, neural networks are especially well-suited [1]. With the use of neural networks with several layers, deep learning has produced impressive outcomes for varied applications, including self-driving cars, medical diagnosis, and game play. As a result of prior work by Warren McCulloch and Walter Pitts, scientist Frank Rosenblatt created an artificial neuron known as a perceptron in the 1950s to 1960s.

Many binary inputs, each of which can be either 0 or 1, are fed into a perceptron, which then outputs a single binary output, likewise either 0 or 1. The inputs are multiplied by weights, which are values that the perceptron learns through a training process. The weighted inputs are then summed together, and a threshold value is applied to the result. If the sum exceeds the threshold, the perceptron outputs 1; otherwise, it outputs 0. Mathematically, this is represented as,

$$output = 0 \; if \; \Sigma \left(w_i x_i \right) \leq threshold$$

$$1 \; if \; \sum (w_i x_i) \leq threshold \tag{1.1}$$

where w_i are the weights associated with each input x_i.

The structure of a perceptron is as displayed in Figure 1.1. A technique for improving the accuracy of the perceptron's output is the perceptron learning algorithm. It involves changing the weights of the inputs. It functions by comparing the perceptron's actual output with the desired output (the right response) and then modifying the weights to get the perceptron's output closer to the desired output. This process is repeated many times until the perceptron can accurately classify the inputs.

The limitation with perceptron is that they are capable of classifying data that can be divided into two classes by a single straight line or data that is linearly separable. For more complex classification tasks, other types of artificial neurons, such as sigmoid neurons, are needed.

Sigmoid neurons are a type of artificial neuron that was first introduced in the 1980s. Unlike perceptron, which can only produce binary outputs (0 or 1), sigmoid neurons can produce outputs that range from 0 to 1, which enables them to model data with more intricate patterns and correlations.

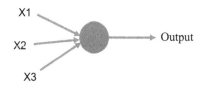

FIGURE 1.1   Structure of a perceptron

Sigmoid neurons work by taking in several inputs, which can be real numbers rather than just binary values. Each input is multiplied by a weight, and the weighted inputs are then summed together. The output of a sigmoid neuron is decided by passing the sum through a sigmoid function, which "squashes" the output to a number between 0 and 1, as opposed to merely applying a threshold like a perceptron. The S-shaped curve of a sigmoid function allows it to model non-linear relationships between inputs and outputs. Mathematically, the output of a sigmoid neuron can be represented as,

$$output = \frac{1}{\left(1 + e^{(-\Sigma(w_i x_i))}\right)} \tag{1.2}$$

where e is the mathematical constant known as Euler's number, w_i are the weights associated with each input x_i, and the sum is taken over all the inputs.

Gradient descent is a method for training sigmoid neurons that involves changing the weights to reduce the cost function, which determines the difference between the desired and actual outputs. This process can be repeated many times with the goal of improving the accuracy of the sigmoid neuron's predictions on new data. Sigmoid neurons are used extensively in modern neural networks, including deep learning models that are capable of learning highly complex patterns in large datasets.

1.2.1 ARCHITECTURE OF NEURAL NETWORKS

Input neurons are the neurons that make up the input layer, which is the leftmost layer in this network. The output neurons, or in this instance, just one output neuron, are found in the rightmost output layer. Since the neurons in the middle layer are neither inputs nor outputs, this is known as a hidden layer.

Some networks contain more hidden layers than the network shown in Figure 1.2, which only has one. The four-layer network shown in Figure 1.3, for instance, has two hidden layers.

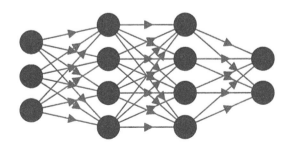

Input Layer $\in \mathbb{R}^3$ Hidden Layer $\in \mathbb{R}^4$ Hidden Layer $\in \mathbb{R}^4$ Output Layer $\in \mathbb{R}^2$

FIGURE 1.2   Neural network architecture

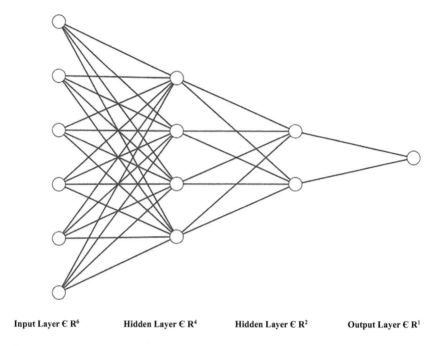

Input Layer $\in R^6$ Hidden Layer $\in R^4$ Hidden Layer $\in R^2$ Output Layer $\in R^1$

FIGURE 1.3   A four-layer neural network

1.3   NEURAL NETWORKS AND ITS REAL-LIFE APPLICATIONS

Applications for neural networks in medicine range from disease diagnosis to patient outcome prediction. Some of the examples are as follows:

1. **Medical imaging** – To find patterns and make diagnoses, neural networks have been used to examine and infer medical images. Medical imaging is a technique that allows for the visualization of the body's interior for clinical examination and medical intervention. It uses a variety of imaging technologies, including X-rays, ultrasound, computed tomography (CT), magnetic resonance imaging (MRI), and positron emission tomography (PET). For example, the neural network can be trained to recognize specific features in an image that are indicative of a certain disease, such as cancer. Advancements in medical imaging technology have also enabled the development of minimally invasive surgical procedures, where doctors can use real-time imaging to guide their surgical instruments and perform precise interventions. However, medical imaging also comes with potential risks such as radiation exposure, contrast agent reactions, and false positive or false negative results. Therefore, it is important to balance the benefits and risks of using medical imaging techniques on a case-by-case basis and to ensure that appropriate safety measures are in place to minimize potential harm.

2. **Disease diagnosis** – Neural networks can also be used to diagnose diseases based on patient symptoms, medical history, and other factors. For instance, the neural network may be taught to spot patterns in patient data linked to a particular illness, like diabetes. Disease diagnosis is the process of identifying the underlying cause of a patient's symptoms and making a definitive determination of the specific disease or condition that is affecting them. Accurate diagnosis is critical to providing appropriate treatment and management of the disorders and ailments of the patient. The past health condition of the patient, a physical exam, diagnostic tests, etc. are frequently used in medical practice to diagnose diseases. Diagnostic methods include testing of blood of the patient for varied parameters, imaging diagnosis, ultrasounds, and other specialized testing methods. In recent years, machine learning algorithms have been increasingly used in disease diagnosis, particularly in medical imaging. For example, deep learning algorithms have shown great promise in detecting and classifying various types of cancerous lesions on medical images such as mammograms or CT scans [2]. However, it is important to note that machine learning algorithms are not a substitute for a trained medical professional, and human expertise is still critical in interpreting the results and making accurate diagnoses. Therefore, the use of machine learning algorithms in disease diagnosis should be seen as a complementary tool that can aid medical professionals in making more accurate and timely diagnoses [3].

3. **Drug discovery** – Finding new medications or therapeutic agents that can be utilized to cure or prevent different illnesses or medical problems is known as drug discovery. The drug discovery process typically involves a multi-step process that begins with the identification of a potential therapeutic target, followed by drug discovery, preclinical testing, clinical trials, and regulatory approval. In recent years, machine learning algorithms have been increasingly used in the drug discovery process to accelerate and improve the efficiency of drug discovery. For instance, preclinical testing can be completed faster and more cheaply by using machine learning algorithms to forecast the effectiveness and toxicity of new drug candidates. Large datasets can be analyzed using machine learning algorithms to find new pharmacological targets and create new medications. New therapeutic targets that are particular to particular diseases or situations can be found by using machine learning algorithms to analyze the genetic and molecular information of patients. Ultimately, applying machine learning to drug discovery has the potential to transform the industry and vastly increase the speed and effectiveness of the discovery process, which could ultimately result in the creation of more potent medications and patient treatments. By evaluating huge datasets of chemical compounds and determining which ones are most likely to be successful against a specific ailment, neural networks have been used to find new medications.

4. **Patient monitoring** – Patient monitoring is the process of continuously monitoring a patient's physiological measurements, such as the heart rate, body temperature, blood pressure, and saturation level of oxygen, to track

their health status and identify any potential health problems. Continuous patient monitoring can help healthcare professionals identify early warning signs of complications and intervene before they become more serious. In order to assess the vast volumes of data produced by patient monitoring devices and assist healthcare professionals in making more precise and timely choices, machine learning algorithms can be utilized in patient monitoring. Using machine learning algorithms to identify patterns and trends in patient data can help healthcare professionals spot early warning signs of health decline or potential future effects. Healthcare practitioners can make better judgements about patient care by using predictive models that predict a patient's health status, which are created using machine learning algorithms. Predictive models, for instance, can be used to estimate a patient's risk of contracting sepsis or other serious infections, enabling medical practitioners to act sooner and stop the emergence of more severe consequences. Overall, the use of machine learning in patient monitoring has a chance to enhance patient outcomes and lessen the strain on healthcare systems by enabling more accurate and efficient patient monitoring and decision-making. Neural networks can be used to monitor patients in real-time, predicting when a patient is at risk for a medical emergency such as a heart attack or stroke. This can allow doctors to intervene early and prevent serious complications.

Overall, neural networks have the potential to revolutionize the field of medicine by providing more accurate diagnoses, predicting patient outcomes, and developing new treatments. However, it is important to note that there are still many challenges to be overcome, such as ensuring the reliability and safety of these systems.

1.4   WORKING OF BACKPROPAGATION ALGORITHM

In an artificial neural network, the weights and biases are initialized with random values. The neural network probably makes faults in producing the right output because of random initialization. The initial weight and bias parameters in an artificial neural network are chosen at random. The neural network most likely produces incorrect results because of random initialization. By using backpropagation, the network is trained to update the weights and biases. Backpropagation is a type of learning by supervision algorithm used for training the neural networks [4]. By modifying its weights and biases, this gradient descent optimization technique enables the network to learn from its errors. Both an onward pass and a recessive transit over the network are used in the backpropagation process. The input data is fed into the network during the onward pass, and the output is calculated. The difference between the output that was expected and what was actually produced is then transmitted backward via the network during the recessive pass. In order to reduce the total error, the weights and biases of the network are updated using the error.

Using the chain rule of calculus, the backpropagation method calculates the gradient of the error with respect to each weight and bias in the network. Using a learning rate parameter, the gradient is then used to update the weights and biases.

The process of backpropagation is repeated over multiple epochs. The process continues towards a minimal convergence of errors. During training, the network gradually learns to map the input data to the correct output by adjusting its weights and biases.

The backpropagation process is illustrated in Figure 1.4. The backpropagation algorithm can be better understood by analyzing the working of an artificial neural network which is comprised of the following steps:

1. **Parameter initialization** – During this step, the parameters of an artificial neuron are initialized using random weights and biases. The network takes the input and feeds it forward, using weights and biases to build relationships that lead to the output. Most likely, the output connected to those random values is incorrect, and hence feed-forward propagation can be used next.
2. **Feed-forward propagation** – As the input layer gets the input after initialization, it propagates the input into hidden units at each layer. The nodes in this system operate without considering whether or not the results are valid; therefore they do not adjust in response to the output. The output layer is where the output is then produced. Feed-forward propagation is the term used to describe the phenomenon.
3. **Backpropagation** – In order to provide the intended output, the backpropagation algorithm aims to reduce the incorrect values in weights and biases that are allocated at random. The supervised learning method is used to teach the system, in which the system is made aware of the gap between its output and a known anticipated output and used to alter its internal state. To have the smallest overall loss, we must update the weights. As shown in Figure 1.5, an increase in weight reduces error when the gradient is negative. The reduction in weight reduces the error when the gradient is positive.

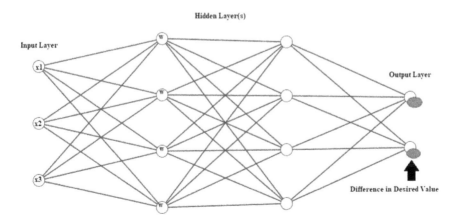

FIGURE 1.4 Backpropagation process

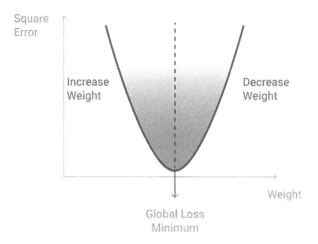

FIGURE 1.5   Error correction using backpropagation

1.5   ENHANCING NEURAL NETWORK LEARNING FOR COMPUTING FUNCTIONS

Neural networks are powerful tools for computing functions. There are several techniques that can enhance their learning and improve their performance. Some of the suggestions are:

1. **Preprocessing** the data simplifies the learning process of the underlying patterns by the neural network. This can include techniques such as normalization, standardization, or feature scaling.
2. **L1 or L2 regularization** approaches can increase the generalization of the neural network and prevent overfitting.
3. During training, the **dropout regularization** approach randomly removes neurons, driving the network to learn more robust representations.
4. **Data augmentation** involves generating additional training data by applying transformations such as rotation, scaling, or flipping to the existing data. This can help the network learn more robust representations and generalize better to new data.
5. **Early stopping** is keeping an eye on how good the model fits for the given data and ceasing it when it stops improving. This prevents overfitting and ensures that the network generalizes well to new data.
6. **Transfer learning** involves using a pre-trained neural network to perform a related task and then fine-tuning it on your specific task. This can save time and improve performance, especially when there is limited training data.
7. **Hyperparameter tuning** – The neural network's performance can be significantly impacted by the hyperparameter choices made, including learning rate, batch size, and number of hidden layers. Tuning these hyperparameters can improve the performance of the network.

By incorporating these techniques, the learning of the neural network can be enhanced and its performance in computing functions is improved.

1.6   DEEP LEARNING AND DEEP NEURAL NETWORKS

Deep learning, a subtype of machine learning, uses deep neural networks, which are neural networks with several layers [5]. Deep learning algorithms can learn from vast amounts of data and can automatically extract complex features and patterns from the input data. The layers of interconnected neurons that make up deep neural networks each process the output from the layer before it. Depending on how difficult the problem being handled is, a deep neural network may have a few, hundreds, or even thousands of layers.

Deep learning has had great success in many different areas, including natural language processing, recognizing images, and recognizing speech [6]. Deep neural networks, for instance, have been applied to create extremely precise image identification systems, such as those used in self-driving cars and facial recognition technology.

Deep learning's capacity to automatically learn valuable characteristics from raw data, as opposed to requiring human experts to manually extract pertinent features, is one of its main advantages [7, 8]. This has eliminated the need for considerable feature engineering and allowed the development of very accurate systems for a variety of applications.

Deep learning does, however, have significant drawbacks, such as the requirement for substantial data and processing resources and the possibility for overfitting to the training data. Deep learning will probably continue to be a significant area of exploration progress in the artificial intelligence field despite these obstacles.

Studying CT scans using neural networks involves training a neural network to analyze the CT images and classify them based on certain criteria. The general overview of the steps involved in the process are:

1. **Collection and preparation of data** – A large dataset of CT scans that are labeled with the appropriate classifications is collected. The data should be preprocessed to ensure that the images are properly formatted and standardized.
2. **Choice of architecture** – The architecture that is appropriate for the task to be undertaken by the neural network is chosen. Normally a convolutional neural network (CNN) is used in the study of images. Figure 1.6 and Figure 1.7 show the architecture of a CNN.
3. **Development process** – Using the dataset at hand, the training of neural network is performed. The network gains the ability to identify patterns in the CT images that correlate to particular categories during training. To reduce the discrepancy between the anticipated and actual classifications, the network's biases and weights must be adjusted.
4. **Testing and evaluation** – Testing is done on a separate dataset to evaluate its performance of the trained neural network. This involves measuring the accuracy, precision, recall, and other performance metrics of the neural network.

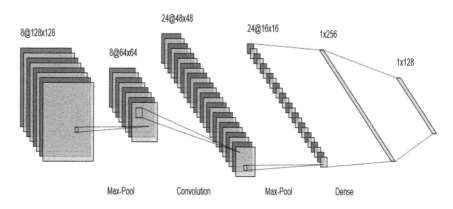

FIGURE 1.6 Architecture of CNN

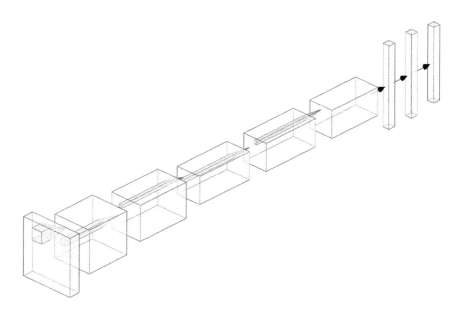

FIGURE 1.7 Convolution layers

5. **Optimization** – On a situation of unsatisfactory performance by the neural network, it can be optimized by changing the architecture or its hyperparameters.
6. **Deployment** – On ensuring optimized and satisfied performance by the neural network, it can be deployed in a clinical setting to assist healthcare professionals in analyzing CT scans and making diagnostic decisions.

Overall, studying CT scans using neural networks involves a complex process that requires expertise in both medical imaging and machine learning. Working with a

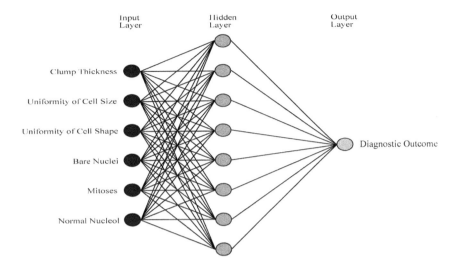

FIGURE 1.8 Neural network architecture for cancer detection

group of professionals that can guarantee the neural network is correctly trained and tested in order to deliver accurate and dependable outcomes is crucial.

A convolutional layer in a convolutional neural network is a typical illustration of a hidden layer in a neural network in medical imaging. In order to extract features that are pertinent to the job at hand from an input image, a convolutional layer applies a collection of filters to the image. In medical imaging, these features might correspond to specific anatomical structures, such as blood vessels or tumors, or to specific imaging characteristics, such as contrast or brightness.

For example, in the task of detecting lung nodules in CT scans, a CNN might use a series of convolutional layers to identify features such as the size, shape, and texture of nodules. Final classification decision is made after single or multiple linked layers receive the output of these convolutional layers. CNN's hidden layer count and structure might change depending on the task at hand and how complex the input data is. It has been demonstrated that deeper networks with added hidden layers are further effectual at extracting complicated information and obtaining greater accuracy in medical imaging tasks. Figure 1.8 shows a similar architecture.

1.6.1 USING DEEP LEARNING TECHNIQUES TO CREATE NEURAL NETWORKS

Deep learning techniques and tools aid in model accuracy improvement, prototype creation speed, and work automation [9]. Some of the most popular choices are listed.

TensorFlow is the most well-known and commonly used deep learning framework created by Google [10]. Being an open-source package, it offers a large selection of tools and features for creating and honing deep neural networks. TensorFlow is intended to be extremely adaptable and scalable, and it enables users to create models for a range of applications, such as reinforcement learning, image and audio recognition, natural language processing, and others. TensorFlow's capability to effectively conduct computations on several GPUs is one of its core characteristics, which enables faster training and inference of large-scale models. It also provides a variety of visualization tools, such as TensorBoard, that allow users to monitor and debug their models. TensorFlow provides support for multiple GPUs, graph visualization, and queues. It was created in C++ using CUDA, NVIDIA's GPU programming language. Another advantage of TensorFlow is its support for multiple programming languages, including Python, Java, R, and Go, which makes it accessible to a wide range of users with different backgrounds and skill sets. The TensorFlow documentation is also extensive and well-organized, with plenty of tutorials, guides, and examples available to help users get started with the framework. Figure 1.9 shows a typical medical application where TensorFlow is used for visualization of medical images featuring in-depth analysis.

In addition to TensorFlow, Theano, and Microsoft Cognitive Toolkit, **Keras** is an advanced API built in Python for neural networks that is intended to operate with them. The goal of its creation is facilitating quick experimentation with deep neural networks and simplifying the creation and training of models. Both novice and expert users can create and train neural networks using Keras' straightforward and user-friendly interface. It has several pre-built layers and models that can be readily modified and extended and supports a broad variety of network topologies, including multilayer perceptrons, convolutional neural networks, and recurrent neural

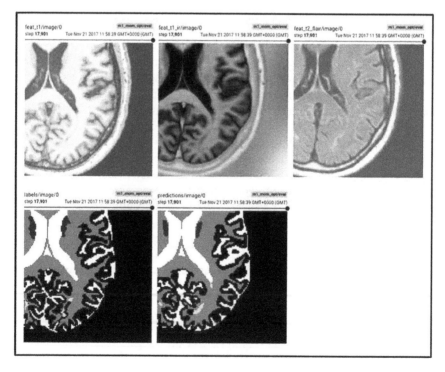

FIGURE 1.9   TensorBoard visualization of medical images featuring in-depth analysis [11]

networks. Keras also supports a variety of useful features, such as automatic differentiation, real-time data augmentation, and easy model saving and loading. Also, Keras has a thriving development community that supports users and contributes to the project. Keras can be used for a variety of applications because it is made to be extremely versatile and modular. Particularly because of its integration with TensorFlow, it is a preferred option for creating and honing deep learning models.

Berkeley AI Research (BAIR) at the University of California, Berkeley, created the open-source deep learning framework **Caffe** (Convolutional Architecture for Rapid Feature Embedding). It can be used for other kinds of neural networks as well, but convolutional neural networks (CNNs) for computer vision applications are a common application. One of the main features of Caffe is its speed, which is achieved through a combination of optimized C++ code and efficient GPU implementation. With a selection of pre-built layers and models that can be quickly modified and extended, Caffe also offers a straightforward and versatile interface for constructing and training neural networks. Many applications, including object detection, picture segmentation, and face recognition, among others, have made use of Caffe. It also includes a number of useful tools for visualizing and analyzing models, such as a graphical user interface for designing and editing networks and a command-line tool for analyzing network performance and visualizing the results. While Caffe has been widely used in the research community, its development has slowed down in recent years, and it may not be as actively maintained as some other deep learning frameworks. Yet it is still a potent and effective technique for creating and honing neural networks, especially in the field of computer vision.

Torch is a lightweight programming language called Lua that is used to create an open-source machine learning library and scientific computing environment. It offers a number of tools and modules for creating and training neural networks, and it was created primarily for numerical computation and deep learning applications. Torch's flexibility and usability, with a clear and straightforward interface for creating and training neural networks, are some of its standout qualities. Torch also includes a variety of pre-built models and algorithms, as well as a number of visualization tools for monitoring and analyzing network performance.

PyTorch, on the other hand, is a Python-based deep learning framework that is built on top of Torch [12]. It provides a similar set of tools and functionalities to Torch but with a Pythonic interface that is more familiar to many users. Moreover, PyTorch is made to be very versatile and configurable, enabling users to quickly define and alter their models and training methods. One of PyTorch's main benefits is its dynamic computational graph, which enables more effective memory usage and simpler model debugging. PyTorch also includes a number of high-level modules and functions for building complex neural networks, such as recurrent and convolutional networks, and it supports a variety of useful features such as distributed training, automatic differentiation and model serialization. Figure 1.10 shows brain MRI image classification using PyTorch.

Overall, while Torch and PyTorch have some similarities in terms of their underlying architecture and functionality, PyTorch is generally considered to be a more user-friendly and flexible framework, particularly for those who are more familiar with Python programming.

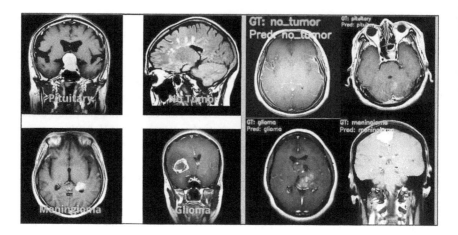

FIGURE 1.10   PyTorch EfficientNetB0 model for brain MRI image classification [13]

CONCLUSION

This chapter has given an overview on the basic concepts of neural networks and deep learning. Real-life applications of neural networks have been discussed elaborately with a thrust on its implications to medical applications. The backpropagation algorithm, which is a fundamental algorithm in deep learning, has been illustrated as a usage for a wide range of neural network architectures that can solve complex problems. Regularization techniques to improve the performance of neural networks have also been explained, which can be improved to perform any sort of function while solving problems. Deep learning is an advancement over neural networks. Its capacity to automatically discover valuable characteristics from raw data, as opposed to requiring human experts to manually extract pertinent features, which is one of its primary advantages, has been explored. This has eliminated the need for considerable feature engineering and allowed the development of very precise systems in a variety of applications.

REFERENCES

[1] Michael Nielsen, *Neural Networks and Deep Learning*, Online Book, http://neuralnet worksanddeeplearning.com/

[2] Phillip Cheng, Emmanuel Montagnon, Rikiya Yamashita, Ian Pan, Alexandre Cadrin-Chênevert, Francisco Perdigón Romero, Gabriel Chartrand, Samuel Kadoury, An Tang, Deep Learning: An Update for Radiologists. *RadioGraphics*. 41, 1427–1445, 2021. https://doi.org/10.1148/rg.2021200210.

[3] Gang Luo, Automatically Explaining Machine Learning Prediction Results: A Demonstration on Type 2 Diabetes Risk Prediction. *Health Information Science and Systems*. 4, 2016. https://doi.org/10.1186/s13755-016-0015-4.

[4] https://intellipaat.com/blog/tutorial/artificial-intelligence-tutorial/back-propagation-algorithm/

[5] Charu C. Aggarwal, *Neural Networks and Deep Learning: A Textbook*, Springer, 1st ed., 2018.

[6] Elham Kariri, Hassen Louati, Ali Louati, Fatma Masmoudi, Exploring the Advancements and Future Research Directions of Artificial Neural Networks: A Text Mining Approach. *Applied Sciences*. 13, 3186, 2023. https://doi.org/10.3390/app13053186.

[7] Ian Goodfellow, Yoshua Bengio, Aaron Courville, *Deep Learning*, The MIT Press, Illustrated ed., 2016.

[8] Josh Patterson, Adam Gibson, *Deep Learning: A Practitioner's Approach*, O'Reilly Media Inc., 2017.

[9] R. Indrakumari, T. Poongodi, K. Singh, Introduction to Deep Learning. In: Prakash, K.B., Kannan, R., Alexander, S., Kanagachidambaresan, G.R. (eds) *Advanced Deep Learning for Engineers and Scientists, EAI/Springer Innovations in Communication and Computing*, Springer, 2021. https://doi.org/10.1007/978-3-030-66519-7_1

[10] Aurélien Géron, *Hands-On Machine Learning with Scikit-Learn, Keras, and TensorFlow*, O'Reilly Media Inc., 2nd ed., 2019.

[11] https://blog.tensorflow.org/2018/07/an-introduction-to-biomedical-image-analysis-tensorflow-dltk.html

[12] Luca Pietro Giovanni Antiga, Eli Stevens, Thomas Viehmann, *Deep Learning with PyTorch*, Manning Publishers, 2020.

[13] https://debuggercafe.com/brain-mri-classification-using-pytorch-efficientnetb0/

2 An In-Depth Analysis of Deep Learning's Multifaceted Influence on Healthcare Systems

L. Dharani and G. Victo Sudha George

2.1 INTRODUCTION

In the modern world, people have different lives and behaviors, including different diets and eating habits, which might be unhealthy. We utilized a number of automated algorithms for sickness detection and treatment to prevent this health issue. In recent years, deep learning has had a substantial impact in a number of scientific fields. Deep learning (DL) algorithms beat cutting-edge methods in a number of applications, including image processing and analysis, which demonstrated this. Deep learning also did better than previous attempts by achieving cutting-edge results in tasks like self-driving cars. Deep learning has even outperformed humans in several tasks, like object recognition and gaming. Another field where this development holds great potential is medicine. Because of the shift toward personalized therapy and the accumulation of vast quantities of patient information and data, there is a pressing need for trustworthy and automated health data processing and analysis. Patient information is obtained by general practitioners, mobile healthcare applications, and online portals, to name a few, in addition to clinical venues like hospitals. Recent years have seen a new wave of important research projects as a result of this tendency. In Q2/2020, PubMed returned almost 11,000 items for the phrase "deep learning," with nearly 90% of these papers coming from the previous three years. Despite being a leading search engine for medical information, PubMed does not encompass all articles related to medicine. As a consequence, obtaining a thorough understanding of the topic of "medical deep learning" and accessing comprehensive reviews in related fields are becoming increasingly challenging. Nevertheless, a number of reviews and research publications on medical deep learning have been released recently. They tend to specialize in one area of medicine, such as the examination of medical photographs featuring a single disease. With these surveys as a starting point, with this publication, we hope to give the first thorough meta-review of medical deep learning surveys.

DOI: 10.1201/9781003343172-2

2.2 DEEP KNOWLEDGE

Deep knowledge is an AI/ML technique that attempts to mimic the way that humans learn new information. Together with data and analytical displaying, in-depth knowledge is a cornerstone of data science. Most people classify it as a subset of machine learning [1]. The foundation of this area is self-improvement and self-learning through the study of computer algorithms. A computer typically uses images, manuscripts, or a wide range of in-depth knowledge to accomplish classification duties. Deep learning algorithms may surpass human performance in front-line accuracy. The technology behind deep learning lies at the core of both common goods and services. Computer power limitations had previously limited the complexity of neural networks [2]. On the other hand, improvements in big data analytics have made it possible for processors to monitor, comprehend, and respond to complex states more quickly than individuals. Deep learning has been useful for speech recognition, language translation, and image categorization.

2.2.1 DEEP KNOWLEDGE VS MACHINE KNOWLEDGE

If deep learning is a division of machine learning, how do they vary from one another? In terms of the types of data it uses and the techniques it employs to learn, deep knowledge is different from out-of-date machine knowledge [1] as shown in Figure 2.1. Machine learning systems generate predictions from structured, labeled

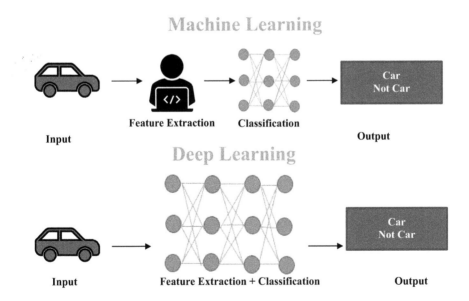

FIGURE 2.1 Machine learning vs deep learning

data, in which specific properties from the model's input data have been specified and are organized into tables. This doesn't mean that it always avoids using unstructured input; rather, if it does, it typically expends energy doing some preprocessing and putting it into a pre-planned format.

2.2.2 BASIC WORKINGS

A youngster learning to recognize a dog goes through the same procedure as deep learning computer algorithms perform. After learning from the data, each algorithm in the hierarchy applies an online transformation to that data and produces a statistical model. The process is repeated until the result reaches an acceptable level of precision. Due to the complexity of the data processing involved, deep learning was inspired by this fact. Like typical machine learning, this approach requires a supervised setting, and the programmer must be extremely explicit about the criteria it should use to determine whether or not an image depicts a dog. The feature extraction method takes a long time.

The first step is to provide the computer with some training data, such as a set of images labeled as "dog" or "not-dog" using metatags. Using the information gathered during the walk, the computer formulates a feature set for the dog and develops a prediction model [3]. In this case, a dog might be anything in the picture with four legs and a tail, according to the computer's initial model. Naturally, the terms "four legs" and "tail" are foreign to the program. Only pixel patterns will be examined in the digital data. With each iteration, the complexity and accuracy of the prediction model increases.

Given a training set, computer software employing deep learning techniques can quickly and accurately sort through millions of photos to find the ones with dogs in them. In contrast, it can take a young child several weeks or months to grasp the idea of a dog. Before the use of cloud computing and big data, programmers lacked the processing capacity and vast volumes of training data necessary for deep learning systems to perform with an acceptable level of accuracy. Intricate statistical models can be generated by deep learning software from its own output, allowing for the development of accurate prediction models from massive amounts of unlabeled, unstructured data as shown in Figure 2.2. It's crucial at this point because of the explosion of Internet of Things (IoT) devices.

2.2.3 WHY DEEP LEARNING

Simply put, accuracy. Credit accuracy is now more accurate than ever thanks to deep learning. It is essential for applications that require high levels of safety, such as driverless vehicles, and it advances customer integrated-circuit technology. In some tasks, including classifying objects in images, recent advancements in deep learning have brought it to the point where it now outperforms human beings. For instance, the number of performance traits could justify the necessity of DL.

Universal Approach to Learning: Universal learning is another name for DL, which excels in almost all application domains.

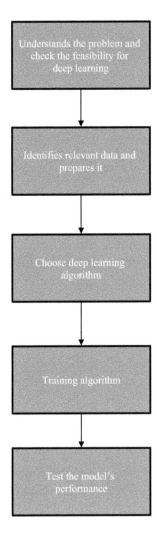

FIGURE 2.2   Deep learning process

Strength: DL approaches typically do not necessitate carefully crafted features. Instead, the best traits are automatically picked up in relation to the work at hand. The input data is hence resistant to common modifications.

Generalization: DL techniques that use transfer learning (TL), which is covered in the next section, applied to many data types or applications. Additionally, it works well when there are few data points.

Scalability: DL scales quite well. ResNet, developed by Microsoft, is typically used on a supercomputer scale; it contains 1202 layers. The vast company Lawrence Livermore National Laboratory (LLNL), which focuses on new network frameworks, employed a similar strategy that can be implemented. Although the concept of deep

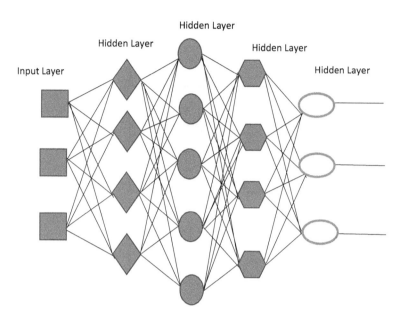

FIGURE 2.3   Basics of neural networks

learning was first introduced in the 1980s, it wasn't until recently that it became feasible.

In a deep neural network as shown in Figure 2.3, using a lot of trained labeled data, millions of images and hundreds of hours of video are required, for instance, to create a driverless car. It takes a lot of computer power to run deep learning programs. The parallel design of modern high-performance GPUs is well-suited to the tasks of deep learning. This helps development teams save the amount of time it takes to train deep learning networks by up to 50% when used in conjunction with clusters or cloud computing.

2.3   DEEP LEARNING ALGORITHMS

Deep learning techniques rely on ANNs to process information in a similar way to how the brain does so while also using self-learning representations. Through the guidance phase, algorithms utilize indefinite distribution of the key in components to take out features and classify things, as well as the finding of interesting information patterns. This occurs through multiple layers within the algorithms that construct the models, akin to teaching robots to develop their own decision-making networks that are pre-trained to fulfill specific tasks.

Many different algorithms are used in deep learning models. While no network is fault-proof, some algorithms are more appropriate for carrying out specific tasks. The classification of deep learning algorithms is show in Figure 2.4.

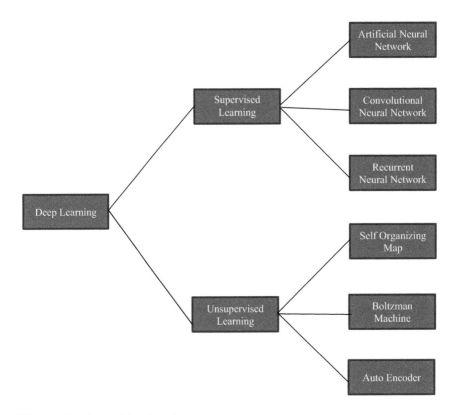

FIGURE 2.4 Types of deep learning

2.4 CONVOLUTIONAL NEURAL NETWORKS (CNNs)

CNN is the most popular and well-known algorithm in the DL space. CNN's primary benefit over its forerunners is that it completes the task without human assistance, automatically recognizing the relevant components. CNNs have found widespread applications in a variety of domains, from computer vision and audio processing to face identification and beyond. The neurons present in the intelligence of human and other nature served as the inspiration for CNNs, which have a structure resembling a typical neural network. Specifically, the CNN is designed to resemble the complex cell structure of the illustration cortex in a cat's brain [4]. Similar representations, sparse interactions, and parameter sharing are cited as three advantages of the CNN. In contrast to traditional fully connected (FC) networks, CNN makes complete use of mains input-data structures, such as visual sign, by utilizing shared weights and local connections. This is possible because of CNN's unique architecture. Because it employs a manageable set of parameters, this technique not only makes training easier but also makes the network run more quickly.

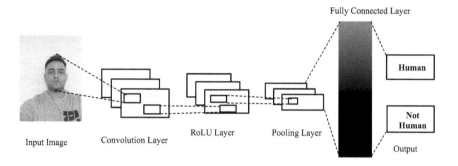

FIGURE 2.5   CNN architecture for image classification

Height (m), breadth (m), and depth (m) are the three dimensions of each layer's input x for a CNN model. In metric terms, the width (m) is proportional to the height (m) (m). The level of depth is equivalent to the channel number in television. The depth(r) of a typical RGB image is 3, for instance. Every convolutional layer's filter option, designated by the letter k, have a total of three dimensions (n, n, qn, qn), however in this case, n must be less, and q must match or be less than r. Additionally, the kernels act as the building blocks for the local connections, which create k feature maps of (mn1mn1) size using the same inputs (bias bk and weight Wk). It was already said that each is convolved with the input. The convolution layer, similar to that used in natural language processing (NLP), produces a dot product between its input and the weights by following the format of Equation 2.1. On the other hand, the inputs in this scenario are scaled-down replicas of the original photograph [5]. The findings that are presented below are obtained by applying a non-linear function production of the convolution layer. Figure 2.5 shows the CNN architecture for image classification.

$$HK = f(Wk * x + bk) \ hk = f(Wk * x + bk) \qquad (2.1)$$

After that, we do a down sampling operation on each feature map that is present in the underlying sub-sampling layers. The overfitting problem can eventually be solved, and faster training is made possible by reducing the number of network parameters. The pooling function is applied to a neighboring region with the size p for each and every feature map, where p is the size of the kernel (such as max or average). After the intermediate and low-level features have been obtained, the FC levels, similar to the final layer in a normal neural network, supply the high-level abstraction. The scores for classification are provided by the last layer, which might employ methods such as support vector machines (SVMs) or SoftMax. The score of a certain instance provides an indication of the class's likelihood of being present in that instance.

2.4.1   Advantages of Using CNN

The CNN's weight-sharing feature helps generalize and prevent overfitting by reducing trainable network parameters. When both the layer for feature extraction and the layer for classification are taught at the same time, the output of the model is highly controlled and significantly dependent on the features that were extracted.

2.5   LONG SHORT-TERM MEMORY NETWORKS (LSTMs)

Recurrent neural networks (RNNs) that make use of LSTMs are able to learn and remember long-standing dependencies. Long-term memory retention of earlier information is the default behavior.

Information is preserved throughout time using LSTMs. Having the ability to recall past inputs makes them effective in time series forecasting. Four interconnected layers work together to form a chain-like structure in LSTMs. In order to communicate in a unique way LSTMs have several applications beyond time series forecasting, including speech recognition, music creation, and the study of drugs.

2.5.1   How Do LSTMs Function?

They begin by losing track of pointless information from the previous situation. Then they output some of the cell-state usages after updating the cell-state data selectively.

Input Gate: The input gate selects the input values that will be utilized to modify the storage contents of the memory.

Entry Gate: The sigmoid function determines whether to pass through 0 or 1 data. The tan function also adds more weight to the information that has been provided, assigning an importance grade on a size ranging from-1 to

$$i_t = \sigma(W_i.[h_t - 1, x_t] + bi)$$
$$C_t = \tanh(W_C.[h_t - 1, x_t] + b_C)$$

Overlook Gate: It recognizes block-removable data. The choice is made using the sigmoid function. It considers the previous state(h_t-1), input (x_t), and cell state C_t-1 to give a number between 0 and 1.

$$f_t = \sigma(W_f.[h_t - 1, x_t] + b_f)$$

Output Gate: The yield of the block is dependent on the input and the memory. The sigmoid function is used to filter out data that is either 0 or 1. In addition, the tanh function limits the range of positive integers to the range 0–1. The tanh function ranks the relevance of the input values from −1 to 1 by dividing them by the sigmoid output. The following Figure 2.6 depicts the LSTM time series.

$$O_t = \sigma(W_o[h_t - 1, x_t] + b_o)$$
$$h_t = o_t * \tanh(C_t)$$

2.6   RECURRENT NEURAL NETWORKS (RNNs)

One of the primary difficulties is the susceptibility of this strategy to the rising gradient and vanishing problem. If numerous major or small derivatives are repeated,

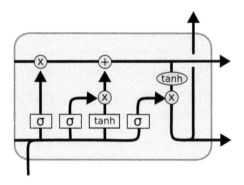

FIGURE 2.6   LSTM time series

the training phase will either inflate or decay. Because of this, the network ceases taking into account the initial inputs when new ones are received, and this sensitivity decreases with time. Additionally, this issue could be resolved with LSTM. This method maintains a steady link to the distributed memory banks. The network's temporal states may be stored in one or more of the memory cells that make up each memory block. Additionally, it features gate elements that control information flow. In extremely deep networks, remaining links can also serve as the backbone. As we'll see later, these measures significantly mitigate the effects of the vanishing gradient problem. It is widely agreed that RNN is not efficient as CNN. The following Figure 2.7 shows the RNN architecture.

2.6.1   How Do RNNs Function?

In the same way, that time's output influences time t+1. Any length of input data can be accepted by an RNN. Although past data is used during the computation, the overall model size remains constant regardless of how much data is fed into it.

2.7   MULTILAYER PERCEPTRONS (MLPs)

MLPs are feed-forward neural networks. They consist of multiple layers of perceptrons, each of which has an activation function. All MLPs have a fully connected output layer and an input layer. They could be implemented in programs for speech recognition, image recognition, and machine translation, all of which would have the same number of input and output layers, in addition to the possibility of having many more hidden levels.

2.7.1   How Do MLPs Function?

Multilayer perceptron (MLPs), delivers the information to the network's input layer. In order to ensure that the signal is only ever traveling in one direction, a graph

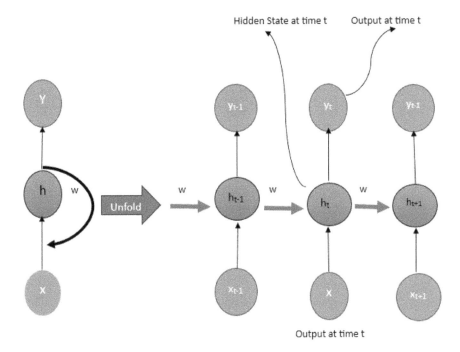

FIGURE 2.7 RNN architecture

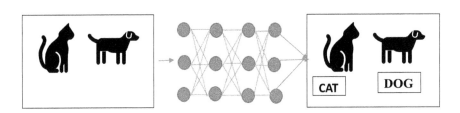

FIGURE 2.8 Multilayer perceptron

depicts the connections between the several layers of neurons. In MLPs, the input is calculated by weighing the connections between the layers of input and hidden information.

For MLPs, the firing of a node is determined by an activation function. Functions like the tanh, sigmoid, and ReLu are all examples of activation functions. By employing a training set of data, MLPs educate the model to recognize correlations and establish dependencies between independent and target variables. Figure 2.8 performs calculations to determine weights, bias, and the necessary activation functions in order to assign categories to images of cats and dogs.

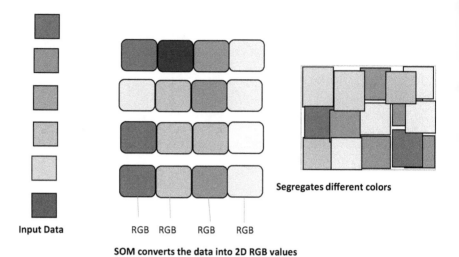

Input Data

RGB RGB   RGB   RGB

Segregates different colors

SOM converts the data into 2D RGB values

FIGURE 2.9   Self-organizing maps

2.8   SELF-ORGANIZING MAPS (SOMs)

2.8.1   How Do SOMs Function?

SOMs randomly choose a vector from the training set and assign weights to each node.

For the best input vector weights, SOMs investigate all of the nodes. The best matching unit is the victorious node (BMU). The number of neighbors eventually decreases as SOMs become more aware of the BMU's surroundings. SOMs favor the sample vector. Weight transitions are faster near a BMU. When a node is in close proximity to a BMU, the rate at which its weight changes are accelerated. The neighbor learns less the more distant it is from the BMU. The SOM will iterate over step two an infinite number of times.

An input vector's color-coded diagram is shown in Figure 2.9. A SOM converts this information into 2D RGB values. Lastly, it sets the colors apart and puts them in order.

2.9   DEEP BELIEF NETWORKS (DBNs)

2.9.1   How Do DBNs Function?

Algorithms for greedy learning are used to train DBNs. The greedy learning approach is used to learn the top-down, generative weights layer by layer. Gibbs sampling is done on the top two hidden layers by DBNs. The RBM that the top two hidden layers have defined are sampled in this stage. DBN takes a sample from the units that can be seen by running a single ancestral sampling run over the remaining components of the model as shown in Figure 2.10. DBNs discover that values may be deduced from a single, bottom-up pass.

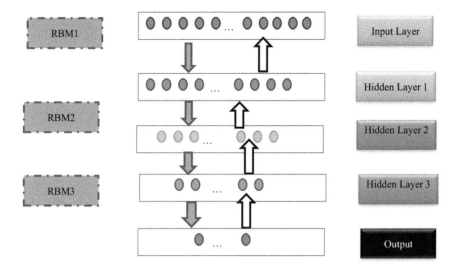

FIGURE 2.10   Deep belief networks

2.10   RESTRICTED BOLTZMANN MACHINES (RBMs)

RBMs are made up of two layers: visible components and covert units. Every visible unit has connections to every hidden unit. Output nodes are absent from RBMs, which instead feature only a bias unit linked to the input and output units.

2.10.1   How Do RBMs Function?

In the forward pass, RBMs transform the inputs into a series of integers. Forward and backward passes are RBM phases. RBMs mix every input with a single global bias and its own weight. The output of the algorithm is sent to the hidden layer. RBMs use that set of integers to convert the reconstructed inputs in the reverse pass. As shown in Figure 2.11, RBMs add the results of all the activations together and send the combined signal to the visual layer, where it can be reconstructed. The function evaluates the visual layer's quality by comparing the reconstructed image to the original input.

2.11   AUTOENCODERS

A feed-forward autoencoder has the same input and output. Autoencoders were created by Geoffrey Hinton in the 1980s to address issues with unsupervised learning [6]. The information fed into these trained neural networks is simply recycled in the next layer. Applications for autoencoders include image processing, medication research, and popularity predicting.

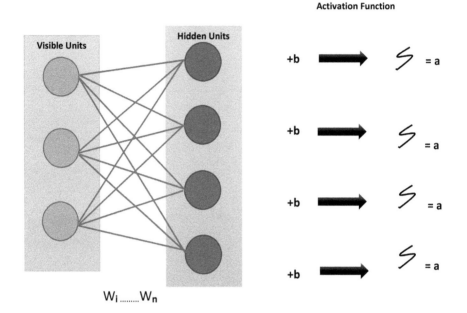

FIGURE 2.11   RBM visual layer quality

2.11.1   The Purpose of Automatic Encoders

Encoder, code, and decoder make up an autoencoder. Autoencoders, as shown in
Figure 2.12, are built in such a way that they can take in a single input and output a whole new representation. Then, they try to faithfully recreate the original
input.

When a digit's image is not clearly visible, the information is sent to an autoencoder neural network. Curative, preventative, rehabilitative, and palliative care are
all provided by different parts of the healthcare or medical industry. Businesses that
deal with sickness prevention, diagnosis, treatment, and rehabilitation make up the
healthcare industry. Charity can be given anonymously or openly and in the form of
goods or services [7]. To meet the needs of individuals and communities in terms
of medical care, the modern healthcare industry is broken up into a wide range of
sub-sectors, all of which rely on interdisciplinary teams comprised of professionals
and paraprofessionals who have received training.

2.12   IMPORTANCE OF HEALTHCARE INDUSTRIES

Around the world, the healthcare sector is held in very high esteem. Manufacturers of
medical equipment, diagnostic labs, hospitals, physicians, nurses, assisted living facilities, pharmacies, and many more businesses make up this sector of the economy [8].
This section offers a concise overview of the healthcare sector. The demand for
lifestyle medical therapies and the growth of the healthcare business are primarily

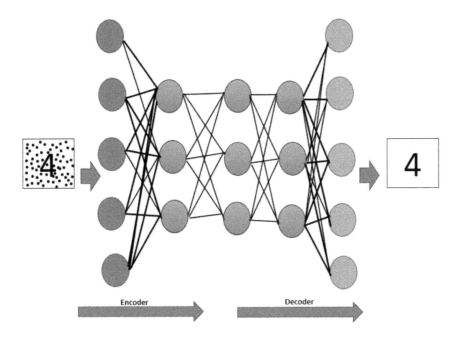

FIGURE 2.12 Autoencoder process

influenced by the ageing of populations and the prevalence of chronic diseases. Products based on medical technology will be in high demand for quite some time.

2.12.1 APPLICATION OF DEEP LEARNING IN HEALTHCARE

Deep learning capabilities have significantly improved the healthcare industry with the digitization of medical data and photos. By applying image recognition software, imaging specialists and radiologists may examine and assess more images in less time. Deep learning is being used by researchers and healthcare professionals to help the uncover and identify untapped potential in data and enhance the healthcare sector [9]. Deep learning in healthcare enables physicians to properly assess any illness and supports better disease treatment, resulting in better medical decisions [3].

2.12.1.1 Drug Research

The development of new medicines is aided by deep learning in the medical profession. The software analyses the patient's health records and suggests the most effective treatment. This technology is also picking up information from test outcomes and patient symptoms.

2.12.1.2 Diagnostic Imaging

Heart disease, cancer, and brain tumors are just a few examples of terrible medical conditions that can be diagnosed with the help of medical imaging procedures like MRI, CT, and ECG.

2.12.1.3   Insurance Theft

Claims for medical insurance fraud are analyzed with deep learning. Claims of future fraud could be predicted using the aid of predictive analytics. Deep learning helps the insurance industry reach its target customers with discounts and offers.

2.12.1.4   Alzheimer's Disease

Alzheimer's disease is a significant problem that the medical disease sector confronts. Using deep learning algorithms, Alzheimer's disease is diagnosed early.

2.12.1.5   Genome

Deep learning systems analyze a genome to help patients identify ailments. The insurance industry and the field of genetics have a bright future for deep learning. Enlitic believes deep learning improves medical professionals' accuracy and efficiency [10]. With Cells Cope, parents can monitor their children's health in real-time via a smart smartphone, avoiding the need for frequent doctor visits. Clinical staff and patients alike may benefit greatly from the use of deep learning in healthcare, which will raise the standard of treatment.

2.13   DEEP LEARNING IN CANCER PROGNOSIS AND SURVIVAL

Prognosis prediction is a crucial component of clinical oncology since it can influence treatment decisions based on the expected course of the disease and the likelihood of survival. Deep learning has the ability to calculate the prognosis and survival rate of patients when used by genomic, transcriptomic, and other forms of data [11]. The Cox proportional hazard regression model (Cox-PH) is the gold standard for predicting survival; it is a multivariate linear regression model that uses predictor variables to establish a relationship between survival time and the variables being studied. Cox-linear PH's structure when applied to genomic and transcriptomic data might potentially ignore intricate and perhaps nonlinear relationships between elements. Deep neural networks, on the other hand, are inherently non-linear and might, in theory, perform this task better than others.

For DL survival analysis, it's interesting to note that several studies have used Cox regression. These models were trained utilizing transcriptome data to provide better prognostic predictions.

Cox-net was a ground-breaking technique that transformed the Cox regression model into the output layer of the neural network by utilizing the millions of deep characteristics obtained by hidden layers as input. Cox-net was trained using RNA-use data from ten TCG A cancer types and was the n compared to two Cox-PH variants (Cox-PH and Cox Boost). Cox-net was the only model capable of differentiating between critical pathways like p53 signaling, endocytosis, and adherent junctions. Its higher accuracy demonstrated that Cox-PH and neural networks may be utilized to collect biological data related to prognosis.

2.14   DEEP LEARNING IN HEART DISEASE PREDICTION

Heart conditions, sometimes referred to as cardiovascular diseases (CVDs), have overtaken cancer as the most dangerous disease not just in India but worldwide in recent decades. A number of heat-related disorders can be referred to as heart disease [12]. A lot of factors in your body might potentially cause heart disease, making it one of the hardest diseases to predict. Heart disease detection and prognosis are challenging tasks for both doctors and researchers. Therefore, a trustworthy, efficient, and useful technique for identifying such life-threatening illnesses is needed, as well as the necessary medication.

2.15   IMAGING ANALYTICS AND DIAGNOSTICS

Convolutional neural networks (CNNs) and other deep learning approaches are particularly successful at analyzing X-ray and MRI data. According to Stanford University computer science experts, CNNs are created with the intention of processing images and increasing network efficiency and image size. As a result, certain CNNs are becoming more accurate at identifying key traits in diagnostic imaging investigations than human diagnosticians and are even surpassing them.

Convolutional neural networks trained to analyze dermatological pictures correctly identified melanoma with 10% more accuracy than human doctors, according to research published in the *Annals of Oncology* in June 2018. Despite the availability of patient histories to human clinicians, CNN outperformed dermatologists by almost 7% in the body location of the problematic trait, including age, gender, and marital status. The research group from the various German universities concluded that "our data clearly imply that a CNN algorithm may be a suitable tool to aid physicians in melanoma detection independent of their specific degree of experience and training." Deep learning technologies are incredibly accurate as well as quick.

At Mount Sinai's Icahn School of Medicine, researchers contain developed a deep neural network that is 150 times faster than human radiologists at identifying life-threatening neurological disorders like stroke and brain hemorrhage. "Our results demonstrate a CNN method may help clinicians diagnose melanoma, independent of their specific level of experience and training," the researchers write. The software examined the image, analyzed the data, and reported a concerning clinical finding in 1.2 seconds.

Dr. Joshua Bederson, who heads the department of neurology and is a professor at the university, claims that "any strategies that minimize time to diagnosis may contribute to improved patient outcomes since the early reaction is critical in the treatment of acute neurological illnesses." Given how well deep learning processes images, some researchers in this field are creating medical images with neural networks. Data scientists at the Mayo Clinic, NVIDIA, and the MGH & BWH Center for Clinical Research, using generative adversarial networks (GANs), a type of deep learning, can automatically create realistic medical images.

2.16   ELECTRONIC HEALTH RECORDS (EHRs)

Deep learning neural networks, such as long short-term memory (LSTM), general recurrent units (GRU), recurrent neural networks, and one-dimensional convolutional neural networks, have proven to be of tremendous assistance in natural language processing. These networks are excellent at handling data that is connected to sequences, such as time series, sentences, and speech. The discipline of computational medicine uses natural language processing technologies to process electronic medical records using neural networks.

Interest in using EHRs has increased rapidly in recent years. An electronic health record contains data about patients' medical care. The data includes unstructured clinical language, structured diagnostic information, structured prescription information, structured information about operations, and structured information about experimental test results [9]. Exploiting electronic medical records can enhance medicine by improving the effectiveness and quality of diagnostics [4]. By using data from electronic health records to foresee sickness, it can, for instance, provide patients with timely treatment. It can also help physicians make decisions by looking at the hidden connections between various diseases, treatments, and pharmaceutical electronic health records. Figure 2.13 shows the EHR cycle process.

Given the sequential nature of an EHR, recurrent neural networks like LSTM and GRU find many uses in the medical industry. While comparing recurrent neural networks to more conventional approaches, the latter fail miserably when processing electronic medical records.

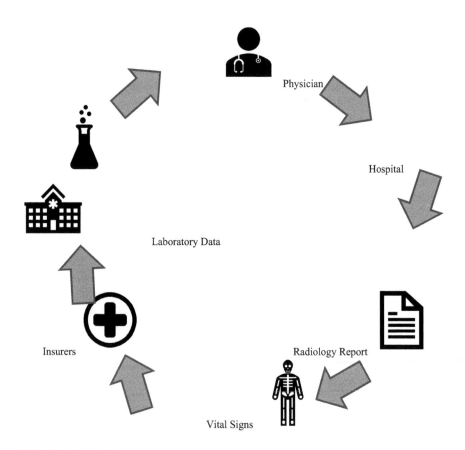

FIGURE 2.13   EHR cycle process

Most deep learning approaches used to retrieve EHR data are supervised. Some researchers analyze electronic health data using unsupervised learning. The electronic health record is analyzed by using deep learning algorithms to look for patterns. The use of the learned patterns in tasks such as disease prediction, event prediction, incidence prediction, and others is clearly the path that deep learning applications in the field of electronic medical records will head in the near future.

The usefulness of deep learning in electronic health records has been demonstrated by a significant number of studies. However, some challenges lie ahead for the future implementation of deep learning in electronic health records: Why is it difficult to analyze all of the many types of data included in the electronic health record? [5]. The reason is, there are five distinct data formats for electronic health records: timeseries, like patient history; categories, such as race and international disease code; date-time object, like patient admittance date; and numerical, like BMI. Also, EHRs are large, noisy, complex, and sparse. Deep learning approaches face a challenge in applying the right model to electronic health data.

Deep learning in EHRs is difficult enough that, in practice, the record's coding alters due to differences in medical oncology. The National Drug Code, the Unified Medical Language System, and medical ontology includes ICD-9, ICD-10, and additional codes. The unique implementation leads to nonstandard data since various departments or hospitals do not strictly follow the medical oncology coding rules. Medical ontologies may describe the same illness phenotype. For instance, for the laboratory result of hemoglobin A1C > 7.0, the ICD-9 code 250.00 and the clinical text writing method "type 2 diabetes mellitus" can be used to identify patients in the electronic health record who have been diagnosed with "type 2 diabetes mellitus." Data processing is more difficult because of the aforementioned problems. Researchers are also inconvenienced by the mapping between the seconds.

2.16.1 NATURAL LANGUAGE PROCESSING (NLP)

Many NLP systems used in health care to transcribe documents and convert audio to text involve deep learning and neural networks. Neural networks optimized for categorization can discover linguistic or grammatical features by "grouping" comparable phrases.

To put it another way, this helps the network comprehend more nuanced semantic meanings. However, the effort is complicated by the complexity of natural speech and dialogue [13]. For instance, the meaning of a pair of words that is always used together in an idiomatic expression may change depending on the context, as seen in phrases like "kick the bucket" or "barking up the wrong tree." Converting acceptable speech to text is already a very frequent practice, and technologies are widely available; however, it is far more challenging to derive reliable and practical conclusions from free-text medical data. It is common knowledge that free-text clinical notes in electronic health records (EHRs) are clunky, incomplete, inconsistent, full of arcane acronyms, and crammed to the gills with jargon. In contrast, pictures are made up of specified rows and columns of pixels. Technology outperformed standard methods in detecting unplanned hospital readmissions, estimating the duration of stay, and forecasting in-hospital mortality.

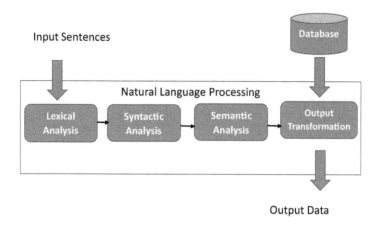

FIGURE 2.14   Natural language processing

Like prior deep learning EHR applications, researchers said this prediction was accurate and was reached without the manual selection of criteria assessed to be signed by an expert. Instead, our program took into account tens of thousands of variables, including free-text notes, to determine each patient's prognosis. This is only a proof-of-concept study; the researcher's searches at Google think the results could have far-reaching consequences for healthcare organizations looking to enhance patient outcomes and be more proactive in giving necessary therapy. The following Figure 2.14 depicts the concepts of Natural Language Processing.

2.17   INFLUENCE OF DEEP LEARNING IN HEALTHCARE

Health care is a clear application area for AI. It generates enormous amounts of data, spends a lot of money on it, and has plenty of room for improving the quality of its offerings by making them more intuitive and sophisticated. Thinking of health care as a single entity is foolish. One of the three branches of AI outside of the IT giants that is making the biggest advancements is robotic process automation (RPA). (While not all RPA makes use of AI [5], it is becoming more common.) RPA would be a logical application because the healthcare systems in the majority of nations are huge, bureaucratic processes. Smart says that it would be challenging to identify several healthcare issues [7].

2.17.1   Diagnostics

The two AI applications that are now being continuously tested and implemented at scale, together with RPA, are chatbots and analytics. Contrary to popular belief, chatbots are less common in most healthcare systems, while other forms of analytics are being extensively researched for diagnosis. Almost every day, a new articles report that robots have outperformed human radiologists or physicians in diagnosing some ail mentor.

2.17.2   Change Is Difficult

The healthcare industry struggles to execute change [10]. There are many powerful entrenched interests, and occasionally there is no efficient market to encourage innovation and promote efficiency. The Food and Drug Administration (FDA) approved a robotic anesthetic system developed by Johnson & Johnson for routine operations like colonoscopies in 2013 [14]. Hundreds of surgeries were performed in Canada and the United States with the help of this machine at a cost of about $150 for each procedure, compared to $2,000 with a human anesthetist. However, resistance from the profession led to sluggish sales.

2.17.3   Medical AI in Consumer Strategies

In Poland others think the medical industry will undergo a transformation as a result of consumer technology advancements. Apple watches can already do an electrocardiogram, monitor your heart rate, and identify atrial fibrillation. Our blood glucose levels will be measured by low-cost, simple sensors that are connected to watches, cell phones, and eventually smart eyewear [15]. Our breath will be taken and examined to look for signs of cancer or possible heart problems. Skin cancer will be detected by our phone's cameras, and Parkinson's disease will be identified by their microphones, which will capture information about our speech. We may have as many sensors constantly monitoring our health in ten years as a Formula One vehicle.

2.17.4   Democratization and Decentralization

The COVID-19 outbreak will leave a lasting impression on the medical profession. Will Smart estimates that 40% of medical visits today involve phone or video calls. Undoubtedly, this saves the patient more time than it does the doctor, but the longer the illness lasts, the harder it will be to get back to your old routines [16]. Development is telemedicine. Chatbots can be used in triage, for instance, to decide which expert and how quickly a patient calling needs to be seen.

It's possible that medicine will become democratic and decentralized. The majority of modern healthcare systems are centered on acute hospitals. They are founded on a Napoleonic paradigm created to unite professionals and improve communication at a high cost of capital. However, it is common knowledge that only 20% of a patient's total well-being is attributable to health care. The remaining factors include income, employment, marital status, and others. Over the past 200 years, doctors have become more and more specialized; AI may allow them to revert to their earlier generalist roles.

2.18   CONCLUSION

Although the pilots and experiments are exciting, their application to healthcare analytics is just beginning. Deep learning is captivating regulators and lawmakers, commercial organizations, medical specialists, and even people. The Office of the

National Coordinator for Health Information Technology (ONC) has high hopes for the future of deep learning and has already honored some outstanding engineers for their contributions to the field.

In a report on AI in healthcare, the agency said deep learning algorithms have provided "transformational" results. Early successes in skin cancer classification and diabetic retinal screenings were mentioned in the report as two applications of deep learning. Due to the established early advantage in many high-value applications, image analytics is expected to overtake other clinical research fields as the dominant area in the near future. Nearly all of the main health IT providers prioritize "cleaning out the garbage" as AI learns user behavior, predicts needs, and displays relevant facts at the right time. Dissatisfied clients seek better solutions from these businesses. There is consensus amongst patients and healthcare professionals that AI has reached a point where it can help facilitate more consumer-focused solutions and interactions in the sector with a surprisingly large number of compelling applications.

REFERENCES

[1] S. Durga; Rishabh Nag; Esther Daniel, "Survey on Machine Learning and Deep Learning Algorithms used in Internet of Things (IoT) Healthcare," 2019 3rd International Conference on Computing Methodologies and Communication (ICCMC), IEEE, 2019.

[2] Riccardo Miotto; Fei Wang; Shuang Wang; Xiaoqian Jiang; Joel T. Dudley, "Deep Learning for Healthcare: Review, Opportunities, and Challenges," Corresponding author: Fei Wang, Department of Healthcare Policy and Research, Weill Cornell Medicine at Cornell University, New York, NY, and USA. Tel.: þ1-646-962-9405; Fax: þ1-646-962-0105; E-mail: few2001@med.cornell.edu

[3] Yiting Wang; Shah Nazir; Muhammad Shafiq, *An Overview on Analysing Deep Learning and Transfer Learning Approaches for Health Monitoring*, School of Business, Central South University, Hunan University of Finance and Economics, 24 March 2021.

[4] Laith Alzubaidi; Jinglan Zhang; Ye Duan, "Review of Deep Learning: Concepts, CNN Architectures, Challenges, Applications, Future Directions," *Journal of Big Data, Research Gate* 31 March 2021, 53.

[5] Gollavilli Srikanth; Nivedita Nukavarapu; Surya Durbha, "Deep Reinforcement Learning Interdependent Health Care Critical Infrastructure Simulation model for Dynamically Varying COVID-19 Scenario-A Case Study of a Metro City," 2021 IEEE International Geoscience and Remote Sensing Symposium (IGARSS), IEEE, 2021.

[6] G. Geetha; J. Thimmiaraja; Chetan Jagannath Shelke; G. Pavithra; Vinay Kumar Sharma; Devvret Verma, "Deep Learning with Unsupervised and Supervised Approaches in Medical Image Analysis," 2022 2nd International Conference on Advance Computing and Innovative Technologies in Engineering (ICACITE), IEEE, 2022.

[7] Abdullah A. Abdullah; Masoud M. Hassan; Yaseen T. Mustafa, "Review on Bayesian Deep Learning in Healthcare: Applications and Challenges," *IEEE Access* 2022, 10.

[8] Song Xue; Karl Peter Bohn; Rui Guo; Hasan Sari; Marco Viscione; Axel Rominger; Biao Li; Kuangyu Shi, "Development of a Deep Learning Method for CT-Free Correction for an Ultra-Long Axial Field of View PET Scanner," 2021 43rd Annual International Conference of the IEEE Engineering in Medicine & Biology Society (EMBC), IEEE, 2021.

[9] Survey Khan Muhammad; Salman Khan; Javier Del Ser; Victor Hugo C de Albuquerque, "Deep Learning for Multigrade Brain Tumor Classification in Smart Healthcare Systems: A Prospective," *IEEE Transactions on Neural Networks and Learning Systems* 2021, 32, 2.

[10] Anish Gupta; Surbhi Gupta; Yogesh Kumar, "A Review on Recent Deep Learning Techniques, Challenges and Its Applications for Medical Helathcare System," 2021 International Conference on Technological Advancements and Innovations (ICTAI), IEEE, 2021.

[11] Khoa A. Tran, Olga Kondrasova, Andrew Bradley, "Deep Learning in Cancer Diagnosis, Prognosis, and Treatment Selection," Jennifer Bresnick, 27 September 2021, 152. https:// healthitanalytics.com/features/what-is-deep-learning-and-how-will-it-change-healthcare

[12] Gouthami Velakanti; Shivani Jarathi; Malladi Harshini; Praveen Ankam; Shankar Vuppu, "Heart Disease Prediction Using Deep Learning," Conference Paper First Online, 15 February 2022.

[13] P. M. Lavanya; E. Sasikala, "Deep Learning Techniques on Text Classification Using Natural Language Processing (NLP) in Social Healthcare Network: A Comprehensive Survey," 2021 3rd International Conference on Signal Processing and Communication (ICPSC), IEEE, 2021.

[14] Mubarak Almutairi; Lubna A. Gabralla; Saidu Abubakar; Haruna Chiroma, "Detecting Elderly Behaviors Based Deep Learning for Healthcare: Recent Advances, Methods, Real-World Applications and Challenges," IEEE Access 2022, 10.

[15] Xianlong Zeng; Simon Lin; Chang Liu, "Multi-View Deep Learning Framework for Predicting Patient Expenditure in Healthcare," *IEEE Open Journal of the Computer Society* 2021, 2.

[16] Haya Elayan; Moayad Aloqaily; Mohsen Guizani, "Deep Federated Learning for IoT-based Decentralized Healthcare Systems," 2021 International Wireless Communications and Mobile Computing (IWCMC), IEEE, 2021.

3 Monitoring and Diagnosis of Health Using Deep Learning Methods

*R. Mothi, M. Mohan, M. Muthuvinayagam,
C. Vigneshwaran, S. T. Lenin, M. Manohar,
and P. Ganesh*

3.1 INTRODUCTION

India had reported a population of 1.39 billion in January 2021; 624 million were internet users noted in the 1.10 billion mobile connections [1]. The development of information technology over the past decades enabled a revolution in scientific, healthcare, and educational infrastructures. Highly configured personal computers, maximum bandwidth, wireless networking systems, and the use of the internet increased connectivity throughout the population. The healthcare systems of India have more obstacles, especially in poor and rural back areas. The country has many medical professionals: more than one million doctors and two million nursing professionals [2]. The ratio of availability of doctors in India is 2.2:1000, whereas in China it is 2.8:1000 [3]. Sixty percent of Indian hospitals are located in cities that occupy 32% of their population. The present healthcare communication system depends on 4G networks for connectivity, but the smart healthcare system based on 5G offers huge services with maximum bandwidth, high reliability, latency, and data delivery [4]. 5G network services comprise URLLC (ultra-reliable low latency communications), eMBB (enhanced mobile broadband), and mMTC (massive machine type communications). Among these, mMTC provides high internet connectivity; eMBB facilitates video calling service, telemedicine prospects, diagnosis, treatment, and augmented reality/virtual reality (AR/VR); and URLLC is responsible for drones and automated vehicles to support surveillance [5]. The World Health Organization (WHO) defines

> a Sustainable Healthcare System as a system that improves, maintains or restores health while minimizing negative impacts on the environment and leveraging opportunities to restore and improve it, to the benefit of the health and well-being of current and future generations. [6]

This chapter consolidates the importance and current requirement of deep learning in electrocardiogram (ECG) signal interpretation, application of LabVIEW and discrete

DOI: 10.1201/9781003343172-3

wavelet transform (DWT), digital pathological findings, and proteomics analysis to find a solution for the pathological condition through the pathway analysis. This will support the researchers to solve present health problems with a holistic approach.

3.1.1 Technology-Driven Healthcare System – Indian Scenario

The expenditure for research and development in India recorded 76% for various priority sectors including health, defense industries, agriculture, forestry and fisheries, industries, space, transport, telecommunication, and infrastructural development. Among this 18.6% of expenditure is utilized for health sectors and 8.7% for transport, telecommunication, and infrastructural development [7]. A positive transition is required in the Indian healthcare system to serve mass health industry requirements. It manages infrastructural set up in the hospital environment, reduces consultation time, and extends service to all corners of the country. Nearly 75% of the Indian population resides outside of the urban environment and accesses limited hospitals.

The main objectives of National Communications Policy 2018 include 1) ensuring broadband to all, 2) creation of four million job opportunities in the area of digital communication, 3) increase of GDP from 6% to 8%, 4) place India in the top fifty countries in the ICT Development Index documented worldwide, 5) promote the contribution of our country to global value chains, and 6) ensure digital sovereignty [8].

Our country is placed in the leading role in fixing optic fiber through the rural area accounts, which is nearly 600,000 villages with the banner of BharatNet. This initiative utilizes the cloud, 5G technology, data analytics, and IoT gearing up digital technology, and it creates more opportunities to compete in the fourth industrial revolution.

The telephone subscription in December 2019 was reported as 1,172.44 million, whereas in December 2020 it was 1,173.83 million. Total internet users increased from 718.74 to 795.18 million. Figure 3.1 shows the telephone subscriptions in India for the years 2016 to 2020 [9].

Next-generation access technologies (NGAT) enable licensed providers of internet connectivity to ensure cost reduction, deliver high-quality service, and maximize revenue. The main aim of the next-generation network (NGN) is to access the range between 3 GHz to 4 GHz. NGN utilizes high-capacity spectrum networks with E-band ranging between 71–76 and 81–86 GHz and V-band with a range of 57–64 GHz.

3.1.2 Biotechnology and Healthcare

After fifty years of elucidation of DNA structure, the completion of the human genome project was achieved. In 2017, the total cost of the sequencing was US$2.7 billion whereas the cost was only US$100 for the whole genome sequencing using Illumina's next-generation sequencing machine. The evolution of molecular medicine was greatly envisaged during the period explaining gene architecture, transcripts, protein, and metabolic processes. The cellular and molecular processes improved the biomarker screening, targeted specific drug designing, and provided well-defined diagnostic methods to maximize healthcare system monitoring.

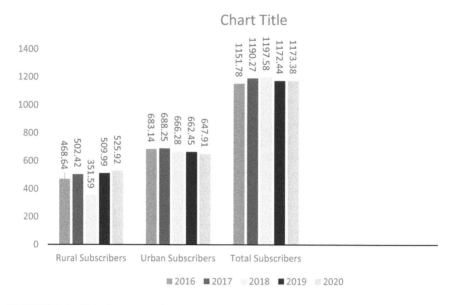

FIGURE 3.1   Telephone subscription in India (Source: TRAI, 2020)

Artificial intelligence and system-based drug designing created many opportunities to find novel drug candidates within a short duration. AI-enabled new drug molecules gave rise to new therapeutic solutions for the present COVID-19 pandemic situation. Computational software was used to interpret bioinformatic data queries. Bioinformatic tools are involved in data mining and the analysis of various omics data [10].

Human physiology is highly complex in nature, and it requires an integrative biological approach to find solutions. HumMod is based on a mathematical model and used appropriate simulations working for 5000 different variable factors including the cardiovascular system; respiratory, neural, nephrological system; muscular system; and metabolic pathways. This mathematical model is derived from empirical data procured from peer-reviewed literature. Data parsing is executed by Extensible Markup Language (XML) and output as simulations describing the physiology of humans. The mathematical model navigator for the physiological analysis is given in Figure 3.2. The accuracy of the model extends quantitative and qualitative changes noted during clinical trials [11].

The data available in various databases can be utilized to perform analysis through supervised and unsupervised learning methods. The statistical significance of proteins was identified with the service of peer-reviewed tools like MetaboAnalyst 5.0 [12] and Reactome [13]. By using the tool, we can find statistically proven protein molecules and their metabolic pathway analysis. It caters to PCA (principal component analysis), PLS-DA (partial least squares discriminant analysis), and FCA (fold change analysis), and it graphically represents heat maps and volcano plots. The results recorded in the tools when we utilized the secondary data enable us to proceed with further research in the field of cancer proteomics.

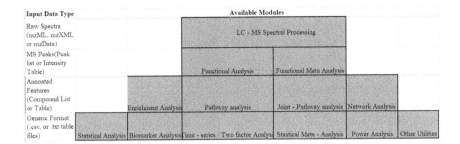

Input Data Type	Available Modules					
Raw Spectra (mzML, mzXML or mzData)			LC - MS Spectral Processing			
MS Peaks(Peak list or Intensity Table)		Functional Analysis		Functional Meta Analysis		
Annoated Features (Compound List or Table)	Enrichment Analysis	Pathway analysis		Joint - Pathway analysis	Network Analysis	
Generic Format (.csv. or .txt table files)	Statstical Analysis	Biomarker Analysis	Time - series / Two factor Analysis	Stastical Meta - Analysis	Power Analysis	Other Utilities

FIGURE 3.2   Front view of MetaboAnalyst v5.0

3.1.3 MACHINE LEARNING AND HEALTH CARE

Smart health care is mediated by AI, machine learning, and the Internet of Health Things (IoHT) enabling the prevention of diseases, accurate diagnosis of different ailments, and appropriate therapy. Machine learning represents a cutting-edge artificial approach for establishing personalized medication pathways. Artificial intelligence-bound clinical decision support is facilitated through machine learning (ML). ML techniques are particularly focused on electronic health records and timely data recognition, highlighting their importance in this area. The huge data maintained for each patient is handled by many successful ML algorithms. ML can be involved in many areas of the healthcare system, which includes the classification of the patient based on their diseases, recommendation of possible treatments, clustering of similar groups of patients, and prediction of possible outcomes. ML can serve automation in the hospital management system. Machine intelligence-based healthcare system includes trustworthiness, explainability, usability, and transparency [14].

3.1.4 MACHINE LEARNING FOR PATHOLOGY

The majority of artificial intelligence applications in pathology are still in the rudimentary stage. Only a limited number of Food and Drug Administration (FDA) approved medical devices are supported by artificial intelligence, and they assists in blood/fluid cell classification and the screening of cervical cytology. Machine learning (ML) is used in research settings for the classification and diagnosis of lung cancer [15, 16], classification of polyps of the colorectal area [17], diagnosis and categorization of lymphoma [18] and measurement of breast tumor growth [19], as well as to find lymph node metastases [20–22], analyze bladder cancer recurrence [22], identify tumor stroma [23], and estimate prognosis in lung and brain cancers [24, 25]. A review of applications of machine learning in pathology was performed [26]. A machine learning application, in Chameleon, was noted [27, 28], which compared the functioning of algorithms used by many research teams. Genetics and prognosis of cancer cells using histological sections to find lymphocytic inclusions can be carried out automatically [29, 30]. The area of interest and slide contents can be identified [31, 32]. Various machine learning algorithms have been developed to diagnose pathological conditions, including analyzing morphological features of cancer cells, cell division and nucleus patterns, blood vessels, and the condition of blood flow in ducts. Machine learning has also been applied to cardiac risk analysis [33], clinical diagnosis of liver disease and anemia [34], diagnosis of the endocrine system [35], and many other specific disorders [36]. Machine learning enables comparison of existing results with test results [37] facilitating auto-validation of GC-MS studies and potentially eliminating the need for testing [38].

Nowadays artificial detection is increased and being used in a variety of sub-specializations with distinct sample types [39]. According to early studies on the accuracy, AI-based systems show the ability to identify accurate data [40], laying a milestone for the adoption of pathological findings in a computational approach [41]. Three kinds of cancer, prostate cancer, carcinoma of cells, and breast cancer, were classified and categorized with 44732 images of the slides validated using the deep neural network method. They found the accuracy of five times magnification of whole slide images. For each tissue type, they adopted a ML-based statistical model for the classification of different types of cancer. They observed the area under curve (AUC) above 0.98 when used clinically, which permits pathologists to elim-inate 65–75% of study slides during the maintenance of 100% of sensitivity [42]. Wildeboer et al. presented deep learning algorithms related to various imaging methods such as CT (computed tomography), EUI (echogenicity in ultrasound imag-ing), and MRI (magnetic resonance imaging) function as a computer-aided meth-odology for the diagnosis of prostate cancer [43]. The following colorectal polyps viz., 1) hyperplastic (HP), 2) sessile serrated (SS), 3) traditional serrated (TS), 4) tubular (T), and 5) villous polyps (VP) can be accurately identified using a variety of deep-learning techniques developed by Korbar et al. Out of 2074 images, 90% of images were used for training model data, and 10% of the images were consigned for validation. The accuracy for the classification of colorectal polyps reported a 93% confidence interval (CI) value between 89–96% [44]. Combined recurrent neural net-works (RNN) and convolutional neural networks (CNN) were designed to predict the outcome based on microarray samples of tissue obtained from 420 patients bear-ing colorectal cancer [45]. According to the findings, the hazard ratio for the deep neural network (DNN) based prediction of outcome noted 2.3 (confidence interval: 1.79–3.03), and the AUC was 0.69. Wang et al. achieved the CAMELYON16 and uti-lized the input patches with 256 x 256 pixels from the negative and positive portion of the pictures of lymph nodes to train different kinds of models such as AlexNet, GoogLeNet, FaceNet, and VGG16. GoogLeNet has the best performance and is gen-erally stable and faster among the various algorithms. Using the deep learning (DL) system, the diagnosis accuracy observed by the pathologists was improved signifi-cantly as the area under the curve (AUC) increased from the value of 0.966 to 0.995, and it represents the reduction of 85% human error [46]. Telemedicine (TM) and computer-aided medicine (CAM) are quickly spreading across the market during the COVID-19 outbreak. The maximum contagious condition and risk in systemic and social isolation brought unexpected challenges for traditional medical practices. The application of artificial intelligence in computer-aided medicine, coupled with clinical data from electronic health records (EHRs), allows for the identification of risk factors affecting the population. This approach enables proactive management of public health issues while maintaining high quality and safety standards [47].

3.2 PROTEOMICS STUDIES

3.2.1 METABOANALYST V5.0

Proteomics data processing, visualization, statistical analysis, and extracting high-lighting proteins for further analysis are performed in MetaboAnalyst, a web-based tool. The tool is employed in the analysis of statistics, enrichment pathways, and mass spectrometric peaks to the pathway. Data upload was carried out in MetaboAnalyst using comma-separated value (CSV) files. The file comprises control and experi-mental data. The uploaded data can be analyzed by the tool as per the requirement.

Proteomic data can be cured and normalized for getting statistical significance, and normalization is an important step in proteomic analysis [48]. The key factors considered during normalization include the differences noted in the magnitude of sample concentration, fold changes, and technical features [49].

MetaboAnalyst v5.0, a user-friendly tool, contains downloadable images of the statistical analysis. It has affordable analytical data like univariate parametric and non-parametric analysis, multivariate unsupervised and supervised data analy-sis, and parametric and non-parametric correlation analysis [50]. Figure 3.3 shows the front view of the MetaboAnalyst v5.0 tool. Supervised analysis by partial least squares discriminant analysis (PLS-DA) and multivariate unsupervised analysis per-formed employing PCA (principal component analysis) can be performed. PCA can be calculated by using a data covariance matrix, and PLS-DA is based on multiple linear regression enable to find the covariance to the maximum [51].

3.2.2 REACTOME

Reactome is an online tool used to find possible pathways by using the data obtained from MetaboAnalyst v5.0 (www.reactome.org). The tool works with the CSV file, and it generated a PDF report. Pathways generated in Reactome can be studied to

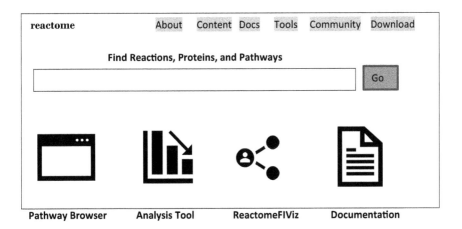

FIGURE 3.3 Front view of the Reactome tool

understand biological pathways. Protein-protein interaction and mass spectroscopy mediated biomarker finding can be carried out by using Reactome [52]. This tool provides data related to the genes and proteins based on their ID. Uniprot, GeneBank, OMIM, EMBL, and many other databases support the Reactome tool. Possible analysis methods available in the Reactome tool are given in Figure 3.3.

3.3 HEALTH MONITORING SYSTEM USING DEEP LEARNING

Deep learning, a machine learning method, is crucial to data analysis, which also involves statistical and data-analytical modeling. Gathering and analyzing a lot of data is beneficial for data analysis. This method will be used to forecast both structured and unstructured data employed in mathematical models that are designed to function like the human brain. Deep learning has been employed in every part of human life, and health-related data is becoming increasingly important to discover great facilities for patients' health records and to recognize disease symptoms. Figure 3.4 shows the role of deep learning in health care.

3.3.1 ADVANCED HEALTHCARE SYSTEM

In the coming years, the healthcare system will witness further advancements in deep learning techniques, enhancing clinical decision-making systems. Technology

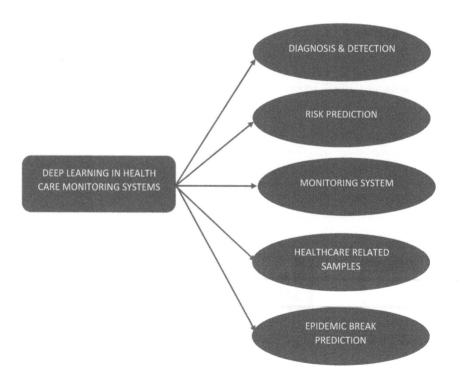

FIGURE 3.4 Role of deep learning in health care

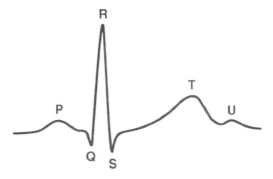

FIGURE 3.5 Graphical representation of ECG waveform

can help medical professionals by enhancing the capabilities of integrated AI technology-based tools that implement and easily analyzing complex data and improve the methods for early diagnosis to lower the death rate and increase the accuracy of disease predictions in this scenario. To provide additional clinical support, unconscious conditions are immediately diagnosed and made a priority for patients thanks to the close communication between medical professionals and their environment.

Deep learning or neural network have many features and levels of variables that are the most crucial types of machine learning. They foresee results. Beyond what the human body can recognize, deep learning can boost the detection of clinically relevant elements in data. Deep learning and neural networks work together to achieve a higher level of diagnostic accuracy than the previous generation of automation tools and analytical detection (Figure 3.5).

3.3.2 Natural Language Processing

Natural language processing, statistical modeling, and speech recognition are three main areas where deep learning is being used more and more.

Healthcare information creation, understanding, and classification are one of the NLP domain applications. Machines can identify and classify patient data for use in developing health reports, interacting with patients, and having a discussion using deep learning systems. In healthcare systems, NLP is a method for extracting information from unstructured data.

NLP has been applied to process unstructured or non-quantitative clinical data in the medical industry for classifying or predicting the health records of patients through extracting the information transformation and outcome-based data [53].

3.3.3 Electrocardiogram (ECG)

The disease caused by the heart is investigated by the electrical pulse recorded from the heart and it is called an electrocardiogram (ECG). The impulses obtained from those electrical pulses are recorded in terms of waves such as PQRST as shown in Figure 3.5. The cells present in the heart are known as cardiac cells; they are surrounded and filled with solution. In comparison with the outside cell membrane, all the cell membranes present inside are negatively charged at the time of resting position. The inner cardiac cell becomes positively charged with that of the outside membrane only when the heart is initiated with an electrical pulse. The change of polarity in the cell membrane is due to the electrical pulses, and the polarity change is named depolarization. The stimulated cardiac cell returns to resting condition once the depolarization happens, and it is called repolarization [54].

3.3.3.1 Analysis of ECG Signal

The ECG is a tool to analyze and identify the abnormal rhythms of the heart, and with the help of the ECG signal one can easily find the disease caused by the heart. The ECG signals are expressed using isolated pulses or isolated pulses with a quasi-periodic sequence in nature. Due to baseline drift, power line interferences, and noises, the analysis of the ECG signal results in complications. These disturbances can influence the visual interpretation of the signal with that of the results obtained by computer-based offline analysis.

To filter the baseline drift available in the ECG signal, a high-pass linear phase filter may be used, but usage of a non-linear filter may be avoided, which results in the introduction of distortions to the filtered ECG signal. Baseline drift is majorly used in PQRST waveform changes and influences the accurate diagnosis of heart diseases. The instantaneous heart rate [55] can be calculated with the help of the R-wave, and it is detected by slope detection in R-wave.

The computer-based ECG signal analysis is needed to find the disease quickly caused by the heart. In this connection, the signal may be analyzed using MATLAB®, LabVIEW, and many other tools.

3.3.3.2 LabVIEW-Based ECG Signal Analysis

The patient affected by a cardiac problem needs to be monitored regularly. If the patient is in a remote area and it takes a lot of time to reach the hospital, the patient can be monitored from their home with any monitoring system to check and analyze the condition of the patient in regular intervals of time. The system will be used to monitor cardiac activities and send the obtained results to the doctors through the mail. The aim is to monitor the patient utilizing a low-cost design and effective implementation of an ECG monitoring system from the non-clinical environment with the doctor sitting in their chamber. The ECG signal obtained from the monitoring system can extract the parameters like amplitude and period of the PQRST waveforms to be analyzed. Also, with the help of a GUI-based system (LabVIEW), they can be displayed for monitoring [56].

The ECG signals are acquired through the output terminals of the sensors. The data from the sensors are acquired to the LabVIEW tool with the help of the DAQ system connected, and the data is stored in NITDMS file format for offline analysis. The ECG data collected from the electrodes are processed in the LabVIEW and used for proper diagnosis of the patient compared with the normal values of ECG signals as given in Table 3.1 [57].

Initially, the patient data are collected using the front panel (Figures 3.6–3.9) designed in LabVIEW, and the data collected by the front panel are processed

TABLE 3.1

Normal ECG Parameters and Abnormal ECG Parameters with Their Effects

Parameters	Duration (sec)	Abnormal parameters	Heart diseases
P wave	0.06–0.11	P wave absent	Atrial ectopic beats
PR Interval	0.12–0.20	Increased PR	AV block
QRS Complex	0.06–0.10	QRS < 0.12	Atrial fibrillation
ST Segment	0.12	ST elevation	myocardial infarction
QT Interval	0.36–0.44	Prolonged QRS duration	ventricular conduction abnormal
T wave	0.16	–	–

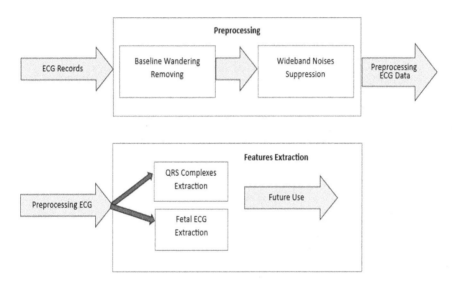

FIGURE 3.6   ECG signals using LabVIEW

in the circuit diagram created in the back panel; it is used to process the data collected [58].

The details of both patients as well as the doctor are already stored in the file directory and are initialized. The front panel is used to display the details of both doctor and patient from the file and shows in their respective columns. Once initiated the controls and indicators are set in the default values. To monitor the range of electrodes that falls from the minimum and maximum value the code has been generated, and once the electrode value of a patient exceeds a certain value or it falls below the average of the given range, the patient history automatically moves to critical condition. The values of the electrodes are stored in an Excel sheet for further process. The values of the electrodes in the Excel sheet are sent to the doctor through the mail if necessary.

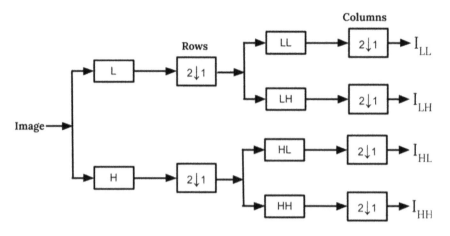

FIGURE 3.7   DWT wavelet transform flowchart

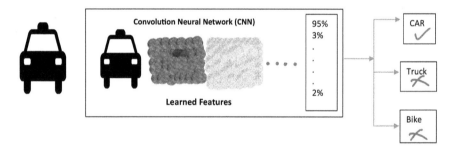

FIGURE 3.8   Block diagram of deep learning (Courtesy: MATLAB® Tool)

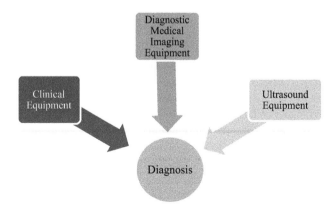

FIGURE 3.9   Methods of diagnostics

3.4   MEDICAL DIAGNOSTIC STRATEGY BY USING COMMUNICATION TECHNOLOGY

At present, the healthcare system gives rise to an open statement on health care, treatment methods, the nature of health complications, and pioneering in biomedical research for the betterment of human beings. The broad impacts of COVID-19 have introduced the world to concentrating on digitally functioning devices and switching to the more integrated development of products. Maximum accessibility and flexibility are provided by digital technologies in the healthcare system [59].

Advancements noted in AI data are recorded from patients making use of wearable devices and smartphones with the presence of Google platforms, Apple, and Amazon networks [60]. This increases communication between patients and healthcare experts. Nowadays, hospitals are more dependent on ICT, which decreases the gap between urban and rural sectors [61].

3.4.1   ECG SIGNAL ANALYSIS USING WAVELET TRANSFORM IN MATLAB

The analysis of ECG signals becomes more difficult due to the variation of morphological factors in the waveform in large numbers not only with different patients but also with the same patient at different time intervals. On analysis, the resultant ECG waveforms are different for the same patient, and they are the same for different types of beats.

The transform is mostly used in a wavelet-based transform, which is used to denoise and detect the trends among signals, breakdown points, and discontinuity of higher derivatives in signals [62, 63]. Here db4 wavelet is used on the ECG signal for the detection of impulse and its discontinuity of frequency elements. The impulse signal here is generated artificially with the predefined data of the ECG signal for our analysis purposes [64]. The db4 wavelet is used for the analysis of the signal in the frequency domain. Here third level decomposition is applied to the signal.

The denoising of the signal is achieved by DWT, and it can be done by the decomposition of the signal at a certain level and applying the threshold to the obtained DWT coefficients and finally reconstructing the signal to its original signal. Three procedures are carried out for denoising the signal; initially, the wavelet analysis method is applied to a noisy signal with level N, then thresholding is applied on each coefficient from 1 to N level, and finally the signal is synthesized with the help of altered detail coefficients with 1 to N level and approximation coefficients of even N. It is not possible to remove noisy signals with corruption.

We calculate the global threshold value for all levels by:

$$\delta = \sigma \sqrt{2 \log L}$$

Where the standard deviation of the DWT coefficients is expressed as σ and also the number of pixels or samples of the signal processed is expressed as L and the threshold values are estimated using the MATLAB tool.

The ECG signal is decomposed up to the third level by convolving it with a db2 filter, which involves down-sampling by a factor of 2. This process extracts both the detail and approximate coefficients. Normally approximation and detailed coefficients are obtained by low pass and high-pass filter g(.) at each level and further decomposed for the next level.

Analysis of the HRV (heart rate variability) signal with different resolutions is carried out on decomposition with elementary function both in time and frequency domains. These elementary functions are called wavelets. We performed a multilevel decomposition of the IHR (instantaneous heart rate) signal by DWT. Although the lowest frequency components of the IHR signal are used for the analysis of long-term modulation in the ANS (automatic nervous system), it leads to an effect on the power spectra of HRV signals. We used the wavelet transform method to de-trend the IHR signal.

The method proposed here can detect transients and artifacts in the signal. It provides a multi-resolution analysis. Since the behavior of the ANS can be tracked using DWT [65], this technique improves the understanding of how to interact with cardiovascular activity by automatic control systems. Since the wavelet technique gives better time-frequency resolution, we can also apply it to pattern recognition of ECG.

3.4.2 MONITORING AND ANALYSIS OF ELECTROCARDIOGRAM SIGNALS USING LabVIEW

ECG is one where the signal is generated since it is due to the electrical parameter present in the function of the heart, and it is recorded by the tool and conveys useful information when there is a change happened in PQRST waves. ECG signal analysis is widely used to diagnose diseases that happened in the heart, especially cardiac attacks. In this chapter, the function of the heart is analyzed by calculating the heart rate with (P, Q, R, S, & T) intervals while using ECG signals. Patients, especially those who suffered from cardiac issues, need to have regular and routine checkups to monitor their cardiac activities. During an emergency, if a patient requires first aid and needs to be rushed to the hospital, but there are no facilities available or the hospital is located in a remote area, it can make the patient uncomfortable and pose a risk to their life. In this situation, a monitoring system shall be needed to monitor the health condition, especially the cardiac-related disease, and update the doctor through email or any other mode. The mail received by the doctor acts as a tool to suggest to the patient when to take necessary safety measures and what first aid needs to be done. This work concentrates on implementing a low-cost and effective ECG monitoring system for frequent monitoring of the patient's cardiac activity at any time from any location, and the doctor can treat the patient from the place where he or she is located. The ECG parameters, such as amplitude level and period of the PQRST wave, are acquired and displayed on the GUI of LabVIEW. The ECG signals observed in the LabVIEW are given in Figure 3.6.

3.4.3 BIOMEDICAL IMAGE COMPRESSION BASED ON WAVELET TRANSFORM

Image compression is important in various applications including commercial, research, defense, and medical fields. Mostly the medical data are in the form of multidimensional data, which constitutes a large amount in data size, so in this connection an efficient system is created to process these types of data to store, retrieve, manage, and transmit. Hence compressing images while maintaining the maximum quality possible is very important for real-world applications. The data size can be reduced by compression on the medical data so that the diagnostics capabilities are not compromised. To compress the image by maintaining the quality of the image with less medical tolerance, the DWT-based system is proposed. Using this technique the noises like speckle, salt, and pepper noises in the ultrasound images can be reduced [66, 67]. The images are compressed with an emphasis on maintaining the quality rather than focusing on diminishing file size. The Huffman encoding technique is applied to the quantized coefficients, and the bits obtained are used to represent the compressed image that is stored and retrieved whenever it is needed. The DWT algorithm is best suited for a more efficient way to compress an image in a lossless technique [68]. Figure 3.7 describes the wavelet transform workflow. As the wavelets are used in this compression, all the elements in the image are compressed while retaining the quality.

3.4.4 Deep Learning for Cardiac Imaging

Deep learning is an algorithm that enables the study of information, estimate or prediction of future happening, decision-making, or the usage of the dataset (called training data) that is used to identify complex patterns.

A machine learning technique becomes a powerful tool for the extraction of useful knowledge and making suitable decisions from big data. As it has increased in technical aspects, deep learning supports machine learning and is a connecting bridge to integrating big machinery data with that of intelligent machine mediator health monitoring. Deep learning attempts modeling data with high-level representations and predicts patterns by arranging multiple layers of information using hierarchical architectures. Nowadays deep learning is adopted in a variety of applications like bioinformatics, computer vision, audio recognition, and automatic speech recognition.

Neural network architectures are widely used in deep learning algorithms, and they use more than 150 hidden layers rather than traditional neural networks. Convolutional neural networks (CNN) are mostly used as deep neural networks, and the input data are convolves with learned features, and 2D data are processed using 2D convolutional layers.

Using CNN the ECG signal may be easily classified for detection and diagnosis of the signals. It is proved that deep learning is widely used to detect R waves for the analysis of ECG arrhythmia classification.

The big challenge for researchers is the implementation of the deep learning technique in ECG signals. Deep learning extends the limitation in access to the raw dataset and also needs huge training and a specific platform for the computational process.

The different input data combinations for the ECG signal analysis were the raw ECG signal and extracted QRS complexes, along with entropy-based features calculated both in raw signals of ECG and also the extracted QRS complexes. In research aspects normally entropy-based features with neural networks act a significant role in the analysis of ECG signals.

CNN can be proposed to use the extracted QRS complexes and entropy-based features. Normally 12-lead signal can be used for the detection and estimation of R-wave using the R-wave detection algorithm and K-mean algorithm. With the help of these algorithms, the r-peak position estimation can be generated.

3.5 APPLICATION OF MACHINE LEARNING FOR CARDIAC IMAGING

According to the data published by the WHO, cardiovascular diseases (CVDs) are the major cause of morbidity and death globally. In the year 2019, around 17.9 million people lost their lives due to CVDs, which represented 32% of all global death. The death rate was recorded due to heart attack and stroke [69]. The mortality rate is increasing every year. Advances in the identification CVDs enable perfect assessment and treatment of cardiovascular diseases. Medical imaging techniques such as CT, MRI, and ultrasound methods are widely used to find out the anatomy of cardiac structures, their movement patterns, and functional aspects and to provide support for prognosis, monitor the disease, diagnose and find better options for therapy [69]. The use of artificial intelligence, deep learning, and machine learning demonstrated a powerful tool for interpreting and analyzing medical images, identifying and predicting diseases, and treating diseases. Echocardiography serves as the first line of diagnostic imaging, and it typically acts as an integral part of cardiac medical practice [70]. Many echocardiographic variables, together with speckle tracking and vector flow mapping have made it difficult for physicians to evaluate the outcomes [71]. The use of a variety of algorithms with many modalities has grown exponentially. A CNN was employed to evaluate the 14035 ECGs over the period of ten years [72]. Using the random forest ML method, Samad et al. predicted survival after ECG in a population of 171510 patients [73]. Motwani et al. investigated the usage of a machine learning algorithm to prognosticate five-year mortality in CT scans in comparison to traditional cardiac measures for patients of 10030 with possible CAD [74]. For predicting five-year all-cause death, the machine learning algorithm showed a statistically significant higher AUC when compared to the fractional flow reserve. A team of experts predicted cardiovascular problems in 8844 patients using a ML algorithm [75]. There are some research works that exhibit the application of machine learning. Bai et al. performed a fully convolutional network to examine the CMR images [76]. To assess cardiac mass and function metrics from various datasets, Winther et al. performed a deep learning machine learning system to segment the right ventricular, left ventricular, and epicardium [77].

3.6 DIAGNOSTIC CHALLENGES IN HEALTHCARE SYSTEM APPLICATIONS

Today, the diagnosis of a patient by a physician depends on aided medical equipment: clinical, medical imaging, and ultrasound machines. Also, the development of ICT maximizes the nature of care, extends patient security, and decreases the expense for working and regulatory aspects.

FIGURE 3.10 Use of ICT in health care

The ICT gadgets were made easy to understand and are used by a huge population around the globe thus reducing the communication gap. Consequently, openness to data has become straightforward utilizing ICT, and individuals end up more relaxed while availing themselves of medical care services.

The use of ICT in health care can be categorized into four main streams as shown in Figure 3.10, such as 1) Health & Education, 2) Hospital Management System, 3) Health Research, and 4) Health Data Management.

3.7 A POTENTIAL SOLUTION TO COMMUNICATION CHALLENGES IN THE HEALTHCARE SYSTEM

The WHO defined electronic health (eHealth) as "the cost-effective and secure use of information and communications technologies in support of health and health-related fields, including health-care services, health surveillance, health literature, health education, knowledge and research" [78].

Physicians can observe and predict the treatment system using computer-based technology. From cosmetic-related reconstructive to dental care, modeling provides the appropriate solution to patients. Many of the medical instruments are incorporated with software, and the results of the medical observations are documented properly. The laser technology and drug administration involved a more system-based work-force. ICT gives support to the healthcare system in a remarkable manner. More areas of ICT tools engaged in healthcare system includes electronic records of medical and health system, health cards of patients, mobile phone and sensor-linked technology to monitor health system, and educational and health networks based on the IoT.

The demand is expected to exceed 100 billion connections within ten years. There has been a huge shortage of data faced during recent years that can be fulfilled by fifth-generation networks, and it is considered to be ultra-fast, reliable, with high transmitting capacity and low latency. This facility is provided with 5G and leads to the Worldwide Wireless Web (WWWW) [79].

3.8 CONCLUSION

Health care in the global community is undergoing profound, unimaginable changes at the grassroots level. The coordination and consolidation of technology to the public is essential to know the patterns of development and proper usage by the population. The present days are almost all fields blended with totally computer-based diagnosis, documentation, and knowledge sharing. This chapter encompasses the possible interchanging of novel technologies giving way to understanding the needs of society catered by experts from various disciplines. A holistic approach in the field of the healthcare system is to provide important decision taking points to meet the current requirement in the point-specific outcome.

REFERENCES

[1] Digital India. 2021. https://digitalindia.gov.in/ebook/5_years_of_Digital_India_Book.pdf.
[2] National health profile of India, 2018, Central Bureau of Health Intelligence; Young A, et al. A census of actively licensed physicians in the United States, 2016. J Med Reg. June 2017;103(2).
[3] WHO. *Global health workforce statistics*. World Health Organization, 2016.
[4] Li, D. 5G and intelligence medicine – how the next generation of wireless technology will reconstruct healthcare? Precis Clin Med. 2019;2:205–208. https://doi.org/10.1093/pcmedi/pbz020
[5] Ahad A, Tahir M, Yau K-LA. 5G-based smart healthcare network: architecture, taxonomy, challenges and future research directions. IEEE Access. 2019;7:100747–100762. https://doi.org/10.1109/ACCESS.2019.2930628.
[6] WHO. 2020. www.who.int/publications/i/item/environmentally-sustainable-health-systems.
[7] DST (Department of Science and Technology), India. *Research and Development Statistics, 2019–2020*. Government of India Ministry of Science & Technology Department of Science & Technology. December 2020.
[8] National Commissions Policy. 2018. https://dot.gov.in/sites/default/files/EnglishPolicy-NDCP.pdf.
[9] TRAI. *Yearly performance indicators Indian telecom sector*. Fifth edition. Telecom Regulatory Authority of India, 2020.
[10] Ambrosino L, Colantuono C, Diretto G, Fiore A, Chiusano ML. Bioinformatics resources for plant abiotic stress responses: state of the art and opportunities in the fast evolving-omics era. Plants. 2020;9:591. https://doi.org/10.3390/plants9050591.
[11] Hester RL, Brown AJ, Husband L, Iliescu R, Pruett D, Summers R, Coleman TG. HumMod: a modeling environment for the simulation of integrative human physiology. Front Physiol. 2011 April 13;2:12. https://doi.org/10.3389/fphys.2011.00012. PMID: 21647209; PMCID: PMC3082131.
[12] Pang Z, Chong J, Zhou G, de Lima Morais DA, Chang L, Barrette M, Gauthier C, Jacques P-É, Li S, Xia J. MetaboAnalyst 5.0: narrowing the gap between raw spectra and functional insights. *Nucleic Acids Res*. 2 July 2021;49(W1):W388–W396. https://doi.org/10.1093/nar/gkab382.

[13] Fabregat A, Sidiropoulos K, Viteri, G, et al. Reactome pathway analysis: a high-performance in-memory approach. BMC Bioinform. 2017;18:142. https://doi.org/10.1186/s12859-017-1559-2.

[14] Cutillo CM, Sharma KR, Foschini L, et al. Machine intelligence in healthcare – perspectives on trustworthiness, explainability, usability, and transparency. npj Digit Med. 2020;3:47. https://doi.org/10.1038/s41746-020-0254-2.

[15] Wei JW, Tafe LJ, Linnik YA, Vaickus LJ, Tomita N, Hassanpour S. Pathologist-level classification of histologic patterns on resected lung adenocarcinoma slides with deep neural networks. Sci Rep. 2019;9(1):1–8.

[16] Coudray N, Ocampo PS, Sakellaropoulos T, et al. Classification and mutation prediction from non – small cell lung cancer histopathology images using deep learning. Nat Med. 2018;24(10):1559–1567.

[17] Korbar B, Olofson AM, Miraflor AP, et al. Deep learning for classification of colorectal polyps on whole-slide images. J Pathol Inform. 2017;8:30.

[18] Achi HE, Belousova T, Chen L, et al. Automated diagnosis of lymphoma with digital pathology images using deep learning. Ann Clin Lab Sci. 2019;49(2):153–160.

[19] Veta M, Heng YJ, Stathonikos N, et al. Predicting breast tumor proliferation from whole-slide images: the TUPAC16 challenge. Med Image Anal. 2019;54:111–121.

[20] Liu Y, Kohlberger T, Norouzi M, et al. Artificial intelligence-based breast cancer nodal metastasis detection: insights into the black box for pathologists. Arch Pathol Lab Med. 2019;143(7):859–868.

[21] Steiner DF, MacDonald R, Liu Y, et al. Impact of deep learning assistance on the histopathologic review of lymph nodes for metastatic breast cancer. Am J Surg Pathol. 2018;42(12):1636–1646.

[22] Hasnain Z, Mason J, Gill K, et al. Machine learning models for predicting post-cystectomy recurrence and survival in bladder cancer patients. PLoS One. 2019;14(2):e0210976.

[23] Brinton LA, Fan S, Karssemeijer N, et al. Using deep convolutional neural networks to identify and classify tumor-associated stroma in diagnostic breast biopsies. Mod Pathol. 2018;31(10):1502–1512.

[24] Yu KH, Zhang C, Berry GJ, et al. Predicting non-small cell lung cancer prognosis by fully automated microscopic pathology image features. Nat Comm. 2016;7:1–10.

[25] Mobadersany P, Yousefi S, Amgad M, et al. Predicting cancer outcomes from histology and genomics using convolutional networks. Proc Natl Acad Sci USA. 2018;115(13): E2970–E2979.

[26] Bera K, Schalper KA, Rimm DL, Velcheti V, Madabhushi A. Artificial intelligence in digital pathology – new tools for diagnosis and precision oncology. Nat Rev Clin Oncol. 2019;16(11):703–715.

[27] Bejnordi BE, Veta M, Van Diest PJ, et al. Diagnostic assessment of deep learning algorithms for detection of lymph node metastases in women with breast cancer. JAMA. 2017;318(22):2199–2210.

[28] Serag A, Ion-Margineanu A, Qureshi H, et al. Translational AI and deep learning in diagnostic pathology. Front Med (Lausanne). 2019;6:185.

[29] Fu Y, Jung AW, Torne RV, et al. Pan-cancer computational histopathology reveals mutations, tumor composition and prognosis. Nat Cancer. 2020;1:800–810.

[30] Kather JN, Heij LR, Grabsch HI, et al. Pan-cancer image-based detection of clinically actionable genetic alterations. Nat Cancer. 2020;1:789–799.

[31] Acs B, Hartman J. Next generation pathology: artificial intelligence enhances histopathology practice. J Pathol. 2020;250(1):7–8.

[32] Colling R, Pitman H, Oien K, et al. Artificial intelligence in digital pathology: a roadmap to routine use in clinical practice. J Pathol. 2019;249(2):143–150.

[33] Goldstein BA, Navar AM, Carter RE. Moving beyond regression techniques in cardio-vascular risk prediction: applying machine learning to address analytic challenges. Eur Heart J. 2017;38(23):1805–1814.

[34] Richardson A, Signor BM, Lidbury BA, Badrick T. Clinical chemistry in higher dimensions: machine-learning and enhanced prediction from routine clinical chemistry data. Clin Biochem. 2016;49(16–17):1213–1220.

[35] Wilkes EH, Rumsby G, Woodward GM. Using machine learning to aid the interpretation of urine steroid profiles. Clin Chem. 2018;64(11):1586–1595.

[36] Cabitza F, Banfi G. Machine learning in laboratory medicine: waiting for the flood. Clin Chem Lab Med. 2018;56(4):516–524.

[37] Luo Y, Szolovits P, Dighe AS, Baron JM. Using machine learning to predict laboratory test results. Am J Clin Pathol. 2016;145(6):778–788.

[38] Yu M, Bazydlo LAL, Bruns DE, Harrison JHJ. Streamlining quality review of mass spectrometry data in the clinical laboratory by use of machine learning. Arch Pathol Lab Med. 2019;143(8):990–998.

[39] Landau MS, Pantanowitz L. Artificial intelligence in cytopathology: a review of the literature and overview of commercial landscape. J Am Soc Cytopathol. 2019;8:230–241.

[40] Houssami N, Kirkpatrick-Jones G, Noguchi N, Lee CI. Artificial intelligence (AI) for the early detection of breast cancer: a scoping review to assess AI's potential in breast screening practice. Expert Rev Med Devices. 2019;16:351–362.

[41] Jang HJ, Cho KO. Applications of deep learning for the analysis of medical data. Arch Pharm Res. 2019;42:492–504.

[42] Campanella G, Hanna MG, Geneslaw L, Miraflor A, Werneck Krauss Silva V, Busam KJ, et al. Clinical-grade computational pathology using weakly supervised deep learning on whole slide images. Nat Med. 2019;25:1301–1309.

[43] Wildeboer RR, van Sloun RJG, Wijkstra H, Mischi M. Artificial intelligence in multiparametric prostate cancer imaging with focus on deep-learning methods. Comput Methods Programs Biomed. 2020;189:105316.

[44] Korbar B, Olofson AM, Miraflor AP, Nicka CM, Suriawinata MA, Torresani L, et al. Deep learning for classification of colorectal polyps on whole-slide images. J Pathol Inform. 2017;8:30.

[45] Bychkov D, Linder N, Turkki R, Nordling S, Kovanen PE, Verrill C, et al. Deep learning based tissue analysis predicts outcome in colorectal cancer. Sci Rep. 2018;8:3395.

[46] Wang DY, Khosla A, Gargeya R, Irshad H, Beck AH. Deep learning for identifying metastatic breast cancer. arXiv. 2016. https://arxiv.org/abs/1606.05718

[47] Niazi MKK, Parwani AV, Gurcan MN. Digital pathology and artificial intelligence. Lancet Oncol. 2019;20:e253–e261.

[48] Turck CW, Mak TD, Goudarzi M, Salek RM, Cheema AK. The ABRF metabolomics research group 2016 exploratory study: investigation of data analysis methods for untargeted metabolomics. Metabolites. 2020;10(4):128. https://doi.org/10.3390/metabo10040128

[49] Van den Berg RA, Hoefsloot HC, Westerhuis JA, Smilde AK, van der Werf MJ. Centering, scaling, andtransformations: improving the biological information content of metabolomics data. BMC Genom. 2006;7(1):142. https://doi.org/10.1186/1471-2164-7-142.

[50] Pang Z, Chong J, Zhou G, Morais D, Chang L, Barrette M, Gauthier C, Jacques P-É, Li S, Xia J (Jeff). MetaboAnalyst 5.0: narrowing the gap between raw spectra and functional insights. Nucleic Acids Res. 2021;49. https://doi.org/10.1093/nar/gkab382.

[51] Xia J, Psychogios N, Young N, Wishart DS. MetaboAnalyst: a web server for metabolomic data analysisand interpretation. Nucleic Acids Res. 2009;37(suppl_2):W652–W660. https://doi.org/10.1093/nar/gkp356.

[52] Haw R, Hermjakob H, D'Eustachio P, Stein L. Reactome pathway analysis to enrich biological discovery in proteomics data sets. Proteomics. 2011;11(18):3598–3613. https://doi.org/10.1002/pmic.201100066.

[53] Davenport T, Kalakota R. The potential for artificial intelligence in healthcare. Future Healthc J. 2019;6(2):94–98.

[54] Rashid F, Khalid A, Design and implementation of real-time electrocardiogram monitoring system for telemedicine services. Indian J Sci Technol. 2019;2(16). https://doi.org/10.17485/ijst/2019/v12i16/141689.

[55] Aydın SG, Kaya T, Güler H. Heart rate variability (HRV) based feature extraction for congestive heart failure. Int J Comput Electr Eng (IJCEE). 2016;8(4):275–285. ISSN: 1793-8163, https://doi.org/10.17706/IJCEE.

[56] Ay AN, Yildiz MZ, Boru, B. Real-time feature extraction of ECG signals using NI LabVIEW. Sakarya Univ J Sci. 2017. https://doi.org/10.1698saufenbilder.287418.

[57] Hernandez AI, Mora F, Villegas M, Passariello G, Carrault G. Real-time ECG transmission via Internet for nonclinical applications. IEEE Trans Inf Technol Biomed. 2016;5(3):253–257. https://doi.org/10.1109/4233.945297.

[58] Deshmukh A, Gandole Y. ECG feature extraction using NI lab-view biomedical workbench. Int J Recent Sci Res. August 2015;6(8):5603–5607.

[59] Senbekov M, Zhanaliyeva M, Saliev T, Bukeyeva Z, Aitenova N, lmabayeva A, Toishibekov Y, Fakhradiyev I. The recent progress and applications of digital technologies in healthcare: a review. Int J Telemed Appl. 2020;2020:18. Article ID 8830200. https://doi.org/10.1155/2020/8830200.

[60] Castro GM, Schrandt S, Improving diagnosis through technology. Health Manag. 2020;20(6).

[61] El-Kareh R, Hasan O, Schiff GD. Use of health information technology to reduce diagnostic errors. BMJ Qual Saf. https://qualitysafety.bmj.com/content/22/Suppl_2/ii40.

[62] Kumar A, Komaragiri R, Kumar M. Design of wavelet transform based electrocardiogram monitoring system. J Adv SOTA Sci Eng Meas Autom. 2018;80:381–398.

[63] Rashid F, Khalid A. Design and implementation of real-time electrocardiogram monitoring system for telemedicine services. Indian J Sci Technol. 2019 Apr;12(16):1–6.

[64] Nagai S, Anzai D, Wang J. Motion artefact removals for wearable ECG using stationary wavelet transform. J Healthc Technol Lett. 2017;4:138–141.

[65] Mothi R, Karthikeyan M. Protection of bio medical iris image using watermarking and cryptography with WPT. Int J Meas. 2019;136:67–73. Elsevier Publications.

[66] Eben Sophia P, Anitha J. Contextual medical image compression using normalized wavelet-transform coefficients and prediction. IETE J Res. 2017 Sep 3;63(5):671–683.

[67] Mothi R. Biometric image protection using optimal crypto-watermarking system. Int J Imaging Sci Eng. 2020;11:1–7.

[68] Vaishnav M, Kamargaonkar C, Sharma M. Medical image compression using dual tree complex wavelet transform and arithmetic coding technique. Int J Sci Res Compu Sci. 2017 May;2(3):172–176.

[69] Chen C, Qin C, Qiu H, Tarroni G, Duan J, Bai W, Rueckert D. Deep learning for cardiac image segmentation: a review. Front Cardiovasc Med. 2020;7:25. https://doi.org/10.3389/fcvm.2020.00025

[70] Seetharam K, Kagiyama N, Sengupta PP. Application of mobile health, telemedicine and artificial intelligence to echocardiography. Echo Res Pract. 2019;6:R41–R52.

[71] Cho JS, Ashraf M, Shrestha S, et al. The classification of intracardiac vortex structure and function using the patient similarity analysis. J Am Coll Cardiol. 2019;73(Suppl 1):1436.

[72] Zhang J, Gajjala S, Agrawal P, et al. Fully automated echocardiogram interpretation in clinical practice. Circulation. 2018;138:1623–1635.

[73] Samad MD, Ulloa A, Wehner GJ, et al. Predicting survival from large echocardiography and electronic health record datasets: optimization with machine learning. JACC Cardiovasc Imaging. 2019;12:681–689.

[74] Motwani M, Dey D, Berman DS, et al. Machine learning for prediction of all-cause mortality in patients with suspected coronary artery disease: a 5-year multicentre prospective registry analysis. Eur Heart J. 2017;38:500–507.

[75] Van Rosendael AR, Maliakal G, Kolli KK, et al. Maximization of the usage of coronary CTA derived plaque information using a machine learning based algorithm to improve risk stratification; insights from the CONFIRM registry. J Cardiovasc Comput Tomogr. 2018;12:204–209.

[76] Bai W, Sinclair M, Tarroni G, et al. Automated cardiovascular magnetic resonance image analysis with fully convolutional networks. J Cardiovasc Magn Reson. 2018;20:65.

[77] Winther HB, Hundt C, Schmidt B, et al. ν-net: deep learning for generalized biventricular mass and function parameters using multicenter cardiac MRI data. JACC Cardiovasc Imaging. 2018;11:1036–1038.

[78] WHO. *Atlas eHealth country profiles: based on the findings of the second global survey on eHealth*. Global Observatory for eHealth Series 1. World Health Organization; 2010.

[79] Gandewar, Swaroop & Hiware, Rahul & Palekar, Sangeeta. (2017). 5G : World Wide Wireless Web. 10.24001/ijaems.icsesd2017.100.

4 A Survey
Recent Advances and Clinical Applications of Deep Learning in Medical Image Analysis

P. Radha Jayalakshmi and P. S. Rajakumar

4.1 INTRODUCTION

In the field of medical science [1], there has been a tremendous increase of image data from several sources, which includes X-ray, positron emission tomography (PET), ultrasound images, nuclear medicine image, magnetic resonance image (MRI), magnetic resonance angiography (MRA), CT (computed tomography), and fMRI (functional MRI). This enormous amount of data from multiple sources needs to be analyzed, which is a vital step in a clinical diagnosis and also in decision-making in the healthcare industry.

Due to the swift growth of artificial intelligence technology, AI being used to extract medical data has been identified as a significant trend in the healthcare sector. AI includes machine learning, which allows machines to learn from experiences and acquire skills without the need for human intervention. A part of machine learning (ML) is called deep learning (DL), and it offers a powerful method for automatically analyzing medical images for the diagnosis or evaluation of a disease [2, 3].

Earlier, automated approaches for analyzing medical images to diagnose diseases were developed based on conventional machine learning techniques [4]. However, these conventional machine learning methods weren't able to produce the expected results since complex pictures were involved. An evolving technology in machine learning is deep learning, which has been offering several cutting-edge solutions for the most accurate outcomes.

In this chapter, various popular imaging modalities and technologies for particular task classification, recognition, and segmentation in the context of medical image analysis are explained. This chapter also covers the different deep learning algorithms like self-organizing maps (SOMs), convolutional neural networks (CNNs), radial basis function networks (RBFNs), restricted Boltzmann machines (RBMs), recurrent neural networks (RNNs), generative adversarial networks (GANs), multilayer perceptrons (MLPs), autoencoders, long short-term memory networks (LSTMs), and deep belief networks (DBNs).

DOI: 10.1201/9781003343172-4

4.1.1 UNDERSTANDING THE CONCEPT OF DEEP LEARNING

Deep learning, occasionally called "deep structured learning", is a more extensive group of artificial neural network-based machine learning methods. This topic is illustrated diagrammatically in Figure 4.1.

Artificial intelligence: The name artificial intelligence, or AI, is employed to describe systems or robots that imitate human intelligence in order to carry out tasks and can fine tune themselves based on the data they gather.

Machine Learning: Artificial intelligence includes machine learning, in which researchers study how computers may learn on their own. Algorithms used in machine learning produce predictions based on data and gain expertise from it.

Deep Learning: Deep learning is a section of machine learning algorithms that employ neural networks to identify patterns in the information that is collected from various sources and predict outcomes.

Deep learning systems process a lot of data and include several intricate mathematical computations; they demand strong hardware. However, even with such advanced hardware, training a neural network can take weeks.

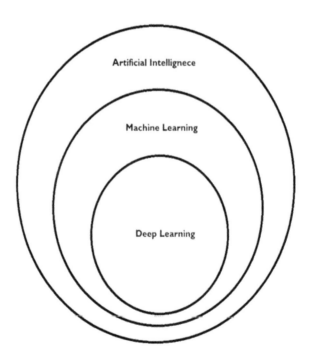

FIGURE 4.1 Artificial intelligence/machine learning/deep learning

From raw input data, DL can automatically extract key features. Cognitive and information theories served as the foundation for the development of DL algorithms. The two main traits of DL are as follows:

1. Several processing layers, each of which is capable of learning distinct data aspects at varying levels of abstraction
2. Learning of feature presentations on each layer may be unsupervised or supervised.

4.1.2 Why Deep Learning

Deep learning techniques are more effective than machine learning techniques because of the following reasons.

Data must be preprocessed in typical machine learning methods, a process called feature extraction. Preprocessing is a challenging task since it necessitates a thorough understanding of the problem domain. For the best results, this preprocessing layer needs to be modified, examined, and improved across numerous iterations.

Artificial neural networks for deep learning don't entail the feature extraction stage. The layers have the ability to directly and independently learn an implicit representation of the raw data. Figure 4.2 represents the aforementioned.

Complex issues like picture categorization, object detection, or NLP tasks can be resolved using deep learning. Deep learning truly takes advantage of the deep neural network, which allows for the mining of increasingly complicated information and characteristics from a problem statement as it gets deeper (Figure 4.3).

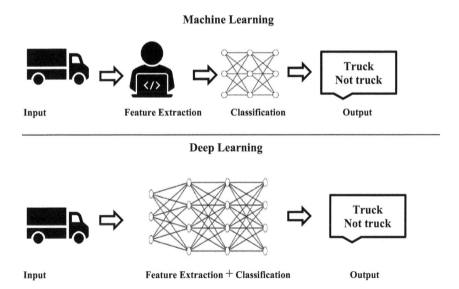

FIGURE 4.2 Comparison of machine learning and deep learning

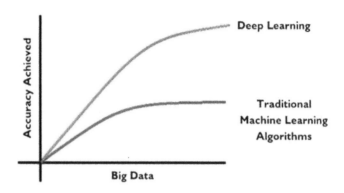

FIGURE 4.3   Machine learning vs deep learning

Deep learning has the great benefit of being fueled by enormous amounts of data gathered through smart phones and various social media platforms like Facebook, Instagram, or WhatsApp. This is a key factor in understanding why deep learning is becoming so popular. We can surely accomplish a lot of things and address a variety of issues by utilizing this vast amount of data. New deep learning techniques will provide huge opportunities for new innovations in the big data era.

4.1.3   How Deep Learning Works

Millions of neurons make up a human brain. Neurons are networked nerve cells that process and transmit electrical and chemical impulses in the human brain. Dendrites are extensions that take information from neighboring neurons. In 1957, an American scientist, Franck Rosenblatt, inspired by these biological processes in a neuron, developed the idea of the perceptron at Cornell Aeronautical Laboratory. A mathematical operation called a perceptron is an artificial neuron that is based on the concept of biological neurons as shown in Figure 4.4. Every neuron collects inputs, weighs each one individually, adds them all together, and then transfers the total through a non-linear function to generate an outcome.

4.2   PERCEPTRON

Perceptron was designed by Mr. Frank Rosenblatt to carry out certain computations to identify input data capabilities or business intellect. The perceptron model is recognized as an outstanding and simplistic form of artificial neural networks. A linear machine learning algorithm called the perceptron is used for supervised learning for different binary classifiers. The four fundamental elements of a perceptron are the input data, weights and bias, net sum, and an activation function. With the help of the algorithm, neurons can learn new elements and process them one by one while training.

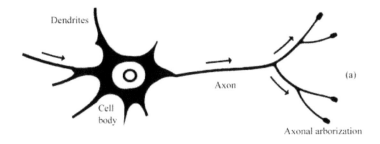

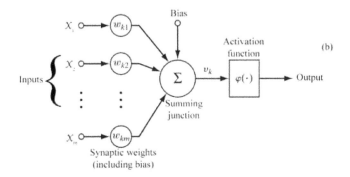

FIGURE 4.4 Similarity between biological and artificial neural networks

A perceptron takes two steps to produce output.

1. The first step involves multiplying the given input values by the equivalent weights and totaling them all up. The result is known as weighted sum, $\Sigma wi*xi$, or $x1*w1 + x2*w2 +\ldots wn*xn$. Additionally, bias is added to this sum, i.e. $\Sigma wi*xi + b$.
2. In the next step, an activation function f is applied to the aforementioned result, i.e. $Y = f(\Sigma wi*xi+ b)$.

There are two kinds of perceptron models:

1. Single-layer perceptron model: The capacity to linearly classify input is the feature of a single-layer perceptron. To pre-classify the input using the learnt weights, this form of model just employs a single hyperplane line.
2. Multilayer perceptron model: The ability of the multilayer perceptron to classify inputs using layers is one of its defining features. This kind of method, which requires a lot of processing power, enables computers to simultaneously classify inputs using many layers.

4.2.1 CHARACTERISTICS OF PERCEPTRON

1. A machine learning algorithm called perceptron is used to learn binary classifiers under supervision.
2. The weight coefficient is automatically learned in a perceptron.
3. Weights are first multiplied by input features to determine whether to fire the neuron or not.
4. To determine if the weight function is larger than zero, a step rule is applied by the activation function.
5. In order to differentiate among the two linearly distinguishable classes, (+1) and (−1), the linear decision boundary is drawn.
6. It must have an output signal if the total of all input values is greater than the beginning value; otherwise, no output will be displayed.

4.2.2 CONFINES OF THE PERCEPTRON

- The hard-limit transfer function of a perceptron limits the output to a binary number (0 or 1) alone.
- Perceptrons can only classify vector sets that can be linearly separated. If a plane or line can be formed to divide the input vectors into the relevant groups, then the vectors are linearly separable. If the vectors are not linearly separable, learning will never advance to the point where all vectors are accurately categorized. However, it has been shown that if the vectors are linearly separable, adaptive perceptrons will always find a solution in a finite amount of time. It is difficult to classify objects accurately when the input vectors are non-linear.

4.3 NEURAL NETWORK

Perceptrons are considered the basic building blocks of artificial neural networks. The first stage in neural networks is defined by the perceptron. Perceptron was intended to produce a single binary output from a number of binary inputs (0 or 1). The concept was that each input should be given a separate weight to signify its relative importance, and that the aggregate of those weights should be above a threshold before a decision, such as true or false, is made (0 or 1). Artificial neurons are combined to form a neural network. These multi-layers perceptrons are capable of making extremely complex decisions.

Layers of nodes comprise neural networks, much like the neurons that make up the human brain. Different layer nodes are connected to neighboring layer nodes. The number of layers in the network determines how deep it is considered to be. In the human brain, a single neuron takes in thousands of signals from other neurons. Signals move between nodes and assign matching weights in an artificial neural network. A node with a higher weight will have a larger impression on the nodes in the layer below it. The weighted inputs are combined to create an output in the final layer.

A simple neural network has three layers: the input layer, hidden layer, and output layer, which are associated by artificial neurons as shown in Figure 4.5.

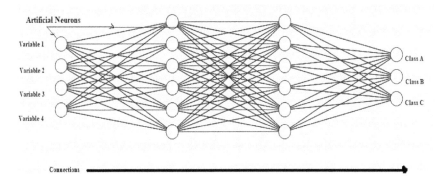

FIGURE 4.5 Artificial neurons

Input Layer: Data entering an artificial neural network is done through an input layer. Data is processed, analyzed, or classified by input nodes before being forwarded to the following layer.

Hidden Layer: The input layer or even additional hidden layers can be used as the input for hidden layers. Artificial neural networks may contain numerous hidden layers. The output from each hidden layer is assessed, refined, and then forwarded to the following layer.

Output Layer: An output layer presents the overall outcome of the artificial neural network's data processing. It may include one or more nodes. For instance, if the classification task is binary (yes/no), the output layer will have a single output node that will indicate whether the outcome is 1 or 0. The output layer could have more than one output node if we are working with a multi-class classification problem.

4.4 CLASSIFICATION OF DEEP LEARNING ARCHITECTURE

Figure 4.6 categorizes deep learning architectures into supervised and unsupervised learning and introduces a number of well-known deep learning algorithms. Deep learning algorithms use nearly any type of data and need a lot of knowledge and processing power to tackle complex problems. The top deep learning algorithms will now be examined in more detail.

4.4.1 SUPERVISED DEEP LEARNING

During the training stage of the machine learning lifecycle, supervised machine learning requires tagged input and output data. A data scientist would frequently label this training data at the preprocessing stage before it is employed to train and evaluate the proposed model. Once the model has learned how the input and output data are related, it may be used to categorize new and unseen datasets and predict results.

Its name, "supervised machine learning", refers to the fact that at least some of this method requires human supervision. Most of the data that exists is unlabeled,

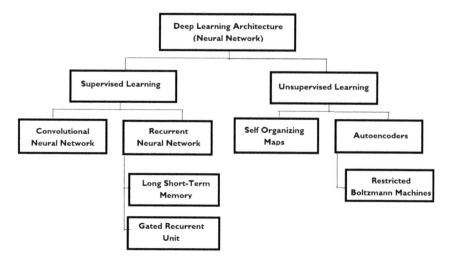

FIGURE 4.6   Deep learning architectures

raw information. Human input is typically needed to precisely label data ready for supervised learning. Naturally, since vast arrays of precisely labelled training data are required, this method can be resource- intensive. Classification and regression issues are two different types of supervised learning issues.

Real-world activities including spam filtering, fraud detection, risk assessment, and image categorization can benefit from supervised learning. For example, if we have a dataset of various shapes, such as squares, hexagons, and pentagons, the model must now be trained for each shape, which is the first stage.

- The given shape will be referred to as a Square if it has four sides and all of those sides are equal.
- A pentagon is the name given to a particular form if it has five sides.
- The given shape will be referred to be a hexagon if it has six equal sides.

After training, we now use the test set to put our model to the test, and the model's job is to recognize the shape. The computer has already been educated on many forms, so when it encounters a new shape, it categorizes it based on the number of its sides and predicts the outcome.

4.4.2   UNSUPERVISED DEEP LEARNING

Unsupervised learning aims to discover the underlying construction of a dataset, classify the data into groups founded on their similarities, and represent the dataset in a compressed style. Unlike supervised learning, models themselves glean insights and hidden patterns from the collected data. It is comparable to acquiring new knowledge in the human brain while learning new information. Three primary tasks – clustering, association, and dimensionality reduction – are carried out via unsupervised learning models.

TABLE 4.1
Study of Different Deep Learning Algorithms

Name of the algorithms	Type	Used Areas	Working	Pros	Cons
Convolutional neural networks (CNNs)	Supervised learning	Image recognition and computer vision	1. Convolutional operation with ReLU activation function 2. Pooling 3. Flattening fully connected layer	Results are more accurate when compared to other ML techniques, notably for image/object recognition use cases	Very high computation power is needed for ConvNet training; consequently, not very economical
Long short-term memory network (LSTM)	Supervised learning	Speech recognition, music composition, and pharmaceutical development	1. They start by forgetting pointless details of the prior condition 2. Then, they update the cell-state values in a selected manner. 3. Lastly, the output of specific cell state components	When compared to RNN, can handle the information in memory for a long time	The model must be trained using a lot of resources and computation power
Recurrent neural networks (RNNs)	Supervised learning	Image captioning [6, 7], time series analysis, NLP, handwritten recognition and machine translation	1. The result at time t-1 sends into the input at time t 2. In a similar manner, the input at time t+1 is fed by the output at time t 3. RNNs are able to handle inputs of any length 4. Older data are taken into account in the computation, and the size of the model does not increase as the input size rises	Time series prediction relies heavily on the ability to retain information over the training period Input size and model size do not scale together inputs of any length can be processed	Computation takes time due to its repetitive nature Retrieving information from a long time ago is challenging

(Continued)

TABLE 4.1 (Continued)
Study of Different Deep Learning Algorithms

Name of the algorithms	Type	Used Areas	Working	Pros	Cons
Generative adversarial networks (GANs)	Supervised learning	Video game developing, creating realistic cartoon character, recreating lower resolution old video games into 4k or higher resolution via image training	1. The discriminator gains the ability to differentiate between the real sample data and the generator's bogus data. 2. The originator creates bogus data during early training, the discriminator quickly picks up on the fact that it is untrue. 3. In order to update the model, The findings are delivered to the generator and discriminator by the GAN	Capable of understanding the internal complex and cluttered distributions of any data Can determine the distance between items as well as identify them	When new data is generated from the old data, there is no evaluation metric to assess the output's accuracy. The training of models requires a lot of computation and time
Multilayer perceptrons (MLPs)	Supervised learning	Speech- identification, digital image-identification, and machine- translation programme	1. Simplest deep learning method (with single hidden layer) 2. A kind of neural feed-forward network	Unlike other models that are based on probability, do not make any assumptions about probability density functions (PDF) Can distinguish between data that cannot be separated linearly	The network may become trapped in a local minimum when updating layer weights, which can reduce accuracy The hard-limit transfer function means that the perceptrons can only produce outputs of 0 and 1

| Radial basis function networks (RBFNs) | Unsupervised learning | Classification, regression, and time-series prediction | 1. The result at time t-1 sends into the input at time t
2. In a similar manner, the input at time t+1 is fed by the output at time t
3. RNNs are able to handle inputs of any length
4. Older data are taken into account in the number of RBF non-linear activation units, and a linear output layer that acts as a summation unit to create the final output. | Compared to MLP, the training phase is completed quickly since there is no backpropagation | Due to the fact that each hidden layer node must determine the rbf function for the input sample vector, classification takes longer than MLP |
| Self- organizing maps (SOMs) | Unsupervised learning | 3D modelling in the healthcare industry. Image analysis, fault finding, process monitoring, and management | 1. Initialize the weights for every node and select a random vector from the training data
2. Investigate each node to determine which weights are the most probable input vector. The best matching unit (BMU) is the node that wins
3. Discover the neighbourhood surrounding the bmu, and that there are less neighbours with time
4. The sample vector is given a winning weight. A node's weight varies depending on how close it is to a bmu. The neighbour learns less the further it is from the BMU. Step two is repeated by SOMs N times in total. | Makes it simple to comprehend and analyze the data

It is easier to look for any similarities in our data after dimensionality reduction

It is easier to look for any similarities in our data after dimensionality reduction | While training SOM, if we provide less or more data, we may not get an informative or very exact output |

(Continued)

TABLE 4.1 (*Continued*)
Study of Different Deep Learning Algorithms

Name of the algorithms	Type	Used Areas	Working	Pros	Cons
Deep belief networks (DBNs)	Unsupervised learning	Picture identification, video-identification, and motion-capture data	1. Uses a layer-by-layer method to learn all generating weights and top-down methods 2. With the help of the greedy algorithm, networks are pre-trained	Can be used with any size labelled dataset Gives classification strength	The training of models require a lot of calculation and time
Restricted Boltzmann machines (RBMs)	Unsupervised learning	Dimension reduction, classification, regression, collective filtering, feature learning, and topic modelling. RBMs create the building chunks of DBNs	Two layers comprise RBMs: 1. Visible units 2. Hidden units All visible units are connected to all hidden ones. There is no Output node in RBMs, and the bias unit is attached to both the visible and hidden units.	Massive amounts of unlabeled data can be used well by learning algorithms, and they can be taught fully unsupervised	It is exceedingly challenging to calculate the energy gradient function when training The CD-k algorithm's weight adjustment is more difficult than Backpropagation.
Autoencoders	Unsupervised learning	Pharmaceutical discovery, popularity prediction, and image processing.	1. The design of autoencoders allows them to take an input and change how it is represented. Then, they make an effort to precisely reproduce the original input. 2. A digit's picture feeds an autoencoder neural network when it cannot be seen clearly. 3. Before compressing the size of the input into a smaller frame, autoencoders first encode the image. 4. Finally, the autoencoder produces the reconstructed image after decoding the original image.	Some functions can be represented computationally more cheaply by using numerous encoder and decoder layers	Not as effective as GANs when it comes to image reconstruction. After encoding, it's possible to lose crucial data from the original input.

For example, let's imagine that the unsupervised learning system is given a dataset containing images of different breeds of dogs and cats. The algorithm has no knowledge of the characteristics of the dataset because it has never been trained on it. The unsupervised learning algorithm's objective is to allow computers to recognize picture attributes by themselves. An algorithm for unsupervised learning will perform this task by classifying the picture dataset into groups according to visual similarity [5].

4.5 DEEP LEARNING: MEDICAL IMAGE ANALYSIS

Table 4.1 represents the digital image classification is an integral component of computer-aided diagnosis and is a significant job in computer vision. A straightforward technique for performing medical image analysis [8] uses image classification to categorize an input image or a group of images as either comprising one of the predefined disorders or free of the diseases. Skin disease detection in dermatology and image categorization issues are frequently used in clinical settings for diagnosing eye illnesses, such as glaucoma, retinopathy caused by diabetes, and corneal conditions. This field also encompasses the classification of pathological pictures for numerous diseases, as well as breast cancer and brain cancer [9].

The most often utilized image modalities for diagnostic evaluation in clinics are projection imaging techniques like X-rays, computed tomography (CT), magnetic resonance imaging (MRI), and ultrasound imaging. T1, T1 − w, T2, T2 − w, diffusion-weighted imaging (DWI), apparent diffusion coefficient (ADC) and fluid attenuation inversion recovery are MRI sequences (FLAIR) [10]. A few examples of clinical uses for various medical picture modalities are shown in Figure 4.7.

CNN, RNN, MLP, SOM, DBN, and autoencoders are the different deep learning algorithms used in image classification and identification [11]. Convolutional neural

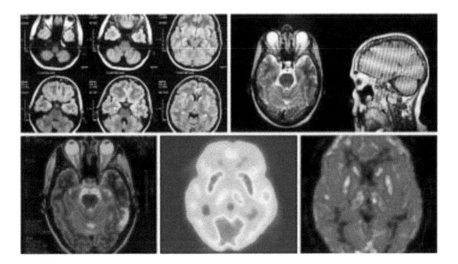

FIGURE 4.7 Medical image modality

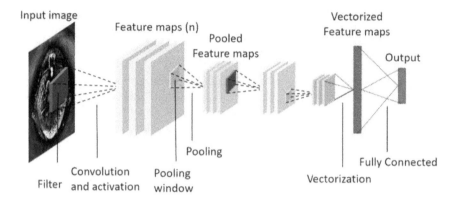

FIGURE 4.8 Typical CNN for medical image analysis

networks (CNN) are the most used classification framework for image analysis. Figure 4.8 shows the CNN framework has improved progressively as deep learning has advanced. The input to a CNN is set up in a grid layout, and it is then passed through layers that maintain these connections, with each layer action using a little portion of the preceding layer. The CNN-based deep neural system is heavily utilized for medical classification [12]. Given that CNN is an excellent feature extractor, using it to identify medical images may avoid complicated and expensive feature engineering. A CNN is trained via backpropagation and gradient descent, similar to typical artificial neural networks, and comprises numerous layers of convolutions and activations, frequently interleaved with pooling layers. Furthermore, CNNs frequently feature fully linked layers at the very end that compute the results.

4.5.1 CONVOLUTIONAL LAYERS

A tensor W(j,i), where j is the amount of the filter and I is the layer, is created by convolutionally combining the activations from the preceding layers with a number of tiny parameterized filters, typically of size 3 x 3. When this is done, the weights of every filter are uniform throughout the entire input domain. A tensor of feature maps is created when a convolutional layer is applied to all of the convolutional filters at every input point.

4.5.2 ACTIVATION LAYER

Non-linear activation functions get the feature maps from the convolutional layer as input. Because of this, the entire neural network may approximatively represent nearly any non-linear function. When the feature maps are fed through an activation function, new tensors, which are typically also referred to as feature maps, are created.

The various components of the model may employ various activation functions. In contrast to the output layer, which frequently employs a different activation function based on the kind of prediction in the dataset, hidden layers typically utilize a similar activation function. Different activation functions are Logistic (Sigmoid), Hyperbolic Tangent (Tanh), Softmax, Rectified Linear Activation (ReLU).

4.5.3 POOLING

This layer applies learned filters to input images to create feature maps that summarize the existence of those features in the input. The size of the feature map must be smaller than the size of the pooling filter. Pooling layers can be divided into two categories: max-pooling and average pooling.

4.5.4 FULLY CONNECTED LAYER

All activations in the previous layer are totally connected to the neurons in FC levels, as is usual for feed-forward neural networks. FC layers are always located near the edge of the network. The following simple architecture demonstrates that one or two FC layers are frequently employed:

INPUT => CONV => RELU => POOL => CONV => RELU => POOL => FC => FC

4.5.5 DROPOUT REGULARIZATION

In reality, dropout is a form of regularization that combats overfitting by increasing testing accuracy, possibly at the expense of training accuracy. It is a method of averaging neural network data that uses stochastic sampling. Using slightly different networks for every bunch of training data is the result of randomly eliminating neurons during instructing, and the resulting weights of network are adjusted based on the optimization of several network variants.

4.6 PROBLEMS WITH CONVOLUTION NEURAL NETWORKS (CNNS)

1. To train CNN to identify any new image, millions of photos are used to teach CNN. Then, CNN develops the ability to recognize each new image that is shown to it by comparing it to similar images that it has previously "seen". Actually, it's not that easy. The premise is essentially the same, but there is a lot of mathematics involved.
2. In order for CNN to learn to function on every potential combination in the training images, each one must be explicitly trained on. For this reason, picture augmentation technology exists, which generates every possible combination and feeds it into the network in order to help it learn better. Naturally, this requires a lot of data and is computationally very expensive.
3. Initial layers of CNN's algorithm detect a few fundamental forms, and as it advances through the layers, activation units are created that react to various portions of the image. As an illustration, a CNN trained on human faces gains the ability to recognize lower-level structures in the earliest layers (such as boundaries, circles, basic shapes, etc.) before progressing to identify higher

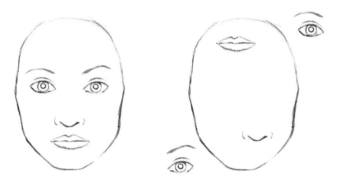

FIGURE 4.9   Human face

level features alike the nose, ears, eyes, mouth, etc. If all three qualities are present, there is a very strong probability that the image is a face.

4. A CNN trained in this manner will recognize the existence of every component and will identify both of the photos in Figure 4.9 as representing a human face. It does not take into account how these parts of an image are arranged.

4.7   FOR MEDICAL IMAGE ANALYSIS, THE NEWEST NEURAL NETWORK

In terms of recognizing images, neural networks have risen tremendously. In terms of image recognition, neural networks have made significant progress. The field of deep learning has developed from a simple neural network to cutting-edge networks like ResNets, GoogLeNets, and InceptionNet to increase the precision of its methods. The algorithms are ingesting an increasing amount of data, the layers are becoming ever-deeper, and as computing power increases, more complicated networks are being deployed.

Despite the fact that all of these have led to a progressive improvement in the exactness and swiftness of image recognition procedures, the fundamental construction parts – pooling layer, regularization (dropouts, etc.), convolution layer and various network architectures – remain largely unchanged. Overall, the improved neural networks [13] used in resolving complications related to image identification are considered different forms of the same traditional CNN. Capsule networks present a completely different approach to solving the problem of image recognition.

4.7.1   CAPSULE NEURAL NETWORK

A new class of networks called capsule networks [14] mimics how the human brain learns by placing a greater concentration on simulating the image's hierarchical relationships. This is totally different from how conventional neural networks operate. A capsule network's brain is dynamic routing [15, 16]. This is why capsule networks are so precise. The feature is learned by a CNN, which then utilizes its presence to determine the overall probability that an image containing the items with the spotted features will exist. In addition to recognizing the qualities, a capsule network also recognizes their orientation and relationships and the probability that they belong to higher-level objects in the hierarchy of parts. Each capsule counts the quantity of lower-level features present and determines the length, thickness, rotation, and position in relation to other features of each feature's activation, as well as the likelihood that the feature will predict a higher-level object. In order for a capsule network to work, each component in a capsule must first be identified, and then the instantiation parameters associated with each component must be communicated to capsules in the layer below.

For instance, in Figure 4.10, when defining a face, we do it without considering the location of the person's body. Instead, we define the place of the eyes in relation to the face. By defining the face's position in relation to the body, we may define a body. Individual parts make up the face, and the body is made up of these objects (the face, hands, and legs). In a capsule network, this hierarchical representation is referred to as the "hierarchy of components" as shown in Figure 4.11. Given that factors like rotation, spatial placements, etc. are also predicting the presence of a face in the capsule in the succeeding layer, there would be separate capsules for each of the slices, and when they were combined, they would predict the presence of a face.

4.7.2 FUNCTIONS WITHIN A CAPSULE NEURAL NETWORK

- Input vectors are multiplied by weight matrices in a matrix. This encodes very significant spatial correlations between the image's high-level features and low-level features.
- Vector inputs are weighted. Which higher-level capsule the current capsule will transmit its output to is determined by these weights. Dynamic routing is used to do this, about which I'll say more in a moment [17].
- The total of the input vectors' weights.
- The "squash" function "squashes" a vector while preserving its orientation, resulting in a vector with a maximum length of 1 and a minimum length of 0.

4.7.3 WHY ARE CAPSULE NETWORKS NOT POPULAR?

On simple datasets like MNIST, CapsNet has attained state-of-the-art performance, but it struggles with more complicated data that could be present on datasets like CIFAR-10 or ImageNet. Because there are so few results that have been demonstrated using capsule nets, they are still in the research and development stage and are not trustworthy enough to be employed in commercial work. The idea is good, though, and further advancement in this field might result in the standardization of Capsule Nets for deep learning image recognition.

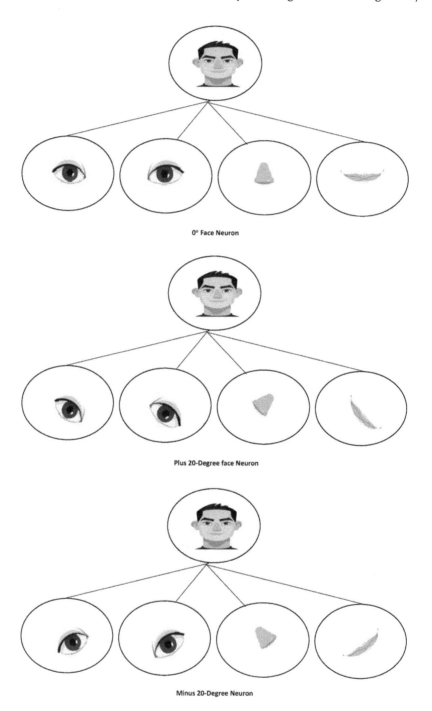

0° Face Neuron

Plus 20-Degree face Neuron

Minus 20-Degree Neuron

FIGURE 4.10   CNN model – needs to be trained on all orientations of a face

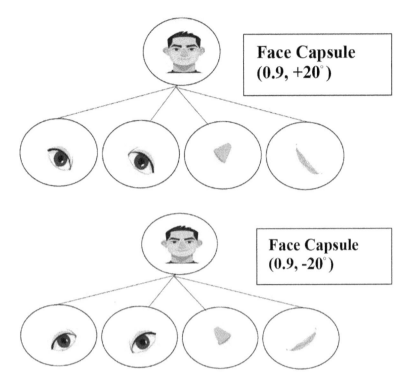

FIGURE 4.11   CapsNet – detects the rotation and leans it as one of the activation vectors

4.8   CONCLUSION

In conclusion, deep learning is a rapidly evolving field of study, and the emergence of sophisticated deep learning techniques has made it possible to analyses medical images with remarkable success and great stability, scalability, precision, and efficiency. The use of CNN in clinical applications such as image classification, object recognition, segmentation, and registration were covered in this chapter, along with a review and summary of current advancements in many CNN-based deep learning techniques. Specifically, CNNs that have been trained on real images have shown unexpectedly excellent results, challenging the accuracy of human professionals in different tasks. Additionally, this chapter addressed the most recent state-of-the-art for capsule networks and clarified current implementations and techniques.

REFERENCES

[1] H. Gu, Y. Guo, L. Gu et al., "Deep learning for identifying corneal diseases from ocular surface slit-lamp photographs," *Scientific Reports*, vol. 10, no. 1, p. 17851, 2020.
[2] S. P. Singh, L. Wang, S. Gupta, H. Goli, P. Padmanabhan, B. Gulyás, "3D deep learning on medical images: a review," *Sensors*, vol. 20, no. 18, article 5097, 2020.

[3] A. Esteva, B. Kuprel, R. A. Novoa et al., "Dermatologist-level classification of skin cancer with deep neural networks," *Nature*, vol. 542, no. 7639, pp. 115–118, 2017.

[4] J. Ker, L. Wang, J. Rao, T. Lim, "Deep learning applications in medical image analysis," *IEEE Access*, vol. 6, 2017.

[5] H. Uzunova, S. Schultz, H. Handels, J. Ehrhardt, "Unsupervised pathology detection in medical images using conditional variational autoencoders," *International Journal of Computer Assisted Radiology and Surgery*, vol. 14, no. 3, pp. 451–461, 2019. https://doi.org/10.1007/s11548-018-1898-0

[6] M. A. Al-Malla, A. Jafar, N. Ghneim, "Image captioning model using attention and object features to mimic human image understanding," *Journal of Bigdata*, 2022, https://doi.org/10.1186/s40537-022-00571-w

[7] A. Maroju, S. S. Doma, L. Chandarlapati, "Image caption generating deep learning model," *International Journal of Engineering Research & Technology (IJERT)*, vol. 10, no. 9, pp. 616–621, 2021, https://doi.org/10.17577/IJERTV10IS090120

[8] X. Chen, X. Wang, K. Zhang, K.-M. Fung, T. C. Thai, K. Moore, R. S. Mannel, H. Liu, B. Zheng, Y. Qiu, "Recent advances and clinical applications of deep learning in medical image analysis," *Journal Medical Image Analysis*, vol. 79, article 102444, 2022. https://doi.org/10.1016/j.media.2022.102444

[9] J. Ker, Y. Bai, H. Y. Lee, J. Rao, L. Wang, "Automated brain histology classification using machine learning," *Journal of Clinical Neuroscience*, vol. 66, pp. 239–245, 2019.

[10] A. S. Lundervold, A. Lundervold, "An overview of deep learning in medical imaging focusing on MRI," *Zeitschrift für Medizinische Physik on Sciencedirect*, vol. 29, no. 2, pp. 102–127, May 2019. https://doi.org/10.1016/j.zemedi.2018.11.002

[11] X. Liu, K. Gao, B. Liu, C. Pan, K. Liang, L. Yan, J. Ma, F. He, S. Zhang, S. Pan, Y. Yu, "Advances in deep learning-based medical image analysis," *Health Data Science*, vol. 2021, article 8786793, 2021. https://doi.org/10.34133/2021/8786793

[12] S. S. Yadav, S. M. Jadhav, "Deep convolutional neural network based medical image classification for disease diagnosis," *Journal of Bigdata*, vol. 6, no. 1, p. 113, 2019.

[13] S. K. Shukla, S. Dubey, A. K. Pandey, V. Mishra, M. Awasthi, V. Bhardwaj, "Image caption generator using neural networks," *International Journal of Scientific Research in Computer Science, Engineering and Information Technology*, vol. 7, no. 3, pp. 01–07, 2021. https://doi.org/10.32628/CSEIT21736

[14] M. K. Patrick, A. F. Adekoya, A. A. Mighty, B. Y. Edward, "Capsule networks – a survey," *Journal of King Saud University – Computer and Information Sciences*, vol. 34, no. 1, pp. 1295–1310, January 2022. https://doi.org/10.1016/j.jksuci.2019.09.014

[15] T. Vijayakumar, "Comparative study of capsule neural network in various applications," *Journal of Artificial Intelligence and Capsule Networks*, vol. 01, no. 01, pp. 19–27, 2019. https://doi.org/10.36548/jaicn.2019.1.003

[16] M. D. G. Mallea, P. Meltzer, P. J. Bentley, "Capsule neural networks for graph classification using explicit tensorial graph representations," 2019. https://doi.org/10.48550/arXiv.1902.08399

[17] S. Sabour, N. Frosst, G. E. Hinton, "Dynamic routing between capsules," *31st Conference on Neural Information Processing Systems*, 2017.

5 A Deep Learning Framework to Detect Diabetic Retinopathy Using CNN

R. Kavitha

5.1 INTRODUCTION

A retinal eye condition called diabetes-related retinopathy affects the retina. Diabetes can strike anyone at any time. Diabetes-related retinopathy can cause blindness or vision loss if left untreated. This occurs when damaged retinal blood nerves are the outcome of more blood sugar. They have the potential to expand and leak. Alternately, they could close, preventing blood flow. On the retina, aberrant new blood vessels can occasionally form.

The diabetic eye disease has two stages, the earliest stage of diabetic retinopathy is called nonproliferative diabetic retinopathy (NPDR) and the later stage is called proliferative diabetic. There are many persons who have diabetes and the more severe form of diabetic retinopathy is called proliferative diabetic retinopathy(PDR). When the retina continues to develop new blood vessels, it occurs. PDR can damage both the central and peripheral(side)vision, which is a very significant issue.

5.1.1 CAUSES OF DIABETIC RETINOPATHY

A variety of vision problems and diabetic retinopathy, which are recognized as harm to the retinal blood nerves of the eye, can be driven on by diabetes. Over time, possessing too much sugar in the blood can cause the minuscule blood capillaries that feed the retina to become blocked, severing that organ's blood supply. The eye makes an effort to develop new blood vessels as a result. However, these new blood vessels don't fully develop and are highly susceptible to leaks. Failing treatment, these damaged arteries could lead to ischemia, inflammation, and eventually legal blindness.

A person with diabetic retinopathy can still have good distance vision; treatment options include infusion of medications, laser therapy, and surgery; prompt treatment can help repair the damage caused by diabetic retinopathy and help prevent blindness. Diabetic retinopathy directly impacts 50 percent of the population with diabetes and is the top reason for irreversible visualization loss.

DOI: 10.1201/9781003343172-5

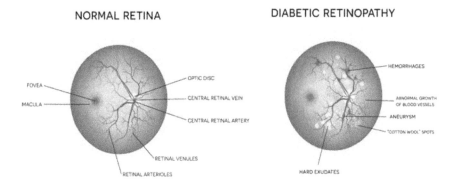

FIGURE 5.1   Diabetic retinopathy

5.1.2   EFFECTS OF DIABETIC RETINOPATHY

Diabetes can cause diabetic retinopathy in anyone with the disease (Figure 5.1). Many complications can elevate the likelihood of getting the eye illness. This is because in its initial phases, it generally shows no symptoms. The symptoms of diabetic retinopathy develop, including seeing an increasing number of floaters.

Vision problems include lost vision, blurry vision, vision that occasionally shifts from hazy to clear, blank or dark spots in your field of vision, poor night vision, and the perception that colours are faded or washed out. Diabetic retinopathy symptoms usually affect both eyes. DR does not show symptoms in the beginning. Until it reaches a certain severity, the vision will not show any difference. A checkup will help to analyze the change in the vision. This is why periodic checkup is necessary.

5.1.3   DIAGNOSIS OF DIABETIC RETINOPATHY

Through a very simple test the diabetic retinopathy can be detected by an eye practitioner.

- **Vision sharpness:** This refers to your visual clarity.
- **Eye tissue activity:** How well your muscles work affects how easily you can move your eyes.
- **Perimeter perception**: Peripheral vision is the ability to see with your peripheral vision.
- **Pupil reply:** This examination examines how your pupils respond to light.

During this examination, irregular blood nerves, flow in the core of the eye, expansion of the blood nerves, and the retina bulge are analyzed.

5.1.4   COMPLICATIONS OF DIABETIC RETINOPATHY

Usually the growth of dysfunctional blood nerves in the centre of the eye is a complication of diabetic retinopathy. Serious eye problems, such as vitreous hemorrhage, might result from complications, such as retinal separation, glaucoma, and or blindness. Glaucoma, or elevated intraocular pressure [1] that might endanger eyesight, is another condition that can result from retinal degeneration. Retinopathy, if left untreated, can cause progressive visual loss. Between the ages of 20 and 60, it is the main cause of blindness [2]. However, blindness can be avoided if retinopathy is identified early. Although many diabetics will experience vision impairment, less than5 percent will experience serious vision loss.

Even with diabetic macular edema, DR's lack of an early warning indication is a well- known problem. Therefore, the ability to identify DR early is greatly desired. Unfortunately, the existing DR detection method practically cannot provide this criterion. The present method specifically calls for a skilled hospital technician to physically assess digital color fundus pictures of the retina [3], and DR is recognized by looking for lesions connected to vascular anomalies brought on by diabetes. Although the existing solution is efficient, it takes more time and heavily relies on the knowledge of skilled practitioners. An automated method of DR detection has been developed during the past several years in an effort to address this problem [4].

5.2   A PRACTICAL APPLICATION OF COMPUTER TECHNOLOGY IN EYE CARE

In a span 50 years, a third of a 600 million people with diabetes globally will also have DR. A comprehensive evaluation of twenty thousand sugar patients from various population-based research work between 1982 and 2010 proves that the incidence of any DR was 40% overall, with 7 percent of occurrences posing a risk to vision. An approved technique for avoiding blindness is to screen for DR and rapidly refer people for therapy. Different healthcare specialists, such as eye surgeon, refractive measure personal, common examiner, viewing professional, and lab photographers, can conduct DR tests. The detection methods are direct ophthalmoscopy, teleretinal screening, retinal video, mydriatic or non-mydriatic retinal photography, dilated slit lamp biomicroscopy with a handheld lens (90 D or 78 D), and others help to accomplish the accessibility of human judges. By examining for lesions connected to the vascular anomalies that occurred due to alignments, clinicians can diagnose DR. Although this strategy works, it has significant resource requirements. Where there is a higher incidence of diabetes among the local population and DR detection is most necessary, there is frequently a scarcity of the necessary knowledge and tools. The infrastructure needed to prevent DR-related blindness will have to increase in order to prevent large number of population with diabetes.

Long-standing efforts have used image classifications, pattern recognition, and machine learning to make better progress towards a more comprehensive and automated DR screening system. The purpose of this challenge is to test the capabilities of an automated detection method using colour fundus photography, ideally producing models with realistic clinical potential. To enhance the effect a winning model can have on increasing DR detection, the winning models will be shared publicly.

5.3 ARTIFICIAL INTELLIGENCE IN OPHTHALMOLOGY

Medical analysis and specialized treatments of eye problems depend on medical imaging. Very high pixel images on anatomical and practical differences can be provided by this technology. Imaging methods have developed quickly in recent years, along with advances in medical science. However, as imaging technology has advanced, it has become more difficult to comprehend and manage eye disease because of the numerous images and observations that may be made for each patient and the concepts as well that the data can support. Every long-suffering person has thus turned into a meta data.

Usual analytical procedures based heavily on the knowledge and training of doctors can contribute to large amount of misdiagnosis and data loss. Intelligent technologies are considered extremely important in the modern world of medical examiners and treatments to direct clinical information carefully and effectively. In several contexts, artificial intelligence (AI) has been used in medication (Figure 5.2). In particular, radiology, dermatology, pathology, and ophthalmology have benefitted immensely from interactions between medical imaging and AI sciences.

5.4 AI TECHNIQUES FOR MACHINE LEARNING

There are four basic methods:

- The supervised learning
- The unsupervised learning
- The semi-supervised learning
- The reinforcement learning.

The kind of data that data scientists need to predict determines the kind of algorithm they use.

- In supervised learning, input data that has already been labelled by humans is often used to train a machine to predict the expected result, leading it to

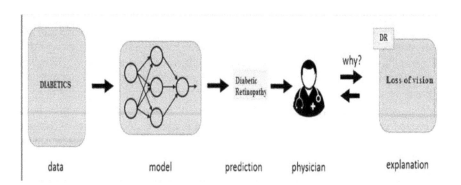

FIGURE 5.2   Predication in ML

resolve categorization and waning issues. However this technique requires a great deal of time because a significant amount of information needs to be manually identified.

- Non-explicit input data in unsupervised learning are not clearly labelled and given to a machine, and the structure is allowed to recognize patterns and structures out from the group of objects, free from people intervention.
- A CNN [5] is a deep NN technique made up of a series of dealing layers that mimic the genetic operations of the visual cortex. Through the use of a differentiable function, the input volume is converted into an output volume. Each nerve in the illustrious cortex would react to a motivation that is precise to an area inside a picture, the same as the way a brain cell will react to vision activity, which will trigger a specific portion of the field of vision, called the reception field, according to Hubel and Weisel [6]. To fill the entire vision area, these reception fields are tiled together. These cells fall into one of two categories: simple cells or complicated cells.

The more complex cells activate if they have a wider receptive field and are distinct from the pattern's position, whereas the simpler cells are active when they detect edge-like patterns. Generally speaking, the input, hidden (also referred to as feature extraction layers), and output layers make up the CNN.

Complication, entirely networked, pooling, and normalizing steps constitute the majority of the hidden layers, and the number of hidden neurons varies between various CNNs. The data layer represents the channels' breadth, width, and number (usually 3 layers – red, green, and blue). The core component of a CNN, which transforms the data by using a group of filters (sometimes referred to as core) that serve as feature finders. To create a feature map, the seizer will move upon the input picture (as the output).

During the training process, a CNN understand the motive of its filter weights, through the precise values.

5.5   FROM ARTIFICIAL INTELLIGENCE TO MACHINE LEARNING

Simply stated, machine learning is revolutionizing health care. Without being specifically programmed to do so, ML, a component of AI, permits computer language systems to be better at making predictions about the future.

In predicting latest outcome standards, ML software use previous values as input. The way in which a prediction-making algorithm learns to achieve high accuracy is a prominent method of classifying traditional machine learning.

ML has increased the routine of many tough tasks in health picture, likely analysis of

- skin images to help to identify cutaneous malignancies
- utilizing chest pictures for lung cancer detection
- risk assessment for cardiovascular disease using computer tomographic imaging (CT)
- CT angiography for pulmonary embolism detection

- analysis of breast histopathology using tissue sections
- polyp detection with a virtual colonoscopy
- utilizing magnetic resonance imaging for a glaucoma diagnosis (MRI)
- use of functional MRI for neurological illness diagnosis.

Artificial intelligence has a significant impact on eye care study as well, mostly from exact and effective picture explanation.

Ophthalmologists must adopt sophisticated software and obtain a deeper analysis of the scope of the methodology in order to evaluate and use AI constructively. This is vital given the rapid growth of ML as shown in Figure 5.2.

On the Weka tool, diabetic illness is predicted using four machine learning algorithms. The four algorithms,

- simple CART
- naïve Bayes
- SVM
- random forest,

are employed to forecast and examine diabetic data. The accuracy of all four algorithms is designed to be compared alongside one another.

5.6 DEVELOPING A DEEP LEARNING MODEL

Using either a supervised or an unsupervised approach, the algorithm can use machine techniques to classify the values that are given to the exercise phase and produce predictions. Utilizing sophisticated mathematical models, ML has been widely used for applications like computer vision and predictive analytics. In supervised learning, also known as ground truth, the computer is educated using labelled examples, whereas in unsupervised learning, the algorithm can discover its own structure in the input without any labelling. SL is used in the majority of artificial intelligence applications in biomedical research.

Naïve Bayes algorithm, random forest (RF), decision tree, support vector machine (SVM), and k-nearest neighbor (KNN) are examples of traditional machine learning techniques [7] (Table 5.1). The ML network architecture are likely to stop the meeting and over fit training values owing to the physical features choice process, which restricts their use even though they achieve good performance with small datasets.

To understand illustrations of the data with varying layers of concept, DL makes use of numerous processing layers. Despite the various fact that deep neural networks have its diagnostic performance has recently been increased in many fields, due to the development of graphic processing units (GPU) with improved processing power, larger annotated datasets, and other variables [8].

A ML or DL system can find complex structures in big datasets via learning techniques like backpropagation and then modifying its internal parameters that are required to compute the depiction in each layer from the preceding one.

In addition to using the entire picture and connecting the whole picture with analytical output, these approaches allow regional samples to enable the network to train

TABLE 5.1

Different AI Algorithms for ML and DL

AI Techniques	Classification	Algorithms
Conventional ML	Supervised learning	SVM, linear regression, naïve Bayesian, logistic regression, neural network, random forest, k-nearest neighbor, decision tree, AdaBoost
	Unsupervised learning	Expectation maximization, K-means, mean shift, hierarchical clustering, principal component analysis, affinity propagation, fuzzy c-means, systems iterative self-organizing data
	RL	State-action, Q-learning, teaching-box systems, temporal difference learning, state-action-reward, maja systems
Deep learning	Deep belief network	Convolutional deep belief network, Boltzmann machine, conditional restricted
	Convolution neural network	Visual geometry group network (VGG), deep residual learning, Inception v4 (v2, v3), Restnet-152 (34, 50, 101), LeNet, AlexNet, GoogLeNet
	Recurrent neural network	Long short-term memory, bidirectional RNN

to detect biomarkers, which eliminates the need for "hand-engineered" acquired images. DL has been broadly used in image detection, audio detection, and NLP due to its significantly enhanced performance.

Convolutional parameter layers are used by deep learning (DL) neural [9] networks to understand filters recursively. From the input photos, these layers extract the hierarchical feature maps, learn the complex relationships between complex features (like shapes) and simpler features (like lines), and produce the expected categorization as a result. Each of these convolution layers is positioned in turn, transforming the basic image and propagating the data into the subsequent steps.

The parameters of the connected nerve are primarily designed to arbitrary values during the training process. The level of discrepancy between the expected value and the actual data of the system is evaluated using the loss function. The output of the activity is then analyzed with training set parameters that are known to exist. Then, the optimizer slightly increases the function's parameters to quickly get to the ideal value, lowering the loss function.

In general, a model's robustness is strengthened by a smaller loss function. The activity learnt how to precisely estimate the parameters from the clarity of the image for all the pictures in the processed set after many repeats of this process. The most popular network, CNN, employs an activity that previously combines neighboring image into ground parameters before aggregating them into global features. Deep learning optimization offers a lot of potential for an ophthalmology diagnosis [10]. These medical facilities have incorporated some of the most recent advancements, including

- AI-driven vision screening technologies that provide machine learning-based point-of-care medical diagnoses for ophthalmological diseases
- Using patient data analysis to detect diabetic retinopathy and give doctors treatment suggestions
- Macular degeneration early-stage diagnosis using deep learning techniques
- Glaucoma and cataract screening with great accuracy.

The abundance of information needed to optimize the model is one difficulty with employing DL models. Different strategies use transfer learning to address this problem without the need for enormous datasets. Through transfer learning, previously chosen model parameters can be improved over a new data distribution domain. Given the most diverse optimal kernels, it is typical to employ a model that was trained using an extremely complicated features dataset like ImageNet for transfer learning.

Table 5.2 shows the difficulties in developing and implementing deep learning (DL) approaches on a clinical and technical level.

5.7 DETECTION PROCESS OF DIABETIC RETINOPATHY USING CNN

DR is classified into five stages according to the severity level.

- Phase0: Not viewable retinopathy
- Phase1: Slightnon-proliferative

TABLE 5.2
Different AI Algorithms for ML and DL

Identification of training datasets	Concerns about confidentiality and patient consent.
	Various institutional review boards have different requirements and rules.
	Small training datasets for uncommon diseases that are not routinely captured, such as eye tumours, or common disorders (eg., cataracts).
Validation and testing datasets	There isn't enough power due to insufficient sample size.
	Lack of generalizability – not extensively tested in many groups or using information gathered from various devices.
Explaining the results	A demonstration of the areas that DL deemed odd.
	Heat maps are produced using a variety of methods, including summarized gradient, ocular tests, class functions, approach, soft concentration map, and others.
Medical operation of DL systems	A suggestion for suitable clinical deployment locations.
	Requesting regulatory permission from the relevant health authorities.
	Conducting clinical trials that are prospective.
	Medical insurance reimbursement programme and medical necessity.
	Ethical challenges.

- Phase 2: Modest NPDR
- Phase3: Rigorous NPDR
- Phase4: Proliferative DR

In the NPDR stage, patients are asymptomatic, and the proliferative process has not yet started. The patients' visual acuity is still intact at the NPDR stage. The patient's NPDR stage must be known in order to forecast the likelihood that proliferative retinopathy will advance.

To stop the disease's progression and lower the risk of visual loss, DR must be accurately and quickly diagnosed. The best possible treatment depends critically on early detection as shown in Figure 5.3. Manual examination of retinal scanning [11] is used to make the traditional diagnosis of DR. The outcome of this time-consuming diagnostic procedure depends on the clinician's experience.

Most image processing researchers in recent years have been involved in the progress of ML, particularly DL methods in the field of reading handwritten digits, like the MNIST collection and ImageNet image categorization.

DL is a sophisticated edition of NN that belongs to the family of ML and AI methods. For low-level feature extraction, DL has numerous hidden layers as opposed to conventional neural networks.

Over time, different architectures have been introduced in the context of DL [12]. Among these architectures, CNNs – feed-forward, multi-layered neural networks

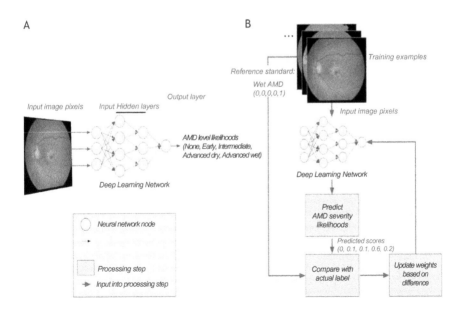

FIGURE 5.3   CNN framework for DR detection

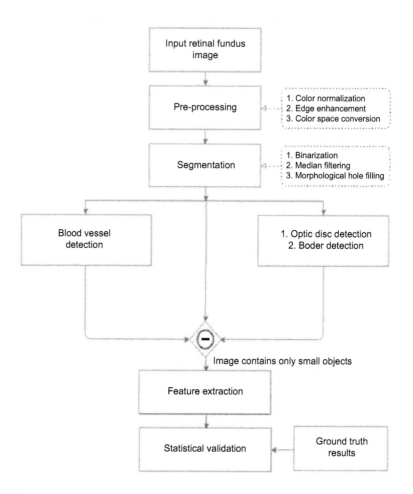

FIGURE 5.4 Flow diagram of the diabetic retinopathy detection system

made up of feature extractor, and classifier components – have achieved notable success, particularly in the classification of medical images (Figure 5.4).

According to the essential distinctiveness of disease vigorous categorization from the fundi picture, the most effective methodology clearly emerged. In general, particularly categorization of diseases is based on these fundamental steps:

- Data enhancement
- Preprocessing
- Starting point of connected system
- Activating training
- Activity decision.

A CNN is made up of one or many fully associated systems like in a typical multilayer neural network, which are then followed by many CNN steps or just single CNN step.

The design of a CNN is created by the input images of two-dimensional tree structure (or other 2D data such as a speech signal). This is accomplished by using tied weights and local connections, followed by some sort of pooling to provide features that are translation invariant.

CNNs also have the advantage of being simpler to train and having a smaller number of features that are completely linked systems with the equal values of hidden units. When training, CNN takes the tree structure by imaging by stacking numerous trainable stages on top of one another.

5.8   THE DATASET

Different types of lesions that are present on a retinal scan can be used to identify DR. These lesions include soft and hard exudates, hemorrhages, and microaneurysms(MA)(EX).

Kaggle offers a significant collection of fundus photographs [13] of the retina that were acquired under various imaging circumstances. On a scale from 0 to 4, a clinically skilled person has given an image a severity rating for diabetic retinopathy as in Figure 5.5.

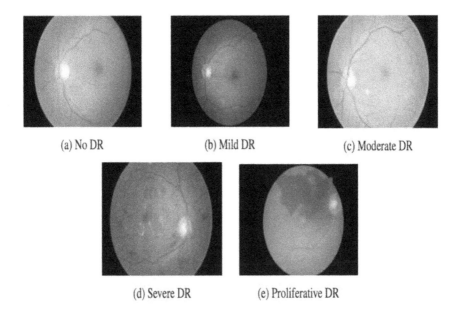

(a) No DR   (b) Mild DR   (c) Moderate DR

(d) Severe DR   (e) Proliferative DR

FIGURE 5.5   Stages of diabetic retinopathy

0 – Absences of DR
1 – Slight
2 – Modest
3 – Vigorous
4 – Proliferative.

The information was derived from the Kaggle Dataset [for Diabetic Retinopathy Detection [14], which is openly accessible. Images from datasets for the diagnosis of retinopathy that are available to the public have been used to generate the database. Images of diabetic retinopathy [15] were gathered from the Messidor-1 dataset, which contains one thousand two hundred fundus images [16], and the Kaggle dataset, that comprises 25,000 images with 5-class labeling [17]. Both datasets are comprised of image features having height and width variations in between low hundreds and multiple thousands as in Table 5.3.

The volume of the information source [18] is an important factor in the effectiveness of the network because deep learning works best on huge datasets. Due to this, the majority of research have employed several datasets to enhance classification performance. Different numbers and frequencies of classes are utilized for DR classification as in Figure 5.6.

Each dataset has a varied number of normal and aberrant photos, as was already mentioned. For example, there is inconsistency in the number of aberrant photos classified by DR severity level. It is challenging to evaluate for more than two classes due to the dataset imbalance and image quality. This is why in the several papers that were examined, binary classification predominated over multi-class classification.

5.8.1 Information Expansion

The picture data [19] are gathered from several resources by employing several cameras by each having a different range of vision, clarity, image noise, contrast, and image size. Adjustments are provided to brightness, contrast, and even image flipping in data augmentation.

TABLE 5.3
Class Allotment in Original Dataset

Class	Name	No. of images
I	Regular	18728
II	Slight	3274
III	Modest	1968
IV	Vigorous	918
V	Proliferative	112

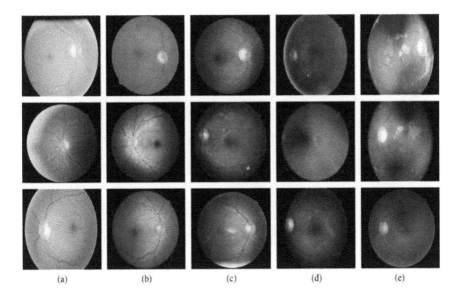

<table>
<tr><td>(a)</td><td>(b)</td><td>(c)</td><td>(d)</td><td>(e)</td></tr>
</table>

FIGURE 5.6   Classification of DR

5.8.2   Data Preprocessing

The spatial data of the fundus images were worked for the deep convolutional neural network [19]. The image data could not be used directly for training owing to the nonstandard image resolutions. To create a uniform dataset, the images were reduced in size to a standard 512 x 512 pixel resolution size as in Figure 5.7. Resizing the images is one of the primary processing phases.

As in Figure 5.8, convert the photos to grayscale before feeding them into the categorization architecture and convert to the L model after that. The microaneurysms and vessels in the fundus pictures [20] are highlighted in a monochromatic image and then single-dimensionally flattened for later processing.

Every picture was normalized by employing Min-Max normalization to avoid the CNN which picks upon the underlying background noise in the image. Zero-padding was used in the convolutional layers to maintain the input and output volumes' spatial dimensions.

5.9   CNN CLASSIFICATION

A CNN, a feed-forward artificial neural network used in image identification, is inspired by the way in which the visual cortex of organisms is organized, with its individual neurons arranged so that they react when the visual field is tiled with overlapping areas. The CNN, which is used in deep learning, employs a sophisticated design made up of piled layers that are especially well-suited to classifying the

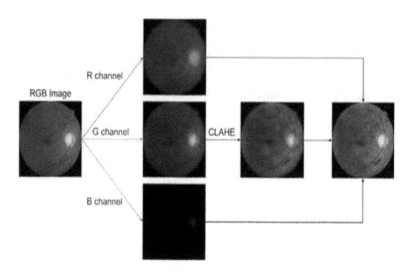

FIGURE 5.7   Preprocessing of data

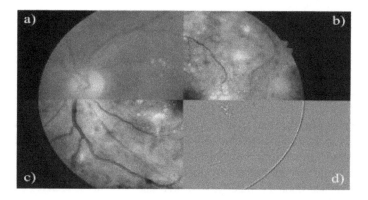

FIGURE 5.8   Grayscale

pictures. This architecture is reliable and responsive to each parameter contained in the images for multi-class classification.

5.9.1   CONVOLUTION LAYER

In order to process the fundus images and generate a dot product, it makes use of many kernels or filters. In this layer, each kernel or filter produces a different set of visual properties as shown in Figure 5.9.

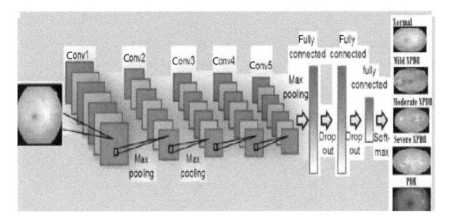

FIGURE 5.9   Convolutional neural network

5.9.2 POOLING LAYER

By lowering the spatial dimension, it offers an abstract representation of convolved characteristics. Although it takes the highest or lowest amount of area depending on the category of pooling from core-overlaid input, it is relatively comparable to the convolution layer.

5.9.3 DROPOUT LAYER

In order to avoid overfitting, neural networks have already been restricted and used the dropout approach. In a 1-dimensional series, flattening sends the data to the subsequent layer.

5.9.4 HIDDEN LAYERS AND FEATURE POOLING LAYERS

In the first model, as shown in Figure 5.10, the amount of entirely associated units in the two concealed layers was set at 450, while it dropped to 256 for the second and third models. A maxout was created after each hidden layer using a characteristic pooling surface with a sieve extent of 3, which collects the parameters of the unseen units and incorporates the advantages of dropouts in model averaging and optimization [21].

5.10 CONCLUSION

Diabetes damages the retina's blood vessels [22], and one of the complications is DR. Blindness may result from DR if it is not addressed. Effectively preventing vision loss starts with early detection of DR. The conventional approach to DR detection is challenging, time consuming, and expensive; as a result, numerous research has been done to automate the recognition activity utilizing machine learning and deep learning techniques. The diagnosis process can be greatly aided by automatic

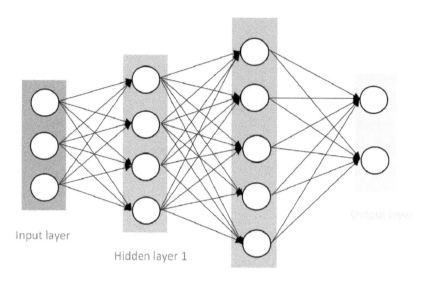

FIGURE 5.10   Deep learning hidden layer

classification of DR images, which also increases the effectiveness of diagnostic procedures.

Recently, investigations involving the analysis and classification of retinal images have extensively used DL methods, primarily CNN architectures. A thorough analysis of several methods for automatically diagnosing diabetic retinopathy and a deep learning strategy for the quick identification of retinopathy utilizing a CNN architecture [23] with numerous deep layers are conducted. Due to insufficiently sized medical data, transfer learning algorithms are used since CNN training necessitates huge datasets for optimal performance. Accordingly, the majority of researchers who used transfer learning techniques for DR detection have had their methods evaluated in terms of the datasets they used, the architectures they used, the performance metrics they used, the optimizers they used, and the preprocessing and augmentation techniques they used. The majority of the conclusions are as follows: The most popular pre-trained CNN architecture is Inception-v3, and the most researched dataset is the Diabetic Retinopathy Detection Dataset on Kaggle [19].

REFERENCES

[1] Zhang Z, Srivastava R, Liu H, Chen X, Duan L, Kee Wong DW, Kwoh CK, Wong TY, Liu J. A survey on computer aided diagnosis for ocular diseases. BMC medical informatics and decision making. 2014 Dec; 14:1–29.
[2] Bernardes R, Serranho P, Lobo C. Digital ocular fundus imaging: a review. Ophthalmological. 2011 Sep 22;226(4):161–81.

[3] Xu K, Feng D, Mi H. Deep convolutional neural network-based early automated detection of diabetic retinopathy using fundus image. Molecules. 2017 Nov 23;22(12):2054.

[4] Bernardes R, Serranho P, Lobo C. Digital ocular fundus imaging: a review. Ophthalmologica. 2011 Sep 22;226(4):161–81.

[5] Pratt H, Coenen F, Broadbent DM, Harding SP, Zheng Y. Convolutional neural networks for diabetic retinopathy. Procedia computer science. 2016 Jan 1;90:200–5.

[6] Hubel DH, Wiesel TN. Receptive fields of single neurones in the cat's striate cortex. The Journal of physiology. 1959 Oct;148(3):574.

[7] Priya R, Aruna P. Diagnosis of diabetic retinopathy using machine learning techniques. ICTACT Journal on soft computing. 2013 Jul 1;3(4):563–75.

[8] Chakrabarti R, Harper CA, Keeffe JE. Diabetic retinopathy management guidelines. Expert review of ophthalmology. 2012 Oct 1;7(5):417–39.

[9] Panwar N, Huang P, Lee J, Keane PA, Chuan TS, Richhariya A, Teoh S, Lim TH, Agrawal R. Fundus photography in the 21st century–a review of recent technological advances and their implications for worldwide healthcare. Telemedicine and e-Health. 2016 Mar 1;22(3):198–208.

[10] Jin K, Ye J. Artificial intelligence and deep learning in ophthalmology: Current status and future perspectives. Advances in Ophthalmology Practice and Research. 2022 Nov 1;2(3):100078.

[11] Gharaibeh N, Al-Hazaimeh OM, Al-Naami B, Nahar KM. An effective image processing method for detection of diabetic retinopathy diseases from retinal fundus images. International Journal of Signal and Imaging Systems Engineering. 2018;11(4):206–16.

[12] Alzubaidi L, Zhang J, Humaidi AJ, Al-Dujaili A, Duan Y, Al-Shamma O, Santamaría J, Fadhel MA, Al-Amidie M, Farhan L. Review of deep learning: concepts, CNN architectures, challenges, applications, future directions. Journal of big Data. 2021 Dec;8:1–74.

[13] www.kaggle.com/c/diabeticretinopathydetection/discussion/15617

[14] Simonyan K. K. Simonyan and A. Zisserman Very Deep Convolutional Networks for Large-Scale Image Recognition. arXiv preprint arXiv:1409.1556. 2014.

[15] Harangi B, Toth J, Baran A, Hajdu A. Automatic screening of fundus images using a combination of convolutional neural network and hand-crafted features. In2019 41st Annual international conference of the IEEE engineering in medicine and biology society (EMBC) 2019 Jul 23 (pp. 2699–2702). IEEE.

[16] Panwar N, Huang P, Lee J, Keane PA, Chuan TS, Richhariya A, Teoh S, Lim TH, Agrawal R. Fundus photography in the 21st century–a review of recent technological advances and their implications for worldwide healthcare. Telemedicine and e-Health. 2016 Mar 1;22(3):198–208.

[17] Taye MM. Understanding of machine learning with deep learning: architectures, workflow, applications and future directions. Computers. 2023 Apr 25;12(5):91.

[18] Taylor R, Batey D, editors. Handbook of retinal screening in diabetes: diagnosis and management. John Wiley & Sons; 2012 Mar 14.

[19] Abràmoff MD, Lou Y, Erginay A, Clarida W, Amelon R, Folk JC, Niemeijer M. Improved automated detection of diabetic retinopathy on a publicly available dataset through integration of deep learning. Investigative ophthalmology & visual science. 2016 Oct 1;57(13):5200–6.

[20] Khan SH, Abbas Z, Rizvi SD. Classification of diabetic retinopathy images based on customised CNN architecture. In2019 Amity International conference on artificial intelligence (AICAI) 2019 Feb 4 (pp. 244–248). IEEE.

[21] Wang X, Lu Y, Wang Y, Chen WB. Diabetic retinopathy stage classification using convolutional neural networks. In2018 IEEE International Conference on Information Reuse and Integration (IRI) 2018 Jul 6 (pp. 465–471). IEEE.

[22] Vengalil SK, Sinha N, Kruthiventi SS, Babu RV. Customizing CNNs for blood vessel segmentation from fundus images. In2016 international conference on signal processing and communications (SPCOM) 2016 Jun 12 (pp. 1–4). IEEE.

[23] Gharaibeh N, Al-Hazaimeh OM, Al-Naami B, Nahar KM. An effective image processing method for detection of diabetic retinopathy diseases from retinal fundus images. International Journal of Signal and Imaging Systems Engineering. 2018;11(4):206–16.

6 Skin Cancer Detection and Classification Using Deep Learning Techniques

R. Rajeswari, P. G. Sivagaminathan,
and A. R. Arunachalam

6.1 INTRODUCTION

Metastasis, the spread of cancerous cells from one place of the body to another, defines cancer as a disease. As the human body is made up of trillions of cells, it is possible for a disease to begin anywhere. Whenever the body requires more of a specific type of cell, the body's existing supply of that cell will undergo a cycle of development and duplication known as cell division. When a cell dies due to age or damage, a new one grows in its place.

Every once in a while, this well-ordered cycle breaks down, and abnormal or damaged cells proliferate when they shouldn't. This type of cell could potentially form the framework for growths, which are specialized tissues. Whether a growth is benign or cancerous can be determined using a scan. Metastasis refers to the process through which cancerous tumors travel to and invade neighboring tissues and even other parts of the body. Malignant tumors are a type of dangerous development. The malignancies of the blood, such as leukemia, typically do not have the same robust malignant development structure as the other cancers.

Cancer cells need sugar as a primary source of fuel, allowing them to multiply rapidly. They are consumed by the disease cells in large quantities, and their multiplication assures the creation of new clones. Humans have microbial cells and microorganisms colonizing them. The number of cells in a microbe appears to be comparable to that of a human, but the genome size of a bacterium is many times that of a human, offering significantly greater genetic diversity. *Helicobacter pylori, Chlamydia trachoma, Salmonella enterica serovar Typhimurium, Fusobacterium nucleatum, enterotoxigenic Bacteroidesfragilis*, and *Koribacteraceae* are some of the bacteria most definitively connected to malignant growth. Cells that have undergone transformation can perish in one of two ways: apoptosis or necroptosis.

The possibility of a cancerous tumor has caused unending anxiety. A note of weak tumor was sprinkled throughout the experts' explanations of the causes of cancer. Recent studies have focused on pain and uncertain safe actuation as possible triggers for illness-related depression. When it comes to developing cancer, city dwellers face a higher risk due to lifestyle choices including nutrition and access to health care that may not be optimal [1].

6.1.1 Skin Cancer

Cancer of the skin is the most well-known form of this disease. It happens when there is a sporadic development of skin cells. The cells are likewise the way in which doctors distinguish the kind of skin malignant growth. The most ideal way to comprehend skin disease is to comprehend its various kinds and what they mean for the body.

6.1.2 Basal Cell Carcinoma

Basal cells start basal cell carcinoma, which are the skin cells that supplant old cells in the lower level of the epidermis. This sort of skin disease ordinarily shows up on the outer layer of the skin. Usually, basal cell carcinoma doesn't spread to different regions of the body.

6.1.3 Squamous Cell Cancer

Squamous cell malignant growth influences the cells on the peripheral piece of the epidermis. Squamous cells can likewise be found in regions like the lungs and mucous layers. When there are squamous cell malignant growth structures in the skin, it's known as cutaneous squamous cell disease.

6.1.4 Melanoma

One more classification of skin malignant growth is melanoma, where the malignant growth is created from the cells that give your skin tone. These cells are known as melanocytes. Noncancerous moles are framed by melanocytes, yet they can become destructive.

6.1.5 Merkel Cell Skin Cancer

Merkel cell skin malignant growth is an intriguing type of skin disease brought about by an excess of Merkel cells. As per a 2019 review by Trusted Source, Merkel cells are a particular sort of cell tracked down in the epidermis.

6.1.6 Lymphoma of the Skin

The body has white platelets that work as a piece of the resistant framework to guard against contamination and sickness. These cells are otherwise called lymphocytes.

6.1.7 Kaposi Sarcoma

Kaposi sarcoma (KS) shows up as red, brown, or purple patches or cancers on the skin. The regions are otherwise called lesions.

6.1.8 ACTı Keratosis

These are usually little patches of red, pink, or earthy colored skin. They're not destructive; however they are viewed as a type of precancer. Without treatment, these skin injuries might form into squamous cell carcinoma.

The fight against cancer can benefit from the use of artificial intelligence. Even the sudden appearances and complexities of diseases have been a cause for concern, calling for greater automation in the healthcare sector and increasing the likelihood of serious injury or death. These skin abnormalities are highly contagious, so they need to be treated quickly to stop the disease from spreading. Almost every known illness may be traced back to an unprotected encounter with harmful ultraviolet radiation (UR). Malignant melanoma is more dangerous than benign melanoma, but treatment is more likely to work for benign melanoma [2].

Medical imaging is only one area where AI, ML, and DL can be used to spot cancer in its early stages and treat patients before it becomes life-threatening. For those interested in a specific branch of machine learning, deep learning is it. When it comes to artificial neural networks, this branch of machine learning is the most cutting-edge option available. These algorithms are modelled after how our brains work. Speech recognition, pattern recognition, and bioinformatics are just some of the many fields that have found use for deep learning techniques. When compared to more traditional forms of machine learning, deep learning systems have proven to be remarkably effective in these contexts. In recent years, DL algorithms have been implemented in computer programmers for the purposes of analyzing and detecting skin cancer. Lack of data is the primary obstacle to the widespread use of deep learning in the medical field at this time. ANN and CNN generalize information from multiple sources to improve task prediction.

6.2 DEEP LEARNING

Warren McCulloch and Walter Pitts spent a great deal of time developing a computational model of the brain's neural networks. By combining the ideas of threshold logic and backpropagation, they were able to create a computational model of human mind. The development of deep learning has shaken up numerous markets and sectors.

For the purpose of simulating human cognition and creating abstract notions from raw data, a subsection of machine learning known as deep learning has been developed. Deep learning is capable of processing data in layers of algorithms, of comprehending human speech, and of recognizing things in images. Each successive layer receives its input from the output of the one above it. An input layer is the first layer in a network as shown in Figure 6.1, and an output layer is the final. Each of these "hidden layers" is really a straightforward algorithm that uses the same activation function throughout. In addition to deep learning, feature extraction is also a part of the field. Automatic feature generation occurs when an algorithm processes data to provide useful characteristics for subsequent analysis, training, and interpretation.

The earliest versions of what would become known as convolutional neural networks were neural networks that incorporated multiple pooling and convolutional layers. The computer was able to learn to recognize visual patterns because of the

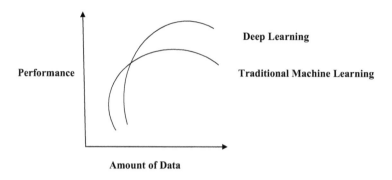

FIGURE 6.1 Deep learning technique

hierarchical, multi-layered structure. The networks were trained by repeatedly activating them over numerous layers, which made them more robust over time and gave them a modern appearance.

A major diagnostic AI application is cancer picture analysis in radiology. An exponential rise in the number of medical photographs being produced every year is leaving professionals behind on a global scale. Therefore, the artificial intelligence medical imaging market is predicted to hit $2 billion by 2023.

Radiologists benefit greatly from image analysis because it allows them to quantitatively aggregate many characteristics of imaging data, including tissue form, size, texture, and density. As a result, medical professionals can spend less time on mundane tasks like segmenting structures like CT scans, while receiving better analysis for each individual instance.

6.2.1 Deep Learning Approaches

To a large extent, deep neural networks can learn new information, recognize patterns, and make judgments with little to no help from a human operator. Because models may learn on their own when presented with new data. DL includes hybrid, supervised, unsupervised, and reinforcement.

6.2.1.1 Supervised Learning

In supervised learning, the algorithm is provided with a defined objective function. Labeled datasets, which include pairs of observable inputs (X) and their corresponding outputs (Y), are used in supervised learning. This data collection "trains" the machine learning algorithm to deduce input-output patterns. To rephrase, the method achieves its desired results by solving the equation. The Y-variable is the dependent one, while the X-variables are the characteristics.

6.2.1.2 Types

Depending on the kind of the target variable, supervised learning presents itself as either a classification or a classification problem. Classification and regression are two such methods.

6.2.1.2.1   Classification

Y represents a set of options, like "blue," "red," "illness," and "no disease." A spam filter is an application of a classification problem since it must decide if an incoming email is safe or suspicious and file it accordingly.

6.2.1.2.2   Regression

Predictions of continuous variables are at the heart of regression analysis. Examples of regression problems include attempting to estimate the future performance of a stock market or the amount of goals a team will score based on its past perform.

6.2.1.3   Unsupervised Learning

Unsupervised learning generates relevant labels (targets). What this means is that there is no end goal to be compared the inputs (Xs) against (Y). When given no labelled training data, unsupervised learning attempts to simulate the data's underlying structure or distribution in order to gain insight into it. Therefore, it can be helpful for investigating novel, complicated, and huge datasets.

6.2.1.4   Types of Unsupervised Learning

Unsupervised learning generates relevant labels (targets). To rephrase, the analysis begins with a set of inputs (Xs). Dimensionality reduction and clustering are two key forms of unsupervised learning.

To "dimensionally reduce" means to reduce the amount of inputs (features) while keeping the structure and utility of the information contained in the variation. Data scientists decrease a big dataset's dimension to ease modelling and reduce file size.

Clustering, on the other hand, aims to organize data by creating groupings of comparable observations called clusters, while separating out data that doesn't belong to any particular cluster. Clustering is used by asset managers, for instance, to classify investments into subgroups that are based on hard data (such as financial statements) rather than subjective factors (such as industry or geography).

6.2.1.5   Reinforcement Learning

By making mistakes and correcting them, a computer learns through reinforcement learning. In order to maximize an outcome, it learns dynamically by modifying its actions in response to ongoing feedback. Deep learning and reinforcement learning use neural networks (NNs) (ANNs). Non-linear and interactive tasks have been effectively tackled using ML techniques like those found in NNs.

Deep learning and reinforcement learning help computers solve issues on their own. With deep learning, computers may "learn" by analyzing and making predictions based on massive volumes of data without being explicitly programmed to do so. Complex algorithms solve problems including image classification, face identification, audio recognition, and natural language processing.

6.3   DEEP LEARNING ARCHITECTURES

In DL, deep and neural networks of different topologies make up the framework. Neural networks are built on the concept that data is fed into an input layer, then

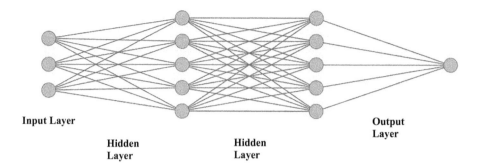

Input Layer

Output Layer

Hidden Layer   **Hidden Layer**

FIGURE 6.2   Layers of deep learning architecture

processed and combined in hidden layers, and then outputted from an additional layer to produce a final result, estimate, forecast, etc.

It's very similar to the framework used in machine learning. This reduces the time and effort required to create an ML algorithm from scratch, allowing for greater practical use of the technology and opening the door to new possibilities. The foundation of deep learning architectures is these neural networks. RNN, LSTM, GRU, CNN, DBN, and DSN are the six most popular deep learning architectures (Figure 6.2).

6.3.1   RNN: RECURRENT NEURAL NETWORKS

It is a foundational network architecture used in the development of other deep learning architectures. An extensive variety of deep learning architectures may be found in RNNs. To handle sequences of inputs of varying lengths, they can access their internal state memory. Information processed by RNNs' memories is recorded, retained, and used in the final calculation, which is helpful in applications such as speech recognition. In addition, the present network may have ties that feed back into earlier levels or even the same layer itself. This feedback makes it possible to remember past data and act on it immediately. When the order of data presentation is crucial, RNNs shine. Useful in natural language processing (i.e. chatbots), speech synthesis, and machine translation. The three types of RNN:

> **Bidirectional RNN**: They are bidirectional, and the output layer can access data as of both the past and the future.
>
> **Deep RNN:** There are several distinct levels. Due to this, the DL model can now extract additional hierarchical information.
>
> **LSTM: Long Short-Term Memory**: Short-term memory (LSTM) is an implementation of neural network topologies that uses the idea of a memory cell. The memory cell remembers what is most important, rather than only the most recently computed value, based on the inputs to the cell. Similarly, this is a form of RNN. The presence of feedback links in LSTM allows it to handle not only individual data points like pictures, but also complete progression of data like video or audio recordings.

For a cell, the output gate, a forget gate, and input gate are the basic building blocks of a conventional LSTM design. The cell can store values for indefinite periods of time thanks to these three gates, which also control the egress and entry of information.

The input gate determines what times data can be written into storage. The information contained within the cell is utilized in the output at predetermined times determined by the output gate. The forget gate determines when data can be forgotten so that the cell can move on to processing fresh information.

LSTMs are used to caption images, recognize handwriting, speak, compress text, and detect gestures. For less frequent and smaller datasets, a gated recurrent unit (GRU) may be preferable due to its superior performance.

6.3.2 CNN: CONVOLUTIONAL NEURAL NETWORKS

CNN is able to process an incoming image, prioritize different features or objects within it, and identify which ones are most important. An operation in mathematics known as "convolution" is responsible for giving the term "convolutional" to describe the combination of two or more functions. The layers of a convolutional neural network include not only an input and an output layer, but also several hidden layers. The convolutional layers that make up the CNN's hidden layers are what it relies on to do its job. It is widely employed in fields including linguistics, computer vision, and the visual arts.

CNNs Process: The process begins when the network takes in the information. A sequence of convolution layers equipped with different filters will be applied to each input (for example, an image). The signaling between the various layers is regulated by the control layer. Next, the output is flattened and sent into the fully connected layer, where every node in the network communicates with every other node in the layers below it. It's now possible to sort the results in several ways.

6.3.3 DBN: DEEP BELIEF NETWORK

Each pair of connected layers in a deep DBN is a restricted Boltzmann machine, making it a multilayer network with numerous hidden layers (RBM). Structured as a hierarchical network of interconnected but independently operating latent variables (or "hidden units"), it has no interlayer connections but does have connections between units within the same layer. DBNs produce results based on probability and unsupervised learning. In DBN, the input is shared between each tier. When it comes to CNNs, the first layers do nothing more than filter the inputs for simple features, whereas the last layers recombine all the basic patterns that were discovered in the first. DBNs function as a whole and are self-regulating. DBNs have several potential applications, including those in the fields of image recognition and natural language processing.

6.3.4 DSN: DEEP STACKING NETWORK

The architecture of deep learning used by DSN is unique. You may also hear DSNs referred to as deep convex networks. While a DSN/DCN is indeed deep, it is composed of many smaller networks rather than one single large one. Different

data-processing levels exist within each network in DSN. Because the training problem is so challenging with conventional deep learning models, a new architecture has
been developed to address it. When it comes to DSNs, training is seen as a collection
of issues, rather than one.

The original proposal for DSN architecture involved the idea of stacking, in which
"simple modules of functions or classifiers are created, and then piled on top of each
other, to learn complex functions or classifiers." There are at least three individual
parts. There are three distinct layers in each module: the input, the hidden, and the
output. Since these modules are layered upon one another, the output of one module
informs the input of the one above it. DSNs with this architecture can learn more
nuanced categorization tasks than they could with a lone module.

6.3.5   DEEP LEARNING AUTOENCODERS

One subset of feed-forward neural networks is known as autoencoders. Both the
input and the output share similar characteristics. A lower-dimensional code is generated from the input by an autoencoder. The result is derived from the input. The
model's code is an abbreviated form of the original data. Autoencoders have the
important job of separating "normal data" from "aberrations" [3].

Three parts make up an autoencoder:

- Code
- A decoder reconstructs the input from the code
- Encoder condenses the input and produces the code.

Autoencoders, for instance, are typically put to use in dimensionality reduction
and, naturally, anomaly detection. Consider the case of fraud. When provided with
sufficient quantities of authentic, representative training data, it's simple to construct
and train. The autoencoder's output could be unclear or skewed.

6.3.6   DEEP LEARNING METHODS

In order to shorten the training time and achieve better model performance, deep
learning algorithms can be taught to employ a gradient-based technique, in which the
gradient of the function being optimized is calculated via backpropagation.

6.3.7   STOCHASTIC GRADIENT DESCENT

To avoid becoming stuck in a local minimum, gradient descent algorithms can use
the convex function to determine the minimum value. Different paths to the optimal
value may be taken depending on the values of the role, learning rate, and step size.

6.3.8   LEARNING RATE DECAY

Stochastic gradient descent algorithms' performance can be improved and their
training time compressed through fiddling with the learning rate. One common

practice is to slow down the training process over time, allowing for dramatic initial alterations before settling into a more manageable pace. This paves the way for later-stage fine-tuning of the weights.

6.3.9 DROPOUT

It is a method for preventing overfitting in deep neural networks. During the training process, this approach randomly eliminates units and their connections. Dropout is a powerful regularization technique for lowering overfitting and raising generalization error. Tasks in computer vision, speech recognition document categorization, and computational biology are examples of supervised learning. Dropout provides superior results.

6.3.10 MAX-POOLING

In max-pooling, an input filter is applied to its overlapping sub-regions, and the input is the largest value from that window. Max-pooling helps lower the dimensionality and the computational cost of learning several parameters.

6.3.11 BATCH NORMALIZATION

To speed up deep neural networks, batch normalization minimizes covariate shift. When the weights are changed during training, it standardizes the layer's inputs for each mini-batch. The training process is shortened, and stability is improved through normalization. By normalizing the output of the previous activation layer, a neural network's stability can be improved.

6.3.12 SKIP-GRAM

For modelling word embedding techniques, skip-gram is a useful tool. According to the skip-grammatical paradigm, if the context of two different words is the same, then the words are the same. Meaningless statements that have the same meaning as "are mammals" include "cats are mammals" and "dogs are mammals."

The skip-gram can be created by skipping one term during neural network training and then using the model to forecast the term that was skipped in a context window comprising n terms.

6.3.13 TRANSFER LEARNING

A model is "transferred" in transfer learning from one task to another that is conceptually comparable to the original task. An additional network can be trained on a similar problem using the information gleaned from solving the original challenge.

6.3.14 Deep Learning Frameworks

If you want to quickly model a network without digging into the underlying techniques, a deep learning framework can help. The various frameworks serve a variety of distinct functions.

6.3.15 TensorFlow

Google developed TensorFlow, and it's now available to the public as an open-source project. It's a flexible and potent instrument for any purpose. It also includes a large and adaptable library of features. Classification models, regression models, and neural networks may all be constructed with the help of TensorFlow. It works well with a wide range of different machine learning models. CPU and GPU are both put to use.

6.3.15.1 Features

The entire iteration of an algorithm's calculations can be viewed in detail using TensorFlow. Its modular design means that you can pick and choose which parts of the framework you need to employ. Distributed training on the CPU and GPU is well supported in TensorFlow.

For the purpose of parallel training of neural networks and graphics processing units (GPUs), it provides pipelines to do so. As a result, it performs admirably in big distributed systems.

6.3.16 PyTorch

Framework based on Caffe2, PyTorch, and Torch library. It is ideal for designing neural networks. PyTorch is free software. It also enables the development of cloud-based software. It supports the user interface development language Lua. It is integral to Python. Additionally, it is compatible with well-known libraries such as Numba and Cython. PyTorch provides a framework for the construction of computational graphs.

6.3.16.1 Features

The utilization of native Python code enables simple execution and greater adaptability.

The transition from development mode to graphics mode is simple. This also contributes to the increased performance and accelerated development of C++ runtime environments.

PyTorch utilizes varying execution intervals for each communication, thereby enhancing the performance of models in both training and production settings. It offers a workflow from beginning to end. This also lets you build models in Python and make them available on iOS and Android.

6.3.17 SciKit Learn

SciKit Learn is a free programme. It is made up of several documents that let the developer change the algorithm's parameters while it is being used or while it is running. This also makes it easy to tweak models and find problems.

SciKit Learn also supports the development of deep learning with a large Python library. It's one of the best tools you can use to mine and analyze data. It also has a lot of functions for preprocessing.

6.3.17.1   Features

It works with most algorithms for learning from examples. SciKit Learn also works with algorithms for learning without supervision. It also checks how accurate new models and data that can't be seen are. SciKit Learn also lets users combine predictions from different models and group data that doesn't have labels.

6.3.18   Keras

The first version was made by François Chollet. Keras is one of the deep learning frameworks and packages that is growing the most quickly. It has more than 350,000 users and 700 people who work on it for free. Keras works with the Python API for high-level neural networks.

6.3.18.1   Features

It also has a clear review in case there was a mistake. It offers modularity as a sequence or diagram and can also be put together with as few restrictions as possible. It is easy to grow because it is easy to add new modules.

6.3.19   MXNet

Apache MXNet is a library for deep learning. The Apache Software Foundation made it. MXNet can be used in a lot of different languages. It works with a number of cloud providers, including AWS and Microsoft Azure. MXNet was also chosen as the best deep learning framework for AWS by Amazon.

6.3.19.1   Features

MXNet works with many different programming languages, such as Scala, Julia, and Python. It also has multi-GPU training and training that is spread out. This lets neural networks be exported into other languages.

6.3.20   Deep Learning 4j(DL4J)

Deep Learning4j is complete with Java, Scala, C++, C, and CUDA. Different neural networks can also be used with DL4J. It works with CNN, RNN, and LSTM. In 2017, Hadoop and Apache Spark were added to DL4J.

Keras is probably the best place to start if you're new to deep learning. PyTorch can be used by an expert researcher who wants to use custom architectures a lot. Table 6.1 shows the deep learning frameworks evaluation.

6.4   DEEP LEARNING TECHNIQUE FOR SKIN CANCER DETECTION

6.4.1   Skin Cancer

Sun exposure causes skin cancer, an abnormal development of skin cells. Because of the fluctuating nature of skin sores in the dermatology field, the ongoing advancements for this assignment have demonstrated that profound learning is the best procedure for addressing the issue.

TABLE 6.1
Evaluate Deep Learning Frameworks

Deep Learning Framework	Language Written in	Release Year	Pre-Trained Models
PyTorch	Python, C	2016	Yes
Keras	Python	2015	Yes
TensorFlow	C++, Python	2015	Yes
Deep Learning4j	C++, Java	2014	Yes

As a matter-of-fact, dermatologists have zero faith in just the image data. They likewise utilize the patient's socioeconomic status to give a more solid testing data. Clinical factors such as the patient's age, gender, nationality, and whether or not the sore is damaged or tingles, among many others, are significant hints toward a better forecast.

Visual inspection is the first step in identifying skin cancer. The dermatologist examines the worrisome lesion both with their own eyes and with the help of a dermatoscope, a handheld microscope that allows low-level magnification of the skin. If the dermatologist still suspects cancer after these tests, a biopsy will be performed. The incorporation of this method into the testing procedure is in line with a current trend in computing that mixes image processing with deep learning, a form of artificial intelligence inspired by the neural networks of the brain. Deep learning has been around for about a decade, but it was not until recently that it was successfully applied to image processing applications.

Each image was provided to the algorithm in its raw pixel form alongside a label indicating the ailment it was meant to detect. This approach to training algorithms has the advantage of requiring less preprocessing or sorting of images before classification, therefore opening up the possibility of using data from a broader range of sources.

6.4.2 DEEP LEARNING METHODOLOGY

Doctors usually utilize biopsy to detect skin cancer in early skin cancer treatment [4]. During this procedure, a skin lesion is sent to a doctor to be checked to see if it is cancerous. This process takes more time and a lot of work from people. Computer-based technology makes it easy, cheap, and quick to find out if someone has skin cancer. Several non-invasive ways have been suggested for checking the skin to see if it has melanoma or not. Figure 6.3 shows the general process used to find skin cancer: image acquisition, picture preprocessing, image segmentation, feature extraction, and classification.

In recent years, computers have been able to find skin cancer with the help of deep learning. Skin cancer detection techniques based on different algorithms are used to look at the image data. Traditional deep learning algorithms used to identify skin cancer include ANN, CNN, KNN, and GAN [5].

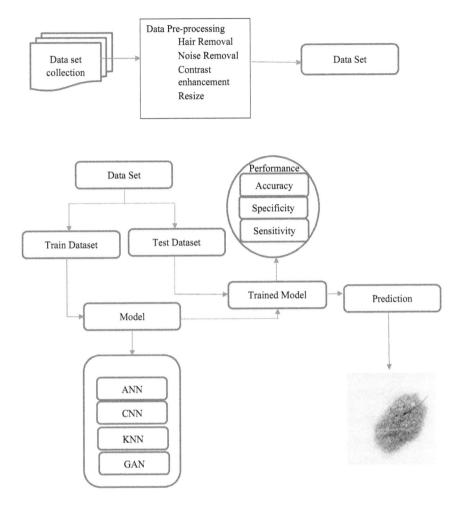

Cancerous Skin

FIGURE 6.3   Deep learning methodology

6.4.3   DATASET SEARCH STRATEGY

Most of the recent progress in deep learning models has been tied to having a lot of different types and sizes of data. For machine learning models to work better, they need to have access to a lot of data. Getting such a huge amount of data is both expensive and time consuming [6]. It is very important to search in a planned and organized way if you want to find useful things in the searched data domain. At this stage, we searched the massive dataset extensively for anything of value. We made an automated search system that gets rid of data from all sources that don't belong to the domain we wanted.

Nevus   Dermatofibroma   Melanoma

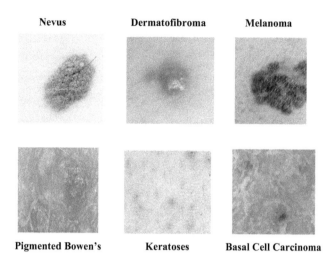

Pigmented Bowen's   Keratoses   Basal Cell Carcinoma

FIGURE 6.4   ISIC2018 skin cancer dataset

Websites with information about skin cancer, its risks, why it happens, and how to find it were looked at carefully.

Ninety percent of all cases were randomly selected from each category and utilized as the training set. The remaining sample (around 10 percent) served as the test group. This means that there were a total of 3060 cells in the training set (1530 good cells and 1530 poor cells) and 340 in the test set (170 benign and 170 malignant).

6.4.4 Deep Learning Techniques

Deep neural networks are a big part of figuring out if someone has skin cancer. It is made up of a network of nodes that are all connected to each other, just like neurons in the brain. All of their nodes work together to solve certain problems. They were taught to classify images and tell the difference between different kinds of skin cancer. The International Skin Imaging Collaboration (ISIC) database was mined to create this image of various skin lesions as shown in Figure 6.4.

For learning, different search methods are used, like KNN, CNN, GAN, and ANN for skin cancer detection systems.

6.5 TECHNIQUES FOR SKIN CANCER DETECTION USING ARTIFICIAL NEURAL NETWORK (ANN)

Malignant melanoma is successfully distinguished from other skin conditions thanks to the classifier's effective application. Effectiveness of the feed-forward multilayer network has been confirmed. Educating individuals makes use of the backpropagation neural (BPN) technique. It should have one layer for input, one layer that stays hidden, and one layer for output [7]. The weight values are fine-tuned at the second- and third-layer nodes based on how well the categories are made. During the

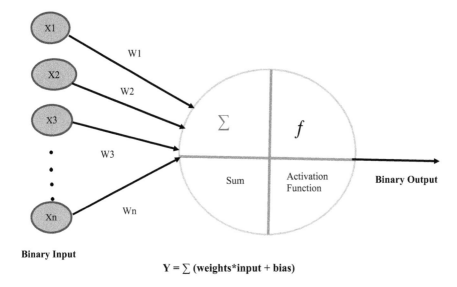

$$Y = \sum (\text{weights*input} + \text{bias})$$

FIGURE 6.5   ANN-based skin cancer detection techniques

BPN process, the signal will move in a forward direction. Any mistakes will be sent backward, and the masses will be fine-tuned to reduce error.

The weights are fine-tuned so that they match the slope of the error curve. So the process of forecasting and classifying is much more consistent. Figure 6.5 shows how ANN is put together. During the BPN process, weights are chosen at random. People will be excited based on what they were taught. Here, supervisory learning is used. The network's output during the signal phase is determined by the inputs of the starting mass and the triggering function. This output has something to do with what was expected to happen. After that, the process stops until the error is 0. It is taught to have certain values. After being trained, the network can make decisions.

ANN is used to classify extracted features in systems that look for skin cancer. After training and classifying the training set, input images are put into two groups: those with melanoma and those without. The number of photos supplied into an ANN determines its hidden layers [8]. Through the input dataset, the first layer of the ANN process is linked to the hidden layer. Depending on the dataset, either supervised or unsupervised learning can be used. Information is transmitted from the input layer to the output layer.

6.6   CONVOLUTIONAL NEURAL NETWORK BASED METHOD FOR DETECTING SKIN CANCER

Deep neural networks include convolution neural networks (CNNs). It is used to sort images into groups, put together a group of images, and do image recognition. CNN is a great way to collect and learn from global and local data. Combining curves and edges creates forms and corners. CNNs use convolution, non-linear pooling, and

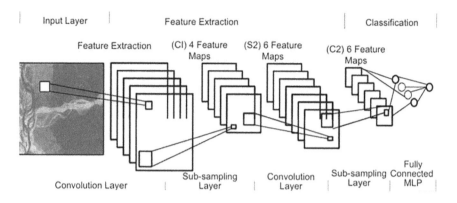

FIGURE 6.6   CNN-based skin cancer detection technique

other related layers [9]. CNN is made up of three different types of layers: convolution layers, pooling layers, and full-connected layers. Figure 6.6 shows how a CNN is put together at its most basic level.

The CNN algorithm was used to find things in medical images, divide them up, and put them into groups. It looked at how to put four different kinds of images of skin lesions into different groups [10]. AlexNet, a deep CNN that had been trained before, was used to pull out features. Then, as a classifier, error-correcting output coding SVM was used. The average scores for sensitivity, specificity, and accuracy were all highest for the proposed system. By classifying input photographs as normal skin or lesion, a deep CNN-based system was developed to detect skin lesion edges [11].

6.7   SKIN CANCER DETECTION METHODS BASED ON KOHONEN SELF-ORGANIZING NEURAL NETWORK (KNN)

It is a type of machine learning that uses a deep network. It is the map of Kohonen putting itself together. Unsupervised learning is used to train CNNs, which don't need any help from developers and don't need to know anything about the properties of the input data.

For the most part, a KNN will have two distinct layers (Figure 6.7). Layer one is the input layer. The second is commonly referred to as "competition." All of the connections between these layers happen between the first- and second-layer dimensions. It is also used to group data without knowing how the parts of the input data are connected. A self-organizing map is another name for this concept. Instead of having a separate output layer, each competitive layer node functions as an output node in KNNs [11].

Most of the time, this organizing map is used to reduce the number of dimensions. It can take data with a lot of dimensions and turn it into a simple format, like a 2D plane, with fewer dimensions. So it gives discrete representations of the dataset it is given. When doing a top-down dimension mapping using KNN, the

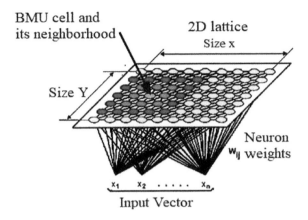

FIGURE 6.7   KNN-based skin cancer detection techniques [12]

topological properties of the original data space are preserved. To preserve anything means to maintain its original state across all of its data dimensions. Variables that are geographically close together in the input data space are mapped to be even closer together, whereas points that are geographically far apart are projected to be even further apart.

As a result, a KNN is the optimal technique for high-dimensional data. One of the most important things about the KNN is that it can't generalize. The network can recognize and sort data that it doesn't know about. The most important thing about a KKN is that it can map hard relationships between data points, including non-linear correlations. Because of these benefits, KNNs are used to find out if someone has skin cancer.

6.8   TECHNIQUES FOR GENERATIVE ADVERSARIAL NETWORK (GAN)-BASED SKIN CANCER DETECTION

As a subset of DNNs, GANs are grounded on the study of zero-sum games. A mathematical analysis of a situation in which one party gains and the other loses exactly the same amount. GANs compete to find and quantify differences in a dataset using a generator and a discriminator neural net (Figure 6.8).

The creation module uses data dispensing to create phony data samples for the discriminator module. The discriminator module's goal is to identify genuine data samples from sham ones. Both neural networks continue to progress through their respective alpha and beta stages as long as they are competing with one another.

The ability of a GAN network to generate realistic-looking images that employ the same data distribution as genuine photographs is a major benefit. Deep convolutional GAN (DCGAN), super-resolution GAN (SRGAN), vanilla GAN, condition GAN (CGAN), and Laplacian Pyramid GAN can address deep learning challenges (LPGAN). GANs can now detect skin cancer [13].

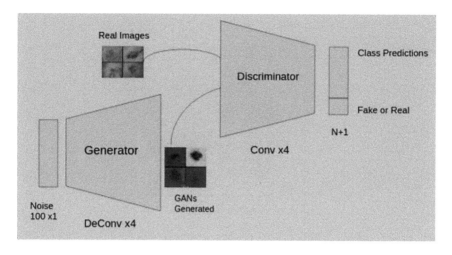

FIGURE 6.8   GAN-based skin cancer detection techniques [12]

6.9   EVALUATION METRICS

The ability to tell if an image is normal or not can be judged by its accuracy, sensitivity, and specificity.

A classifier sorts all the things into their respective categories. Objects are often incorrectly assigned classes due to imperfections in this process. To judge a classifier, you need to know the real class of the objects. To figure out how good the classification is, the class that the classifier gave and the actual class are compared. This makes it possible to divide the objects into four subsets:

- True positive (TP) means the classifier predicts properly.
- The classifier predicts accurately. False positive (FP).
- True negative (TN) means the classifier's negative class is correct.
- The classifier incorrectly assumes the class is negative.

6.9.1   ACCURACY

Using the amount of items in each of these subsets, statistical values may be determined for the classifier. It is only acceptable if the various classes are approximately distributed in the same manner. Precision may be quantified. Accuracy is a common and extensively employed metric, it's advantageous if the dataset's classes are evenly distributed.

$$Accuracy = (TP + TN) / (TP + TN + FP + FN) \qquad (6.1)$$

It says what percentage of objects have been put in the right category.

6.9.2 SENSITIVITY

Sensitivity and specificity are two other important metrics that can be used even if the different classes are not spread out in the same way. When analyzing a dataset, sensitivity is defined as the fraction of positive items that were accurately labelled as such.

$$Sensitivity = (TP) / (TP + FN) \qquad (6.2)$$

6.9.3 SPECIFICITY

Specificity is the percentage of negative objects accurately labelled in a dataset.

$$Specificity = (TN) / (TN + FP) \qquad (6.3)$$

A binary classifier's output can be thought of as a probability distribution over the classes. In a binary classifier, anything with an output value greater than 0.5 is allocated to the "positive" class. An alternative strategy is employed if the receiver operating characteristic can be determined (ROC).

Classification thresholds are continuously varied between 0 and 1, and for each threshold, sensitivity and specificity are calculated. When cancer is still in its early stages, it is easy for a medical professional to figure out what is wrong.

6.10 CONCLUSION

There are various innovative neural network algorithms for the detection and classification of skin cancer. These procedures are all non-invasive. Preprocessing, image segmentation, feature extraction, and classification are only a few of the many procedures involved in skin cancer detection. This work uses ANNs, CNNs, KNNs, and GANs to classify lesion images. Each algorithm has both benefits and drawbacks. Appropriate classification technique selection is essential for optimal outcomes. Due to its closer association with computer vision, CNN outperforms other neural network types when it comes to detecting picture data. Finding out whether or not a lesion in an image is cancerous is the primary focus of skin cancer detection studies.

Existing research is unable to respond to a patient's question as to whether or not a certain skin cancer symptom occurs on any portion of the body. Prior studies have concentrated on the unique difficulty of signal picture classification. Future study can integrate the usage of full-body imaging to uncover the solution to the reoccurring question. Autonomous, full-body photography speeds up the photo-taking process.

The discipline of deep learning has recently seen the development of the idea of auto-organization. Auto-organization is an unsupervised learning method for exploring a dataset's image samples in search of detectable features and previously unknown relationships or patterns. Expert system feature representations are enhanced by auto-organization procedures, which fall under the aegis of convolutional neural networks. One concept that is actively being studied and refined is auto-organization. This study has the potential to improve the quality of future image processing systems, especially in the field of medical imaging where even the smallest of details are vital to making a correct diagnosis of a condition.

REFERENCES

[1] Dildar, M.; Akram, S.; Irfan, M.; Khan, H.U.; Ramzan, M.; Mahmood, A.R.; Alsaiari, S.A.; Saeed, A.H; Alraddadi, M.O.; Mahnashi, M.H. Skin Cancer Detection: A Review Using Deep Learning Techniques. International Journal of Environmental Research and Public Health 20 May 2021, 18(10), 5479.
[2] Lu, X.; Firoozeh Abolhasani Zadeh, Y.A. Deep Learning-Based Classification for Melanoma Detection Using Xception Net. Hindawi Journal of Healthcare Engineering 2022, ArticleID2196096. https://doi.org/10.1155/2022/2196096.
[3] Singh, M.; Kumar, K. *Cancer Detection Using Convolutional Neural Network*. ResearchGate. https://doi.org/10.1007/978-3-030-67187-7_30.
[4] Nahata, H.; Singh, S.P. Deep Learning Solutions for Skin Cancer Detection and Diagnosis. In *Machine Learning with HealthCare Perspective*; Springer, March 2020. https://doi.org/10.1007/978-3-030-40850-3_8.
[5] Medhat, S.; Abdel Galil, H.; Aboutabl, A.E.; Saleh, H. Skin Cancer Diagnosis Using Convolutional Neural Networks for Smartphone Images: A Comparative Study. Journal of Radiation Research and Applied Sciences 2022, 15, 262–267.
[6] Ameri, A. A Deep Learning Approach to Skin Cancer Detection in Dermoscopy Images. Journal of Biomedical Physics Engineering December 2020. https://doi.org/10.31661/jbpe. v0i0.2004-1107.
[7] Aqib, M.; Mehmood, R.; Albeshri, A.; Alzahrani, A. Disaster Management in Smart Cities by Forecasting Traffic Plan Using Deep Learning and GPUs. In *Smart Societies, Infrastructure, Technologies and Applications*; Mehmood, R., Bhaduri, B., Katib, I., Chlamtac, I., Eds.; Lecture Notes of the Institute for Computer Sciences, Social Informatics and Telecommunications Engineering; Springer International Publishing: Cham, Switzerland, 2018; Volume 224, pp. 139–154.
[8] Shyamala Devi, M.; Sruthi, A.N.; Balamurugan, P. Artificial Neural Network Classification-Based Skin Cancer Detection. International Journal of Engineering & Technology 2018, 79(1.1), 591–593.
[9] Yu, L.; Chen, H.; Dou, Q.; Qin, J.; Heng, P.A. Automated Melanoma Recognition in Dermoscopy Images via Very Deep Residual Networks. IEEE Transactions on Medical Imaging 2017, 36, 994–1004.
[10] Rehman, M.; Khan, S.H.; Danish Rizvi, S.M.; Abbas, Z.; Zafar, A. Classification of Skin Lesion by Interference of Segmentation and Convolution Neural Network. In Proceedings of the 2018 2nd International Conference on Engineering Innovation (ICEI), Bangkok, Thailand, 5–6 July 2018; pp. 81–85.
[11] DeVries, T.; Ramachandram, D. Skin Lesion Classification Using Deep Multi-Scale Convolutional Neural Networks. arXiv 2017. arXiv:1703.01402. Available online: http://arxiv.org/abs/1703.01402 (accessed on 13 February 2021).

[12] Rashid, H.; Tanveer, M.A.; Khan, H. Skin Lesion Classification Using GAN based Data Augmentation. In Conference Proceedings: . . . Annual International Conference of the IEEE Engineering in Medicine and Biology Society, 2019; pp. 916–919. https://doi.org/10.1109/EMBC.2019.8857905.

[13] Osualaa, R.; Kushibara, K.; Garruchoa L., et al. A Review of Generative Adversarial Networks in Cancer Imaging: New Applications, New Solutions. 20 July 2021. arXiv:2107.09543v1[eess.IV].

7 Prediction of Epidermis Disease Outbreak Using Deep Learning

K. Uma, C. Ramesh Kumar, and Thirumurugan Shanmugam

7.1 INTRODUCTION

Roughly 10%–12% of the Indian population suffers from some sort of skin disorder. Skin protects and senses the outside world [1]. The skin has seven layers of ecto-dermic tissue that serve to shield the human body's skeleton, muscles, and internal organs. Poor skin care, pollution, climate change, and UV radiation can cause skin problems. Two to three percent more cancer cases can be expected for every 1% of ozone depletion. Benign skin cancer and malignant skin cancer are two types of skin cancer. Image processing advancements enable a non-invasive technique for diagnosis and categorization, as well as an impartial interpretation of skin cancer. Meanwhile, even highly trained dermatologists have trouble telling the difference between a melanoma and a benign mole in their early stages of development [2]. This is why algorithms for computers are constantly being refined.

There are two ways that skin cancer can manifest itself: benign and malignant. Malignant melanoma appears as sores that bleed; benign melanoma has normal moles [2–4]. Malignant melanoma, the deadliest skin cancer, is curable if caught early [5]. There are both non-invasive and invasive methods for diagnosing a condition [3]. Micromorphology can be studied in a non-invasive manner using dermatoscopy, an imaging technique that examines skin lesions with the help of a dermatoscope, but interpretation takes time [6, 7]. The other diagnosis involves the excision of the skin lesion using an invasive technique called biopsy [8, 9]. Image processing allows non-invasive skin cancer detection, classification, and impartial interpretation.

7.2 LITERATURE SURVEY

This study diagnosed skin disorders using adaptive thresholding, edge detection, K-means clustering, and morphology-based picture segmentation. Before processing, the acquired images were polished by removing blur and noise.

A processed image with a disease-related pattern can identify a corresponding input image's disease. This research uses the geometric properties of skin lesions as a diagnostic and categorizing tool for melanoma [10]. The ABCD-rule of dermos-copy is used to extract geometric features of a skin lesion by considering its asymmetry, border, and diameter. Dimensions such as area and perimeter, in addition

DOI: 10.1201/9781003343172-7

to indices such as circularity, greatest and shortest diameter, equivalent diameter, and irregularity index, were utilized as criteria for the classification of the dataset. These indices were also utilized to determine the equivalent diameter [11]. Malignant melanoma, benign melanoma, and unknown melanoma are the three distinct types of skin lesions that are taken into consideration in this research. The k-nearest neighbors (k-NN) algorithm is utilized in the classification of images of skin lesions, with functional testing demonstrating an accuracy of 90.0% [12].

To reduce artifacts, the suggested method preprocesses input clinical photographs that may include lighting and noise effects. The enhanced images are then sent into a previously trained convolutional neural network (CNN), a sort of deep learning model. The CNN classifier, which was developed using a large number of training examples, can distinguish between benign and malignant instances. According to experimental results [13], the suggested strategy outperforms state-of-the-art methods in terms of diagnostic accuracy.

In this chapter, we present an automated, image-processing-based method for identifying melanoma. The device takes a picture of the skin lesion and analyses it with state-of-the-art image processing technology to determine if it is cancerous. Texture, size, and shape analysis can detect melanoma parameters like asymmetry, border, color, diameter (ABCD), and more during image segmentation and feature phases. Using the extracted feature parameters, the image is separated into two classes: melanoma cancer lesion and normal skin. In this chapter, we describe a color-based and shape-based geometry-based automated skin lesion detection and prevention at an early stage through segmentation and analysis. Additional feature sets, such as color, are used by the method to identify the type of lesion. For the development and evaluation of our system, we tapped into Pedro Hispano Hospital's PH2 dermoscopy image database. The 200 dermoscopy images in this collection cover a wide range of lesions, from the common to the rare and even malignant. To spot atypical lesions before they progress into melanoma, our method analyses their color and shape geometry.

Melanoma has replaced basal cell carcinoma as the most feared skin cancer due to its high metastatic potential even when detected early. Medical image processing, or non-invasive medical computer vision, is increasingly used in the clinical diagnosis of many diseases. These methods offer a tool for automatic image analysis that allows for a quick and accurate evaluation of the lesion. Dermoscopy image databases are collected and subjected to preprocessing. A threshold segments, gray level co-occurrence matrix (GLCM), asymmetry, border, color, and diameter features are extracted; features are chosen using principal component analysis (PCA), a total dermoscopy score is calculated, and classes are assigned using a support vector machine (SVM). Classification accuracy was 92.1%.

7.3 MATERIALS AND METHODS

7.3.1 EXISTING SYSTEMS

- For classification, a rule-based approach is utilized, with static range values provided for several classes. As a result, dynamic photos and outlier behavior images are not conceivable.

- The set of features is not normalized. As a result, during the classifier training phase, different features display various outputs and representations.
- Classifiers cannot tell when two features overlap. As a result, the image's pattern is not recognized during the learning phase.
- The class imbalance problem is ignored, and the multi-classification problem is not optimized. As a result, learning is biased because all classes are not considered during the learning phase.
- AdaBoost classifier and PCA are used in the current method to classify data and segment images, respectively.

Disadvantages:

- Precision is lower.
- A technique under supervision is used.
- Also, the precision value is lower.

7.3.2 Problem Definition

- The presence of skin cancer will be predicted using image processing. First-order statistical features are computed by selecting the PCA-generated significant feature vectors for closer inspection, after which the textured top of these slices is extracted.
- To improve accuracy in comparison to other methods.

7.4 PROPOSED METHOD

A Gaussian filter can be used to improve the mammography picture in our proposed method. Fuzzy c segments the mammography image into many segments to easily detect the mass, and DWT extracts characteristics (discrete wavelet features). The CNN classifier has been used to analyze and categorize additional tumors. Due to the convex nature of the optimality problem, CNN offers a special solution. This is a benefit compared to neural networks, which may not be robust across different samples because they have multiple solutions connected to local minima. Figure 7.1 shows the system architecture.

Advantages

- Greater Accuracy
- Decreased time commitment
- Classification can be carried out with a lot more precision.
- **High-Dimensionality:** The KNN is a useful tool in high-dimensional spaces, and it is especially applicable to sentiment analysis and document classification, where the dimensionality can be very high.
- **Memory Efficiency:** Since only a portion of the training points are used in the decision-making process for selecting new members, only these points need to be stored in memory (and used as the basis for calculations).
- **Flexibility:** Class division is frequently very non-linear. Greater classification performance results from the ability to apply new kernels, which gives the decision boundaries a great deal of flexibility.

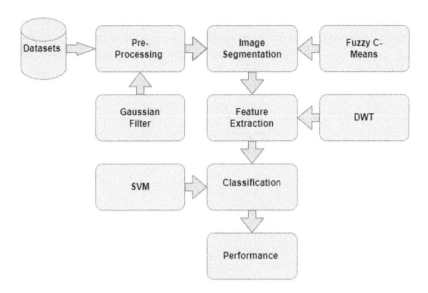

FIGURE 7.1   System architecture

7.4.1   IMAGE PREPROCESSING

Any camera, including a mobile camera, can be used to capture the input image that is provided to the system regardless of the lighting conditions. As a result, pre-processing is required. The preprocessing in this case consists of image resizing as well as brightness and contrast adjustments. This is done to account for the image's uneven lighting. Gamma correction is one of the image processing techniques used in these procedures.

7.4.2   SEGMENTATION OF IMAGES

Our proposed automatic thresholding and masking operation is applied to the R, G, and B planes to perform image segmentation. FCM suggests beginning with an automatic threshold in each plane. Combining the binary masks from each plane yields the lesion mask. Edge detection follows segmentation. Removing features requires separating the lesion from healthy skin. Besides the skin lesion, the segmented image may show many smaller blobs. Fuzzy c-means (FCM) clusters each data point. As a workaround, we look for the image segment with the largest blob. The skin lesion is the only part of the image that was segmented.

7.4.3   FUZZY C-MEAN

Fuzzy c-means (FCM) clusters each data point. Data points closer to the cluster's center have a higher degree of membership.

FCM clustering is used by the FCM function. The initial assumption is made by randomly selecting the centers and the average locations of each cluster. Then, for each cluster, FCM assigns a random membership grade to each data point. FCM iteratively updates cluster centers and membership grades to determine a data point's cluster membership. In this iteration, we minimize a distance objective function between each data point and the cluster center, where each data point's weight in the objective function is determined by its membership in the cluster.

7.4.3.1 Algorithm

FCM clustering assigns each data point to multiple groups. For FCM, the following objective function serves as the basis:

$$F_m = \sum_{i=1}^{D} \sum_{j=1}^{N} Z_{ij}^m \left\| A_i - B_j \right\|^2$$

where
- The number of data points is denoted by D.
- N denotes the number of clusters.
- The fuzzy partition matrix exponent m > 1 determines fuzzy overlap. Fuzzy overlap, the percentage of data points in multiple clusters, indicates group fuzziness.
- The datapoint X^{th} is denoted by A_i.
- The Yth cluster has a nucleus located at B_j.
- Z_{ij} represents A_i's X^{th} cluster membership. The sum of all cluster membership values for X^{th} equals one. fcm clusters:
1. Initialize the cluster membership values at random, Z_{ij}.
2. Determine the cluster centers:

$$A_i = \frac{\sum_{i=1}^{D} Z_{ij}^m A_i}{\sum_{i=1}^{D} Z_{ij}^m}$$

Update Z_{ij} as follows:

$$Z_{ij} = \frac{1}{\sum_{k=1}^{N} \left(\frac{\left\| A_i - B_j \right\|}{\left\| A_i - B_k \right\|} \right)^{2m-1}}$$

3. Determine the objective function, F_m.
4. Repeat steps 2–4 until F_m has improved by the desired amount or until a predetermined limit has been reached in terms of the total number of iterations.

7.4.4 EXTRACTION OF CHARACTERISTICS

Feature extraction, a dimensionality reduction method, compactly represents an image's aesthetic features. This method is useful for image matching and retrieval when large image files require a reduced feature representation. Feature detection, extraction, and matching are used in computer vision problems like object identification, content-based picture retrieval, face detection, and texture classification.

7.4.5 DWT Algorithm

The single-level 2D wavelet decomposition is computed by dwt2. Compare wavedec2 to dwt2 to see which might be better for your application. A specific wavelet or set of wavelet decomposition filters is taken into consideration when performing the decomposition.

The algorithm for the 2D wavelet decomposition of images is analogous to the one-dimensional case. The two-dimensional wavelet and scaling functions are created from the tensor products of the one-dimensional functions. This type of two-dimensional DWT causes the approximation coefficients at level j to be divided into four components: level j+1 approximation, details in three orientations, and level j approximation (horizontal, vertical, and diagonal).

7.4.6 Gaussian Filter

The noise in the input image of the system is reduced using a Gaussian filter. The window size of the Gaussian function is infinite. For tiny windows, it is often best to truncate the filter window and apply the filter directly because it decays quickly, effectively employing a simple rectangular window function.

A co-occurrence matrix, also known as a co-occurrence distribution or GLCM, is a matrix that is defined over an image as the distribution of co-occurring pixel values (colors or grayscale values) at a specific offset. It is a method for texture analysis that has many uses, particularly in the analysis of medical images. Sets of data are referred to as datasets. Let's take a look at the normal and abnormal patient prediction data from skin disease databases. To predict the disease based on the skin disease detection, an input dataset in the form of an image can be obtained here. Based on normal and abnormal conditions, two classes of data will be collected. Data preprocessing techniques may be required for reliable and fruitful analysis. The term "data cleaning" is used to describe processes to identify, eliminate, and replace the inaccurate or missing information. Here, the Gaussian method is used for preprocessing. The system's input image is cleaned up by eliminating noise with the help of a Gaussian filter.

7.5 RESULTS AND DISCUSSION

A process called image segmentation involves dividing an image into several segments (pixel groups, often known as image objects). The goal of picture segmentation is to make an image representation more comprehensible and easier to analyze. Segmenting images is a method for separating different parts of a picture (such as lines, curves, etc.). Segmenting an image involves assigning labels to each pixel in the image with the intention that those pixels sharing the same label will share the same characteristics. Here, segmentation can be applied to the system's FCM. One method for separating the image from the input data is called an FCM. Reducing the number of resources needed to describe a large set of data is the goal of feature extraction. One of the main issues when analyzing complex data is the sheer number of variables that are involved. When a high-dimensional investigation requires lots of memory and processing, a classification algorithm may overfit training examples and underperform on new samples. Feature extraction is a way of creating combinations of variables to avoid these concerns while still accurately describing the data. The DWT and GLCM can be used to extract features in this case.

The term "classification" is used to describe the process of categorizing diseases based on the normal and abnormal characteristics of the patient. The system's network can be trained using a classification process. Here, a classification method can be obtained by using a KNN model to categorize the model's output, which is shown in Figures 7.2–7.4.

The system's performance can then be evaluated. Use cases for a convolutional neural network-based generic model detection algorithm are listed in Table 7.1 (CNN). It will take time to develop the training model and put it through its paces in both training and testing. Transfer learning refines pre-trained models using COCO image task datasets by transferring a generic deep learning model to a specialized one with adjusted weights and outputs. CNN's internal structure is tweaked to improve performance, and the street environment is trained to adapt. The experimental results were compared, and they confirmed the viability of the optimized network.

7.5.1 IMAGE ENHANCEMENT AND RESTORATION

Here, the terms "image sharpening" and "restoration" refer to the processes used to enhance or manipulate images taken with a modern camera to produce desired

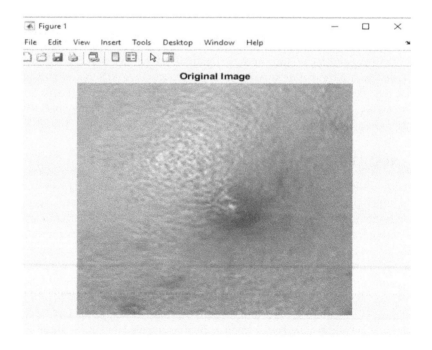

FIGURE 7.2   Skin cancer symptom image

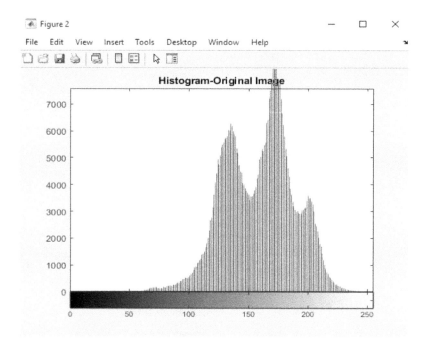

FIGURE 7.3 Histogram of skin cancer symptom image

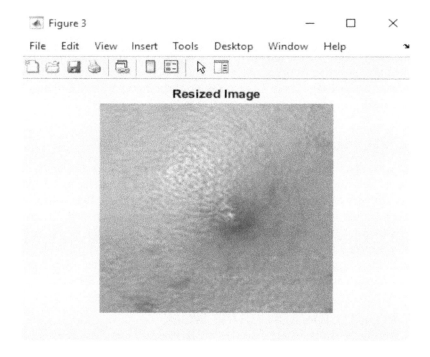

FIGURE 7.4 Resized skin cancer symptom image

TABLE 7.1
List of Application

S. No	Applications
1	sharpening and restoring images
2	clinical setting
3	remote monitoring
4	communication and coding
5	robot or machine vision
6	color gradation
7	pattern recognition
8	video editing
9	miniature imaging

TABLE 7.2
Applications of DIP

S. No	Applications of DIP
1	Gamma imaging
2	PET scanning
3	X-ray Imaging
4	Medical-CT
5	UV imaging

results. They allude to the standard functions of Photoshop. Zooming, blurring, sharpening, converting from greyscale to color, image retrieval, edge detection, and recognition are included. Table 7.2 shows some of the most prevalent DIP uses in the medical field.

7.5.2 UV Imaging

The process of scanning a large area of Earth from space or a great height is known as remote sensing. The detection of earthquake-related infrastructure damage is one specific use of digital image processing in remote sensing. Even when serious damages are the focus, it takes longer for damage to be understood. Because the area affected by an earthquake can occasionally be very large, it is impossible to visually inspect it to determine the extent of the damage. The process is very stressful and time consuming. In light of this, digital image processing offers a remedy. Figures 7.5–7.10 display the histogram results for images of skin diseases.

7.6 CONCLUSION AND FUTURE WORK

To detect and classify skin cancer, this investigation paid special attention to the geometrical features of skin lesions. Using the asymmetry, border, and diameter criteria

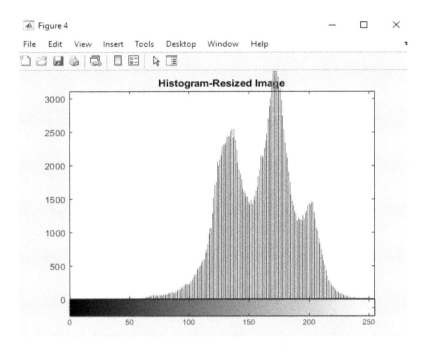

FIGURE 7.5   Shows the histogram of the resized image

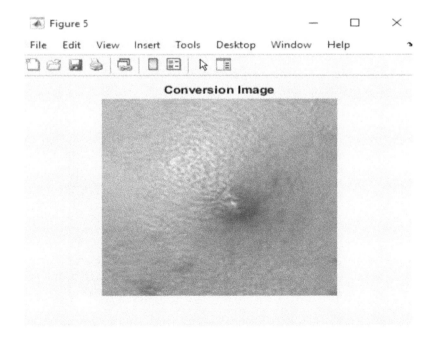

FIGURE 7.6   Conversion image

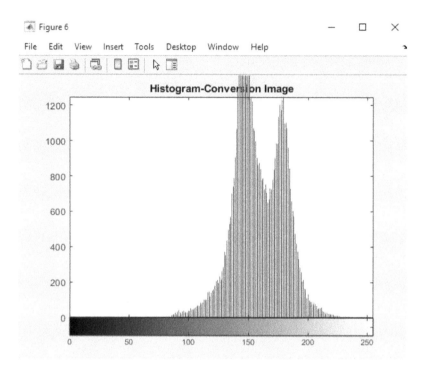

FIGURE 7.7   Histogram conversion image

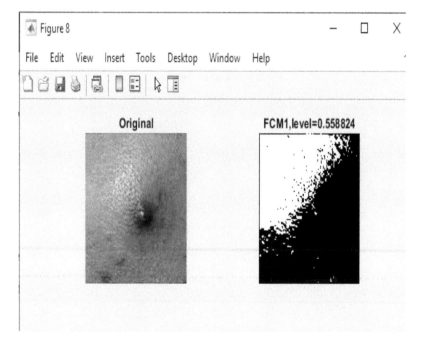

FIGURE 7.8   Original with FCM

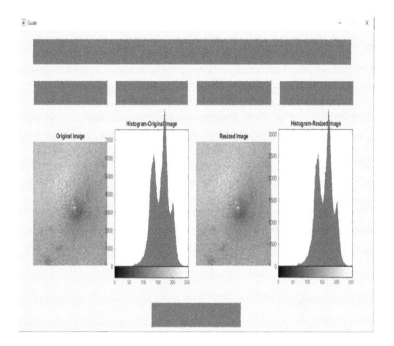

FIGURE 7.9   Final conversion image

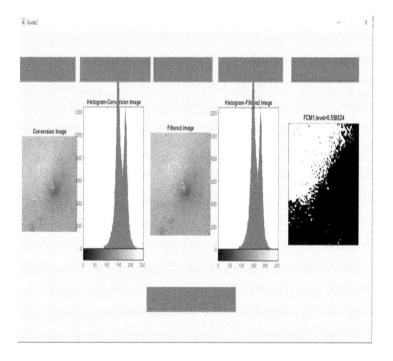

FIGURE 7.10   Final histogram ratio with CNN

of dermoscopy, geometric skin lesion features are extracted. The criteria for categorizing shapes in the dataset include their area, perimeter, circularity index, greatest, and additional dimensions such as shortest diameter, equivalent diameter, and irregularity index. Malignant melanoma, benign melanoma, and unknown skin lesions are all considered in the proposal. In contrast to SVM classification. To classify the skin disease and provide detailed information about the images, we performed four image segmentation techniques. The proposed method displayed the results using machine learning. In this case, pictures of acne, melanoma, and healthy skin were used to create the abnormal condition. The source image is treated as a dataset. MATLAB® software is used to implement and organize the resultant set. Finding the best classification method for the following to identify skin diseases will be made easier. According to the findings of our experiment, SVM is best for skin infection classification. Our performance metrics show experiment results. It offers an analysis of frameworks for deep learning-based object detection. A brief history of deep learning and its illustrative tool, the convolutional neural network, is given before our review (CNN).

7.6.2 Future Work

The term "image processing" refers to a set of procedures that can be applied to a picture to enhance it or get more information out of it. It's a form of signal processing where an image serves as input and the result can be another image or some features or characteristics of the original. One of these rapidly developing technologies is image processing. Both the engineering and computer science communities focus heavily on it as a research topic. Image processing involves the following three steps:

- importing the picture using software for image capture
- manipulating and analyzing the picture
- output, which can be a changed image or a report based on image analysis.

Analog and digital image processing methods exist. Prints and photos can be processed analogously. When using these visual techniques, image analysts employ various interpretational fundamentals. Computer-based digital image manipulation is made possible with the aid of digital image processing techniques. When using the digital technique, all types of data must go through three general phases – preprocessing, enhancement, and display – and information extraction.

REFERENCES

[1] Liu, Yuan, Ayush Jain, Clara Eng, David H. Way, Kang Lee, Peggy Bui, Kimberly Kanada et al. "A deep learning system for differential diagnosis of skin diseases." *Nature Medicine* 26, no. 6 (2020): 900–908.
[2] Patnaik, S.K., M.S. Sidhu, Y. Gehlot, B. Sharma, and P. Muthu. "Automated skin disease identification using deep learning algorithm." *Biomedical & Pharmacology Journal* 11, no. 3 (2018): 1429.
[3] Kshirsagar, Pravin R., Hariprasath Manoharan, S. Shitharth, Abdulrhman M. Alshareef, Nabeel Albishry, and Praveen Kumar Balachandran. "Deep learning approaches for prognosis of automated skin disease." *Life* 12, no. 3 (2022): 426.

[4] Putra, Tryan Aditya, Syahidah Izza Rufaida, and Jenq-Shiou Leu. "Enhanced skin condition prediction through machine learning using dynamic training and testing augmentation." *IEEE Access* 8 (2020): 40536–40546.

[5] Elngar, Ahmed A., Rishabh Kumar, Amber Hayat, and Prathamesh Churi. "Intelligent system for skin disease prediction using machine learning." *Journal of Physics: Conference Series* 1998, no. 1 (2021): 012037. IOP Publishing.

[6] Bhadula, Shuchi, Sachin Sharma, Piyush Juyal, and Chitransh Kulshrestha. "Machine learning algorithms based skin disease detection." *International Journal of Innovative Technology and Exploring Engineering (IJITEE)* 9, no. 2 (2019): 4044–4049.

[7] Verma, Anurag Kumar, Saurabh Pal, and Surjeet Kumar. "Prediction of different classes of skin disease using machine learning techniques." In *Smart Innovations in Communication and Computational Sciences: Proceedings of ICSICCS 2020*, pp. 91–100. Springer Singapore, 2021.

[8] Srinivasu, Parvathaneni Naga, Jalluri Gnana SivaSai, Muhammad Fazal Ijaz, Akash Kumar Bhoi, Wonjoon Kim, and James Jin Kang. "Classification of skin disease using deep learning neural networks with MobileNet V2 and LSTM." *Sensors* 21, no. 8 (2021): 2852.

[9] Aruchamy, Srinivasan, Amrita Haridasan, Ankit Verma, Partha Bhattacharjee, Sambhu Nath Nandy, and Siva Ram Krishna Vadali. "Alzheimer's disease detection using machine learning techniques in 3D MR images." In *2020 National Conference on Emerging Trends on Sustainable Technology and Engineering Applications (NCETSTEA)*, pp. 1–4. IEEE, 2020.

[10] Tien Bui, Dieu, and Nhat-Duc Hoang. "A Bayesian framework based on a Gaussian mixture model and radial-basis-function Fisher discriminant analysis (BayGmmKda V1.1) for spatial prediction of floods." *Geoscientific Model Development* 10, no. 9 (2017): 3391–3409.

[11] Moy, Austin J., Xu Feng, Hieu T.M. Nguyen, Yao Zhang, Katherine R. Sebastian, Jason S. Reichenberg, and James W. Tunnell. "Spectral biopsy for skin cancer diagnosis: initial clinical results." In *Photonics in Dermatology and Plastic Surgery*, vol. 10037, pp. 21–26. SPIE, 2017.

[12] Zhu, Xiangyu, Fatemeh Sobhani, Chunmiao Xu, Li Pan, Mounes Aliyari Ghasebeh, and Ihab R. Kamel. "Quantitative volumetric functional MR imaging: an imaging biomarker of early treatment response in hypo-vascular liver metastasis patients after yttrium-90 transarterial radioembolization." *Abdominal Radiology* 41 (2016): 1495–1504.

[13] Roy, Kyamelia, Sheli Sinha Chaudhuri, Sanjana Ghosh, Swarna Kamal Dutta, Proggya Chakraborty, and Rudradeep Sarkar. "Skin disease detection based on different segmentation techniques." In *2019 International Conference on Opto-Electronics and Applied Optics (Optronix)*, pp. 1–5. IEEE, 2019.

8 Deep Learning-Based Medical Image Segmentation
A Comprehensive Investigation

G. Vennira Selvi, T. Ganesh Kumar, V. Sheeja Kumari, Seema Dev Aksatha, and Priti Rishi

8.1 INTRODUCTION

Images are divided into a sequence of non-overlapping sections during image segmentation. These areas give human tissues completely dissimilar structures and put the tissue through the appropriate method for accurately finding experimental identification. Due to variations in patient structure like shape and size, automatic segmentation of medical images is difficult [1]. Additionally, automated segmentation will be difficult due to the poor contract surrounding the tissue. Recently, methods based on deep learning have made it possible to effectively classify and learn features directly from images. Medical image segmentation has advanced similarly as a result of the improvement of convolutional neural networks (CNNs) [2].

A convolutional neural network consists of sub-examining layers and multiple connectional layers. CNNs are efficient because only a data-driven method can learn an image's hierarchical feature representation [3]. The following describes the difficulties that come with using CNNs:

1. The previously hidden objects that are not included in the training dataset are not simplified by the CNN. Annotations of medical images are important for medical image segmentation because they require more knowledge and more time to give correct information. The skill of CNN to segment the quantified image for observations that are absent from the training dataset is hampered as a result [4].
2. The most current research does not adapt to different test images and needs in-depth image learning to treaty with the great framework differences between dissimilar images.

In machine learning algorithms, deep learning is a set of rules which efficiently and automatically analyzes medical images for disease diagnosis [5]. Deep learning has

DOI: 10.1201/9781003343172-8

expanded approval in current years due to its capability to deliver improved prediction from a given data set at a higher level of abstraction. Image segmentation techniques for medical images based on deep learning are compared and to determine the obstacles that need to be overcome in future research.

8.2 DISTINCT FEATURES OF DEEP LEARNING

A major advantage of deep learning is that driven by huge amounts of data. Deep learning typically requires high-performance hardware compared to conventional machine learning algorithms. In conventional machine learning techniques, domain experts are typically required to identify features to reduce the complexity of the data. However, in deep learning algorithms, high-level features are learned incrementally, enabling the algorithm to automatically extract complex features from the data. This reduces the reliance on domain experts for feature identification. Figure 8.1 shows the differentiation of machine learning with deep learning.

Another important dissimilarity between machine learning and deep learning techniques is the approach of solving the problem. The conventional machine learning divides the problem into small parts that are solved first. The DL gives the end-to-end solution to the given problem.

8.2.1 WHEN TO APPLY DEEP LEARNING

Deep learning could find the solution for a complex problem that necessitates detecting the hidden patterns within the data. Deep learning also finds the relationship between a huge amount of independent and interdependent variables. Deep learning algorithms learn the hidden patterns from data and combine the learned data together to build the effective decision rules. Deep learning plays the most important role for handling lots of unstructured data.

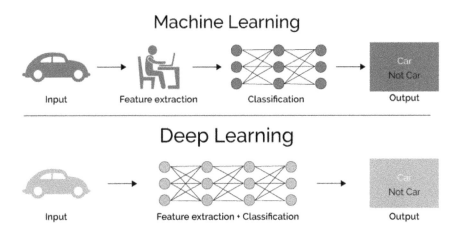

FIGURE 8.1 Differentiation of machine learning with deep learning

In most of the situation, the machine intelligence is better or equal than human experts, which means deep learning can provide a better clarification to the following issues.

- Where people can't make sense of choices made utilizing their expertise, such as medical decisions, etc.
- Where the issue solutions are updated over time. For example, price level prediction, climate forecasting, and object tracing.
- Where the solution necessitates transformation that depends on some precise situations such as biometrics or personalization.
- Where the size of the issue is enormous and surpasses our lacking thinking skills. For example, sentiment analysis, deciding web page ranks, and pattern matching.

8.3   THE PERFORMANCE FEATURES OF DEEP LEARNING

1. **Approach to Universal Learning:** It is possible to learn and implement all applications using deep learning; consequently, it is known as universal learning.
2. **Robustness:** In general, DL techniques do not necessitate precisely designed functions. Instead, the optimized functions are discovered in a way that is automatic and related to the project under consideration.
3. **Generalization:** The same DL method – commonly referred to as switch learning (TL) – can be used by a variety of statistical formats or special software. This method is defined in the following section. In addition, it is a valuable strategy in situations where statistics are inadequate.
4. **Scalability:** The scalability in DL is incredible. Microsoft's ResNet [6] has 1202 layers, is recurrently implemented on a supercomputing measure, and was developed by Microsoft.

8.4   THE CLASSIFICATION OF DL METHODS

There are three main divisions of DL techniques:

- unsupervised
- partial supervised (i.e., semi-supervised)
- supervised.

Another learning method that is frequently seen as being under the group of partially supervised learning methods is deep reinforcement learning (DRL), commonly known as RL.

8.4.1   DEEP SUPERVISED LEARNING

This method utilizes labelled data. While taking such a method, the surroundings have a variety of inputs and subsequent outputs (xt, yt)~ρ. If the input is xt, the smart agent makes a best guess as to what the loss value will be. There are various supervised learning methods for DL available such as RNN, DNNs, etc.

8.4.2 DEEP SEMI-SUPERVISED LEARNING

This method uses semi-labeled datasets as the foundation for the learning process. Occasionally, this method is used in conjunction with DRL and generative adversarial networks (GANs). This method has the benefit of requiring the least amount of labelled possible data. On the other hand, this technique has some drawbacks, including the potential for inaccurate choices due to irrelevant input features included in training data.

8.4.3 DEEP UNSUPERVISED LEARNING

This method makes it probable to carry out the learning procedure even in the lack of readily obtainable labeled data. The agent acquires the essential characteristics or inner illustration mandatory to determine any hidden relationships or structures in the supplied data here. Unsupervised learning typically incorporates methods for clustering, dimensionality reduction, and generative networks.

Several members of the DL family perform non-linear dimensionality reduction and clustering tasks, including the most recently developed limited Boltzmann machine methods, autoencoders, and GANs, and have demonstrated promising results. Unsupervised learning has also been used in a range of ways with RNNs.

8.5 DEEP REINFORCEMENT LEARNING

While supervised learning uses sample data that has already been provided, reinforcement learning works by interacting with the environment. Google Deep Mind was used to create this method [7]. Many improved strategies based on reinforcement learning were subsequently developed. If the input environment samples, for instance, the environment might query the agent. xt-p, as predicted by the agent: and the agent's received cost is, where P is the unidentified probability distribution. It responds with a loud score. This process is also known as semi-supervised learning. Several supervised and unsupervised strategies were created on the basis of this idea.

Because the reinforcement learning method lacks a simple loss function, performing this learning is far more challenging than typical supervised procedures. Additionally, there are two major differences between reinforcement learning and supervised learning. First, the function cannot be accessed fully, necessitating optimization and interaction. Second, the state that is being manipulated is based on an environment, and the input xt is based on the actions that came before it [8].

The sort of reinforcement learning that must be used to complete a job is chosen depending on the problem's scope. DRL, for instance, offers the best solution for issues with a large number of factors. Derivative-free reinforcement learning, on the other hand, is a method that works well for problems with constrained parameters. Reinforcement learning's primary flaw is that learning speed can be affected by settings. The following are the key reasons to use reinforcement learning:

- It helps you choose which activity yields the greatest reward over the long term.
- It helps you identify the situations that call for action.
- It also helps it to choose the most effective strategy for achieving significant benefits.
- Reinforcement learning is time-intensive and computer-intensive, especially if it is a vast workspace.

8.6   DEEP LEARNING ARCHITECTURE

This section looks at the various deep learning architectures that were created and used for medical image segmentation. This demonstrates that the whole field of medical image segmentation is saturated with deep learning technologies [9]. It places an emphasis on the specific contributions that shed light on or circumvent the challenges that arise when segmenting medical images. Medical image segmentation aims to arrange voxels in a way that evokes the structure of the object of interest's contour or interior. Segmentation, which is also the method that is naturally observed to be the most stretched out, is the method that is most frequently used to apply deep learning to medical images. In this section, the following significant and current profound learning models are examined.

8.6.1   RNN: RECURRENT NEURAL NETWORKS

A wide variety of deep learning architectures make up RNNs as shown in Figure 8.2. They can process input sequences of various lengths by processing them using their

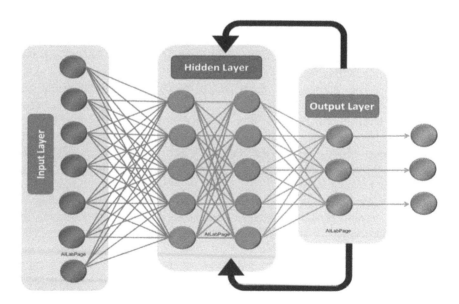

FIGURE 8.2   Recurrent neural networks

internal state (memory). Assume RNNs have a memory. Every piece of processed data is recorded, saved, and used to compute the result. As a result, they are helpful for things like speech recognition [1]. Additionally, links within the recurrent network may provide input into earlier levels (or even into the same layer). By receiving feedback, they are able to keep track of previous suggestions and quickly find solutions to issues.

When it comes to domains where the presentation of information is crucial, RNNs are quite helpful. They are frequently employed in speech synthesis, machine translation, and NLP (including chatbots).

Currently, we can distinguish between two RNN types:

1. **RNN in two directions:** They function in two different ways, allowing the output layer to concurrently gain data from historical and future conditions [2].
2. **Deep RNN:** There are several layers. The DL model can therefore extract more hierarchical data as a result.

8.6.1.1 How RNN Operates

Let's look at an example of an NLP application as shown in Figure 8.3, to better grasp how RNN functions. This method, named entity recognition, finds names in a text.

For each training (sentence) instance in the aforementioned examples, each word is mapped to an output; for example, if the word is mapped to 1. If not, we map it to 0 instead. As a result, the RNN architecture would look something like Figure 8.4 to train it on sentences to recognize names within them.

Forward propagation: Because there are five words or steps in this training example, we use the shared weights W_a, W_x, W_y, and b_a to calculate a, y for each step t.

$$a_1 = \tanh(w_a * a_0 + w_x * x_1 + b_a)$$
$$\hat{y}_1 = \text{sigmoid}(w_y * a_1 + b_y)$$
$$a_2 = \tanh(w_a * a_1 + w_x * x_2 + b_a)$$
$$\hat{y}_2 = \text{sigmoid}(w_y * a_2 + b_y)$$

$$.$$
$$.$$
$$.$$

$$a_5 = \tanh(w_a * a_4 + w_x * x_5 + b_a)$$
$$\hat{y}_5 = \text{sigmoid}(w_y * a_5 + b_y)$$

Typically, the equations would be as follows:

$$a_t = \tanh(w_a * a_{t-1} + w_x * x_t + b_a)$$
$$\hat{y}_1 = \text{sigmoid}(w_y * a_t + b_y)$$

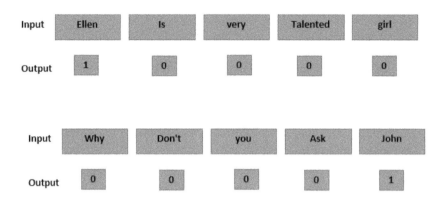

FIGURE 8.3 Example of RNN

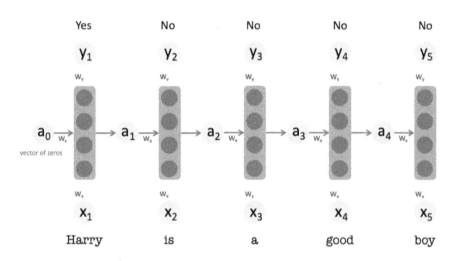

FIGURE 8.4 Forward propagation

The cost function that reflects the correlation between the actual output y and the predicted output is then determined for each time step t:

$$cost\left(\hat{y}_t, y_t\right) = -y_t * log(\hat{y}_t) - \left(1 - y_t\right) log(1 - \hat{y}_t)$$

We'll now add up each word's cost function to determine the loss function:

$$Loss\left(\hat{y}, y\right) = \sum_{t=1}^{5} Cost\left(\hat{y}t, yt\right)$$

Backpropagation: By employing the chain rule to make the calculus simpler, backpropagation is the procedure of computing the derived of the loss function regarding the strictures W_a, W_x, W_y, and b_a. After obtaining the derivatives, we use a descent gradient to update the parameters:

$$w_a = w_a - \frac{\alpha * \partial Loss(\hat{y}, y)}{\partial Wa}$$

$$w_x = w_x - \frac{\alpha * \partial Loss(\hat{y}, y)}{\partial Wx}$$

$$w_y = w_y - \frac{\alpha * \partial Loss(\hat{y}, y)}{\partial Wy}$$

$$b_a = b_a - \frac{\alpha * \partial Loss(\hat{y}, y)}{\partial ba}$$

$$b_y = b_y - \frac{\alpha * \partial Loss(\hat{y}, y)}{\partial by}$$

After much iteration using various training instances, we would be able to reduce the loss function, and the expected output would converge to the actual output. We will therefore employ the optimized weights to identify names in upcoming sentences.

8.6.2 LONG SHORT-TERM MEMORY (LSTM)

It is also a subtype of RNN. However, LSTM has feedback connections. This indicates that it is capable of processing audio or video files as well as whole data sequences [3]. Neural network topologies are the inspiration for LSTM, which is based on the conception of a memory cell. The responsibility of a memory cell is to remember important information rather than just its most recent calculated value because it can hold its value for a time depending on its inputs.

In typical LSTM architecture, the cell can keep values for any length of time because these three gates control how information enters and exits the cell. The LSTM recurrent unit is shown in Figure 8.5.

The input gate controls the new data that can enter the memory, and the output gate decides when the cell's data will be used in the output. The cell can process new data by controlling when a piece of information can be forgotten. Image captioning, handwriting recognition, speech recognition, gesture recognition, and text compression all make use of LSTMs frequently [4].

8.6.3 CNN: CONVOLUTIONAL NEURAL NETWORKS

This architecture, as shown in Figure 8.6, is frequently applied to NLP, video analysis, image processing, and image recognition.

CNN consumes the capacity to analyses an input image, rank numerous features and objects within the image, and distinguish between them [9]. The term "convolutional" refers to a mathematical operation that combines many functions. Convolutional layers often make up the hidden layers of a convolutional neural network.

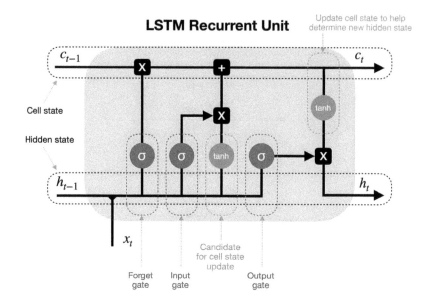

FIGURE 8.5   LSTM recurrent unit

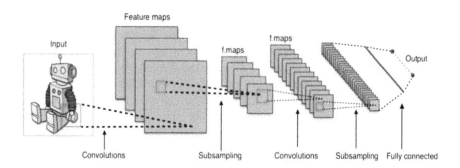

FIGURE 8.6   Convolutional neural network

8.7   DBN: DEEP BELIEF NETWORK

A multilayer network with several hidden layer restricted Boltzmann machines (RBMs), is the name given to each connected layer pair in a DBN (Figure 8.7). So it's true that DBN is a collection of RBMs. DBN is made up of many layers of latent variables called hidden units, and only the units in different layers can be connected to one another [10].

Probabilities and unsupervised learning are utilized by DBNs to generate outputs. The DBN, in contrast to other models, learns every layer of the input. In CNNs, the inputs are only filtered by the first layers for the most fundamental features, and the last levels combine all of the simple patterns that the first layers found. DBNs operate

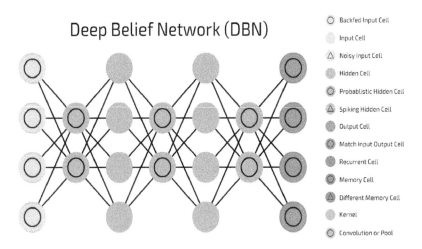

Deep Belief Network (DBN)

○ Backfed Input Cell
◉ Input Cell
△ Noisy Input Cell
◉ Hidden Cell
◎ Probablistic Hidden Cell
△ Spiking Hidden Cell
◉ Output Cell
◎ Match Input Output Cell
● Recurrent Cell
◎ Memory Cell
△ Different Memory Cell
◉ Kernel
○ Convolution or Pool

FIGURE 8.7 Deep belief network

holistically and control each layer sequentially. DBNs, for instance, can be beneficial to NLP and image recognition.

8.7.1 DSN: DEEP STACKING NETWORK

In this, DSN placed last because it is different from the other deep learning architectures. Another common name for DSNs is the deep convex network, or DCN. A collection of distinct deep networks that together constitute a deep network is known as DSN/DCN. The DSN's data processing layers are hidden within each network. The training issue, which presents a significant obstacle for conventional deep learning models, was the focus of this architecture. DSNs view training as a collection of distinct challenges rather than a single issue that must be resolved because of its various levels.

A DSN typically contains three or more modules. Because these modules are stacked one on top of the other, each module's feedback is influenced by the results of the modules below it. DSNs can learn more complex classifications with this design than with just one module (Figure 8.8).

In deep learning at the moment, the six architectures listed earlier are the most common. We should also discuss the final and most fundamental architecture at this point. Let's have a brief conversation about autoencoders.

8.8 DEEP LEARNING ARCHITECTURE – AUTOENCODERS

A particular kind of feed-forward neural network is an autoencoder. This is the basis for producing the result. In this model, the input is condensed into the code. Identification of what constitutes regular data and the subsequent detection of anomalies or aberrations is one of the primary duties of autoencoders.

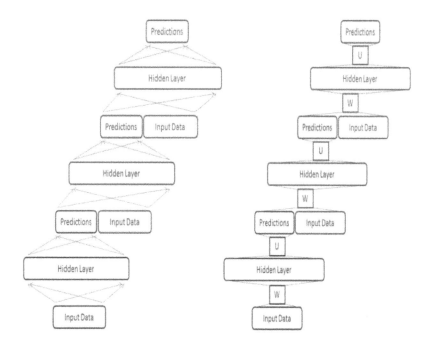

FIGURE 8.8 Deep stacking network [11]

Three parts make up autoencoders:

- encoder (code is produced, which condenses the input)
- code
- decoder (uses the code to recreate the input).

Anomaly detection and dimensionality reduction are the two main applications of autoencoders. One of their biggest benefits is simplicity. They are simple to construct and train. The opposing side of the coin is present as well, though. You require representative training data of the highest caliber. If you don't, the data the autoencoder produces may be skewed or unclear.

8.8.1   U-Net

The FCCN (fully combined convolution network) is the foundation upon which the U-Net [10] architecture is built, and it has been changed in format, and it allows for greater segmentation in medical images. The equal distribution of the upsampling and downsampling layers is one of U-Net architecture's two most significant innovations. There are two ways that the U-Net architecture differs from FCN-8: First, a symmetric connection is used by U-Net, and the concatenate operator is used to expand and contract the path of the skip connection between the layers. Because of the symmetric connection, which makes it possible to transfer information, the sampling layer of U-Net has a lot of feature maps. Figure 8.9 depicts the architecture of the U-Net.

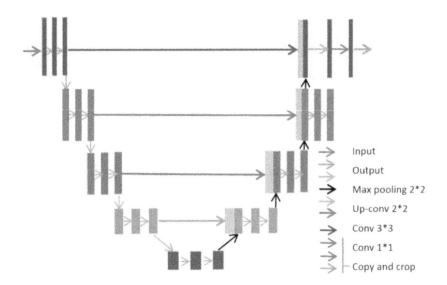

FIGURE 8.9 Architecture of U-Net

The contracting path in U-Net is made up of four blocks, each of which can have an activation function with batch normalization and 3*3 convolutional layers. Sixty-four feature maps are the foundation of U-Net. Each pooling doubles the feature map.

8.8.2 V-NET

Diagnostic images used for medical image segmentation often come in three-dimensional format, allowing for volumetric segmentation by directly assessing the complete volume content, which holds particular significance.

The goal of the V-Net [12] architecture is to segment MRI volumetrically, which is challenging due to changes in intensity distribution across different tests. In V-Net, the intensity of entirely convolutional systems processes MRI images. V-Net, in distinction to other recent approaches, uses dice coefficient maximization rather than slice-wise preparation to achieve precise segmentation. Compared to other networks, V-Net efficiently and quickly segments MRI images.

The relationship between expected segmentation and ground truth annotation is established during training. The decompression path is on the right side, while the compression path is on the left. The convolution at each state is carried out with the help of a volumetric kernel that has a size of 5*5*5 voxels.

8.8.3 GOOGLENET

Google developed the GoogLeNet [13] as shown in the Figure 8.10. It has the novel method of inception module and 22 layers. In order to decrease the amount of required parameters, this module has a small number of convolutional layers.

In comparison to AlexNet, the number of parameters examined in GoogLeNet has decreased from 60 million to 4 million [14]. Many feature extractors in GoogLeNet

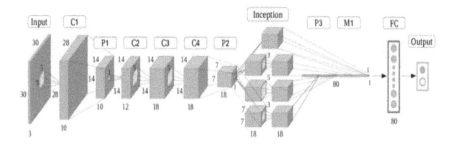

FIGURE 8.10   GoogLeNet architecture

are housed in a single layer, which indirectly improves network performance. In contrast to the other network, the inception modules are stacked in the last architecture, and the topmost layers are made up of their own layer. GoogLeNet converges much more quickly than other networks, and the layer itself performs parallel and joint trainings.

8.8.4 RESNET

The architecture was constructed by ResNet [15] using a novel strategy that combined feature-heavy batch normalization with skip connections. It has lower complexities than previous networks and can simultaneously train a network with 152 layers. ResNet has a number of residual modules that help build the architecture. The following is an illustration of the residual module.

The chemical analysis of images can be handled by the residual module in one of two ways: Either it can complete the task set for this input or it can completely avoid this step. Currently, these modules are laid out in a staked pattern to create a complete, end-to-end network, similar to GoogLeNet. A few of the additional novel techniques that the ResNet has introduced are outlined in the as follows:

- ResNet employs a straightforward SGD (stochastic gradient descent) strategy rather than an intricate adaptive strategy.
- An inexpensive initialization function that keeps the training together can be used to accomplish this.

8.8.5 R-CNN

The R-CNN usages a selective method to extract a huge amount of object applications in order to identify the CNN features of each object. Each image region is classified using class-specific classifier SVMs. By first creating a bounding box for the objects in the image and then recognizing the quantified object in image, it addresses the issue of object detection.

In each region of an R-CNN image, two types of features are extracted. They are full region and foreground features. The image segmentation performance is

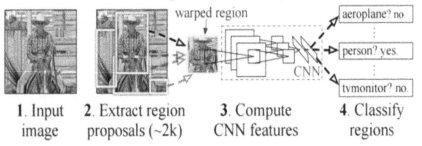

FIGURE 8.11   R-CNN architecture

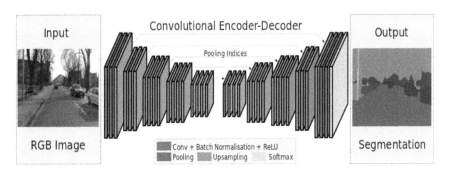

FIGURE 8.12   SegNet architecture

enhanced by combining these two features. Predictions based on pixels replace predictions based on regions during the testing stage. The pixels are categorized according to the region's high score. The architecture of R-CNN is shown in Figure 8.11.

8.8.6   SEGNET

A deep learning architecture for image segmentation known as SegNet as shown in Figure 8.12, [16] includes a pixel classification layer in addition to an encoder and subsequent decoder. The feature map used in the convolution with the filter bank is created by the encoder. The decoder uses max-pooling to transmute the input feature map into an upsample. The feature map decoder triggers the maximum pooling. The sparse feature map is produced as a result.

The decoder filter bank trains these feature maps further to produce dense feature maps. Finally, the feature maps are subjected to batch normalization. The comparative of deep learning based architectures is shown in Table 8.1.

TABLE 8.1

Comparative Study of Various Deep Learning-Based Architectures

Deep Learning Architecture	No. Layers	Advantage	Disadvantage
U-Net	Two convolutional layers with carpooling and ReLU layer	1. To determine high-quality image segmentation, the U-Net merge the local information from deconvolutional layer and context information from convolutional layer. 2. Various size images will be used as input. i.e., there is no dense layer. 3. The usage of huge amount of data growth is important while the quantity of annotated sample is limited.	It takes considerable amount of time for training the data.
V-Net	Two convolutional layers with 3*3*3 kernels	1. The dice loss layer doesn't require any sample re-weighting when the pixels of foreground and background of the image is unbalanced. 2. The V-Net minimizes the resolution and extract the features from data by using suitable stride.	Difficult to insert an unparameterized layer such as ReLU or delete after adding element.
GoogLeNet	22 layers	1. The training of GoogLeNet is faster than VGG architecture. 2. The pre-trained size of GoogLeNet is relatively small when compared with VGG. 3. The GoogLeNet has a size of most effective 96MB, but VGG can have greater than 500MB.	1. Still it has less computational complexity with fewer parameters. 2. There is no use of fully connected convolutional neural networks.
ResNet	152 layers	Hundreds or thousands of residual modules is familiarized to construct a network completely different from normal networks.	1. It takes more time for extracting the features of specified objects. 2. The final performance of image segmentation is affected.
R-CNN	13 sharable convolutional layers	R-CNN attain major enhancement in performing image segmentation by using the high discriminative CNN features.	1. In segmentation, the features are not attuned. 2. The features does not have sufficient spatial information for particular boundary generation.
SegNet	13 encoder layers 13 decoder layers	1. SegNet is best architecture for dealing image segmentation. 2. The trainable parameters are smaller than other networks. 3. SegNet provides more efficient time inference and memory inference compared than other networks.	1. It cannot absolutely separate the result of model vs. optimization in attaining the detailed effect. 2. In training, this network includes gradient backpropagation, which is inadequate for solving image segmented problem.

8.9 DEEP LEARNING ALGORITHMS FOR IMAGE SEGMENTATION

Because it is effective at a variety of tasks, deep learning methods in computer vision have become increasingly popular for image segmentation. With possible user interactions, an effective segmentation technique should be able to quickly obtain results [17]. When managing the image segmentations quality and performance, there are two crucial aspects to take into consideration. Algorithms' foundational representations and user interaction are two examples.

Convolutional networks mostly help to solve computer vision and vision issues that are heavily influenced by user factors. The deep learning technique, on the other hand, offers a different approach for learning the feature of images and stills in video. As a result, understanding the various deep learning algorithms is essential, and selecting the appropriate algorithm for a given problem may be challenging. The following is a discussion of certain currently available image segmentation using deep learning algorithms.

8.9.1 DEEPIGEOS

A 2D and 3D image segmentation framework based on deep learning interaction was proposed in a deep interactive deodisk [18]. A two-stage framework was presented by DeepIGeos to increase user interaction. P-Net is used to automatically obtain the initial segmentation in the first stage, and DeepIGeos uses R-Net in the second stage to filter user interaction and identify miss-segmented regions. R-Net incorporates the converted and filtered user interactions into its input. After the convolutional neural network has been trained based on user interaction, the R-Net considers when to retrain it for a large number of training sets.

8.9.2 DEEPCUT

Deep learning and iterative graphical optimization are combined in DeepCut [19] to achieve pixel-by-pixel segmentation. From image datasets, the medical images are separated, resulting in bounding box observations. A fully connected conditional random file is used to regularize the segmentations, and the CNN technique is used to iteratively update the training outputs. The DeepCut method is easy to use on any kind of medical image because it was made to be very general.

8.9.3 DCAN

Multilevel contextual features from layered architecture are proposed by deep contour-aware networks or discovering gland segmentation with auxiliary supervisor. When a multilevel regularization technique is integrated into the training set, discriminative features of transitional features get better. The segmentation of glands presents three significant obstacles that DCAN can overcome.

First, a single forward propagation generates a straight probability map for a large amount of image analysis. Second, performing a biopsy test, which can distinguish between benign and malignant tumors, is simple. Finally, organ shape and features are freely researched using various task-oriented training systems.

TABLE 8.2

Comparative Analysis of Deep Learning Applications in Medical Sector

DL Applications	Datasets Used	Advantages	Disadvantages
DeepLab	Pascal context, Pascal perform-port and cityscapes	It addresses the atrous convolution and CRF	1. Downsampling causes loss of information in image. 2. The input damages the pixel accuracy.
DeepIGeos	2D fetal MRI, brain tumors, 3D FALIK images	1. It uses underpinning learning methods to learn the knowledge from large amount of training set. 2. It requires a significant amount of user interaction to encode into geodesic distance.	In testing, this method does not connect fully.
DeepCut	Fetal MRI, brain and lungs	Fast and provide optimal results.	1. In testing, it does not interact fully. 2. No refinement for further user interaction.
DeepMedic	Brain MRI, BRATS and ISLES	It minimizes the user interaction and provide the good performance.	Loss of feature map due to multilevel max-pooling and down sampling.
DCAN	MICCAI gland	1. It uses joint multilevel learning method for improving the performance of gland segmentation. 2. It improve the robustness of gland.	This method fails to provide acceptable results in malignant field.

Table 8.2 presents a comparative study of deep learning applications.

8.10 CONCLUSION

The architecture of deep learning and its use for medical image segmentation are briefly discussed in this chapter. This survey aims to provide a clear and understandable description of deep learning's applications for analyzing medical images. The medical field involves a variety of issues for analyzing the disease of various patient types. Subsequently, this chapter is focused on examining the engineering of deep learning and use of deep learning in the clinical field. In addition, the difficulties of analyzing a specific disease in particular organs were discussed in detail. According to the survey, DL can be a useful tool for encouraging medical specialization. In the future, various fields of application will be taken into consideration.

REFERENCES

[1] Li, W.: Automatic segmentation of liver tumor in CT images with deep convolutional neural networks. J. Comput. Commun. 3(11), 146–151, 2015.

[2] Fu, H., Cheng, J., Xu, Y., Wong, D.W.K., Liu, J., Cao, X.: Joint optic disc and cup segmentation based on multi-label deep network and polar transformation. IEEE Trans. Med. Image. 37(7), 1597–1605, 2018.

[3] Wang, S., Zhou, M., Liu, Z., Liu, Z., Gu, D., Zang, Y., et al.: Central focused convolutional neural networks: developing a data-driven model for lung nodule segmentation. Med. Image Anal. 40, 172–183, 2017.

[4] Krizhevsky, A., Sutskever, I., Hinton, G.E.: Imagenet classification with deep convolutional neural networks. Commun. ACM. 60(6), 84–90, 2017.

[5] Bai, W., Suzuki, H., Qin, C., Tarroni, G., Oktay, O., Matthews, P.M., et al.: Recurrent neural networks for aortic image sequence segmentation with sparse annotations. In: Proceedings of the International Conference on Medical Image Computing and Computer-Assisted Intervention (MICCAI), pp. 586–594, 2018.

[6] Khan, A., Sohail, A., Zahoora, U., Qureshi, A.S.: A survey of the recent architectures of deep convolutional neural networks. Artif. Intell. Rev. 53(8), 5455–5516, 2020.

[7] Guo, Y., Liu, Y., Georgiou, T., Lew, M.S.: A review of semantic segmentation using deep neural networks. Int. J. Multimed. Inf. Retr. 7(2), 87–93, 2018.

[8] Milletari, F., Navab, N., Ahmadi, S.A.: V-net: fully convolutional neural networks for volumetric medical image segmentation. In: Proceedings of the 2016 Fourth International Conference on 3D Vision (3DV), pp. 565–571, IEEE, Stanford, CA, USA, October 2016.

[9] Gao, Y., Phillips, J.M., Zheng, Y., Min, R., Fletcher, P.T., Gerig, G.: Fully convolutional structured LSTM networks for joint 4d medical image segmentation. In: Proceedings of the IEEE International Symposium on Biomedical Imaging (ISBI), pp. 1104–1108, IEEE, Piscataway, NJ, 2018.

[10] Zhang, J., Xiaogang, L., Sun, Q., Zhang, Q., Wei, X., Liu, B.: SDResU-Net: separable and dilated residual U-net for MRI brain tumor segmentation. Curr. Med. Imaging. 1, 15, 2019.

[11] Deng, L., Hutchinson, B., Yu, D.: Parallel training for deep stacking networks. *Interspeech*, 2012.

[12] Tang, W., Zou, D., Yang, S., Shi, J.: DSL: automatic liver segmentation with faster R-CNN and DeepLab. In: Proceedings of the International Conference on Artificial Neural Network, pp. 137–147, 2018.

[13] Lee, C.Y., Xie, S., Gallagher, P., Zhang, Z., Tu, Z.: Deeply-supervised nets. Artif. Intell. Statist. 38, 562–570, 2015.

[14] Lei, T., Wang, R., Wan, Y., Zhang, B., Meng, H., Nandi, A.K.: Medical image segmentation using deep learning: a survey. 2020. https://arxiv.org/abs/2009.13120.

[15] Wang, G., Li, W., Zuluaga, M.A., et al.: Interactive medical image segmentation using deep learning with image-specific fine tuning. IEEE Trans. Med. Imaging. 37(7), 1562–1573, 2018.

[16] Ibtehaz, N., Rahman, M.S.: MultiResUNet: rethinking the U-Net architecture for multimodal biomedical image segmentation. Neural Netw. 121, 74–87, 2020.

[17] Chollet, F.: Xception: deep learning with depthwise separable convolutions. In: Proceedings of the IEEE Conference on Computer Vision and Pattern Recognition, pp. 1251–1258, Honolulu, HI, USA, July 2017.

[18] Wang, H., Gu, H., Qin, P., Wang, J.: CheXLocNet: automatic localization of pneumothorax in chest radiographs using deep convolutional neural networks. PLoS One. 15(11), 2020.

[19] Çiçek, O., Abdulkadir, A., Lienkamp, S.S., Brox, T., Ronneberger, O.: 3D U-Net: learning dense volumetric segmentation from sparse annotation. In: Proceedings of the International Conference on Medical Image Computing and Computer-Assisted Intervention, pp. 424–432, Springer, Athens, Greece, October 2016.

9 Unleashing the Potential of Deep Learning in Diabetic Retinopathy
A Comprehensive Survey

R. Lotus, G. Sakthi, B. Bharathi Kannan,
V. Anusuya Devi, and T. Sam Pradeepraj

9.1 INTRODUCTION

Diabetic retinopathy is a progressive eye disease that occurs as a result of long-term diabetes. It is a leading cause of vision loss and blindness in adults and has an impact on the blood vessels in the retina and the light-sensitive tissue at the back of the eye. Blood sugar levels that are consistently raised over time are strongly associated with the onset of diabetic retinopathy. The small blood vessels in the retina are harmed by high blood sugar, which makes them leak fluid or blood. The retina may expand as a result of this aberrant leakage, and abnormal blood vessels may develop [1].

The severity of diabetic retinopathy is typically assessed using a grading system based on the presence and extent of specific retinal abnormalities observed in retinal images or through a comprehensive eye examination. Early diagnosis and prompt treatment are essential for stopping or delaying the disease's course and minimizing visual loss [2]. For people with diabetes, routine eye exams and dilated eye exams are advised to find diabetic retinopathy in its early stages. Different lesions can be identified using a retinal CT scan, including microaneurysms (MA), haemorrhages (HM), and soft and hard exudates (EX). Microaneurysms (MA), which appear as tiny red circulars on the retina due to the brittleness of the vessel's walls, are the initial sign of DR. They have sharp margins and a dimension of less than 125 m [3].

Diabetic retinopathy has two distinct stages. There are two types of diabetic retinopathy: proliferative and non-proliferative.

9.1.1 NON-PROLIFERATIVE DIABETIC RETINOPATHY (NPDR)

Early on, the retina's blood vessels may begin to leak fluid or blood, which can cause microaneurysms, haemorrhages, and retinal edoema. If NPDR is not treated, it can advance to more severe stages even though it may not initially show any symptoms [4].

DOI: 10.1201/9781003343172-9

9.1.2 PROLIFERATIVE DIABETIC RETINOPATHY (PDR)

As the condition worsens, the retina's surface starts to sprout new blood vessels. Further retinal damage results from these new vessels' fragility and propensity for leakage. Scar tissue may also develop, causing the retina to separate from the back of the eye, which could result in blindness or severe vision loss [5].

9.2 IMPORTANCE OF EARLY DETECTION OF DIABETIC RETINOPATHY

For a number of reasons, early identification of diabetic retinopathy is crucial [6].

Vision Preservation: Because diabetic retinopathy is a progressive condition, early detection enables prompt treatments to protect vision. Early illness detection allows medical practitioners to start the right treatments to stop or delay the disease's progression. As a result, there is a much lower chance of vision loss or blindness.

Effective Treatment Options: Early detection offers the chance to put into practise efficient treatment methods. There are many ways to control diabetic retinopathy, including laser therapy, intravitreal injections, and surgical procedures. When these treatments are started early, the disease's underlying causes and complications can be addressed before they worsen, which can increase their success.

Enhanced Quality of Life: Diabetic retinopathy can significantly reduce a person's quality of life by causing vision loss. It may restrict their capacity to carry out daily tasks, jeopardize their independence, and harm their general well-being. A person's quality of life can be maintained, and their visual function can be preserved with early detection and effective management.

Cost Savings: In the long run, early diagnosis and action can result in significant cost savings. Early diagnosis and treatment of diabetic retinopathy can reduce the need for more invasive and expensive procedures like vitrectomy or retinal detachment repair. A reduction in visual loss can also lessen the financial cost of rehabilitation, social support, and lost productivity.

Screening Effectiveness: For those with diabetes, routine eye exams for diabetic retinopathy are advised. Early detection makes it possible to identify patients who are more likely to advance, allowing healthcare resources to be distributed more effectively. While patients with advanced cancer can receive rapid and appropriate therapy, individuals with early-stage disease may need less regular monitoring.

Patient Education and Empowerment: The ability to educate patients about the value of routine eye exams, glycemic control, and other diabetes management techniques is made possible by early identification. Patient empowerment through education about the dangers and effects of diabetic retinopathy can promote proactive self-care and adherence to treatment regimens.

9.3 TRADITIONAL APPROACHES FOR DIABETIC RETINOPATHY DETECTION

Prior to the development of deep learning, a number of conventional methods were employed to identify diabetic retinopathy (DR). These methods relied on traditional machine learning methods and human feature extraction [7]. Some of the conventional methods for DR detection are listed here:

Image Preprocessing: To improve image quality and get rid of noise, preprocessing techniques were used on retinal images. Image resizing, normalization, contrast enhancement, and denoising are some of these methods.

Image Segmentation: To separate the regions of interest in retinal pictures, such as the optic disc, macula, and blood vessels, image segmentation techniques were applied. In order to accurately outline these structures for additional analysis and feature extraction, segmentation techniques were developed.

Feature Extraction: To extract pertinent features from retinal pictures, manual feature extraction techniques were used. Morphological traits, textural features, statistical measurements, and vessel-related features are some examples of features. These characteristics intended to identify the pathogenic DR-related alterations.

Classification Algorithms: After the characteristics were extracted, classification was done using traditional machine learning algorithms. Support vector machines (SVM), k-nearest neighbours (KNN), decision trees, and random forests are examples of frequently used algorithms. These algorithms were developed using labelled datasets, which included expert annotations of the presence and severity of DR [8].

Feature Selection and Dimensionality Reduction: To minimize the feature space and increase computational efficiency, as the number of extracted features may be considerable, feature selection and dimensionality reduction approaches were applied. For this, techniques like feature ranking algorithms, principal component analysis (PCA), and linear discriminant analysis (LDA) were used.

Ensemble Techniques: To increase the effectiveness and resilience of the classification models, ensemble techniques including bagging and boosting were applied. These methods tried to lessen variation and bias by merging many classifiers, producing predictions that were more accurate.

9.4   MOTIVATION FOR DEEP LEARNING APPROACH

Even though conventional methods have produced good results in DR detection, they frequently depended on hand-crafted features that would not have been able to capture intricate and subtle patterns in retinal pictures. By automatically developing discriminative features from the data, deep learning systems have outperformed older methods and eliminated the need for manual feature engineering. Traditional methods still contribute to baseline performance, interpretability, and as a supplementary tool when used with deep learning methods.

Convolutional neural networks (CNNs), a particular advancement in deep learning algorithms, have demonstrated encouraging results in automating the identification and categorization of diabetic retinopathy from retinal pictures. These algorithms can help medical personnel detect diabetic retinopathy patients correctly and intervene when necessary [9].

The use of deep learning techniques in the identification and diagnosis of diabetic retinopathy has numerous justifications. Deep learning algorithms have been proven to perform well in a range of image analysis applications, including medical image analysis. They are able to identify and categorize diabetic retinopathy with high degrees of accuracy because they can learn complex patterns and features from vast volumes of data. This precision is essential for obtaining accurate and consistent diagnoses [10]. The analysis of several retinal pictures is frequently used to diagnose diabetic retinopathy. Deep learning algorithms are excellent at managing enormous datasets and automatically extracting pertinent features. They are capable of processing and analyzing complicated visual data efficiently, picking up minute features and anomalies that can be symptoms of diabetic retinopathy [11]. Deep learning models can automate the screening and detection process, lessening the stress on medical staff, and increasing productivity. They can quickly analyze retinal scans and offer preliminary assessments, which helps identify situations that need urgent treatment. By enabling early intervention, this automation can simplify the diagnosing process and enhance patient outcomes. Deep learning models have the capacity to generalize and scale effectively across various datasets and populations. These models can be applied to new data with similar properties after being trained on a sizable dataset, making them adaptable to various clinical scenarios. Deep learning algorithms are appropriate for large-scale screening programmes and population-wide diabetic retinopathy diagnosis initiatives due to their scalability and generalizability. As they are exposed to additional data, deep learning models can continuously learn and enhance their performance. The accuracy and robustness of the models can be improved over time by routinely updating and optimizing them with fresh annotated photos. Deep learning techniques are particularly suited for long-term diabetic retinopathy monitoring and tracking disease development because of their capacity for continual learning. Deep learning algorithms may be able to identify diabetic retinopathy in its earliest stages, when there are still plenty of curative alternatives available. Deep learning models can help in the early detection of diabetic retinopathy by spotting small changes in the retinal pictures that may go undetected by human observers, resulting in prompt interventions and better results. Deep learning algorithms can be easily adopted in healthcare settings by integrating with current clinical workflows and systems. They can be connected with telemedicine platforms, electronic health records (EHRs), and other systems to provide remote screening and diagnosis. In underprivileged areas and locations with a dearth of ophthalmologists, this integration may make diabetic retinopathy screening more accessible.

Deep learning algorithms are an excellent option for detecting diabetic retinopathy due to their high accuracy, capacity to handle huge and complicated data, automation, scalability, continuous learning, possibility for early diagnosis, and integration with clinical procedures [12]. They have a great deal of potential to enhance patient care, increase screening programme efficiency and efficacy, and lessen the financial burden of diabetic retinopathy on healthcare systems.

9.5 INTRODUCTION TO DEEP LEARNING IN MEDICAL IMAGING

Deep learning has attracted a lot of attention and excelled in many areas, including medical imaging. It has completely changed how medical images are evaluated, processed, and used for planning diagnoses, prognoses, and treatments. Convolutional neural networks (CNNs), in particular, have proven to have extraordinary skills in directly extracting relevant patterns and features from medical images, improving diagnostic accuracy and efficacy. Deep learning algorithms are made up of several interconnected layers of artificial neurons that can learn complicated representations from unprocessed input data [13]. Due to their capacity to recognize pertinent elements at many sizes and capture spatial dependencies in images, CNNs in particular have been frequently used in medical imaging. Enhanced detection, classification, segmentation, and prediction tasks are now possible thanks to the use of deep learning in medical imaging, including diabetic retinopathy.

Deep learning in medical imaging provides a number of benefits, including:

Automatic Learning of Discriminative Features: Deep learning models can learn discriminative features directly from unprocessed medical pictures, doing away with the necessity for manual feature extraction. The models' ability to learn enables them to recognize complex patterns and minute characteristics that may be essential for precise diagnosis but may be difficult to express clearly [14].

Scalability: Deep learning systems are capable of processing enormous amounts of medical picture data with efficiency. This scalability is especially useful for medical imaging, which requires the analysis and interpretation of large amounts of data from sources including radiological scans and retinal images [15].

Generalization: Deep learning models have proven to be quite good at generalization, which enables them to perform well on untried or fresh data. This is essential in the field of medical imaging because of the wide range of patient groups, imaging techniques, and disease presentations that can be seen there [16].

Greater Accuracy: Deep learning models have outperformed conventional machine learning techniques in a number of medical imaging applications. Improved illness detection, classification, and segmentation accuracy is a result of the capacity to learn complicated representations and extract pertinent characteristics from medical images.

Automation and Efficiency: Deep learning makes it possible to automate some medical imaging operations, which eases the workload on medical staff and boosts productivity [17]. With the use of this technology, the analytical process might be sped up, resulting in quicker judgements about diagnosis and treatment.

Integration with Current Clinical Workflows: Deep learning models can be incorporated into current clinical workflows, assisting healthcare practitioners in making decisions. They can support treatment planning with quantitative measurements, help with risk assessment, and aid in the interpretation of medical pictures.

Deep learning in medical imaging faces difficulties despite its many benefits. Some of the important factors are the accessibility of sizable, annotated datasets, the interpretability of deep learning models, and the necessity of thorough validation and regulatory approval. Deep learning, however, is still developing and has significant potential for enhancing the precision, effectiveness, and significance of medical imaging in the diagnosis and treatment of a variety of disorders, including diabetic retinopathy. The detection, diagnosis, and treatment of diabetic retinopathy (DR) have all benefited from the development of deep learning as an effective method. It has demonstrated significant promise in enhancing the precision and effectiveness of DR screening and has the potential to fundamentally alter how this condition is treated.

9.6 OVERVIEW OF DEEP LEARNING APPLICATIONS IN DIABETIC RETINOPATHY

To automatically identify the presence of DR in retinal pictures, deep learning algorithms have been developed. These algorithms can examine the photos and categorize them according to their severity, assisting in the identification of individuals who need additional testing and care. High sensitivity and specificity in DR screening have been achieved using deep learning models, with encouraging results. Deep learning algorithms have been used to identify and classify certain DR lesions like microaneurysms, haemorrhages, exudates, and neovascularization [18]. These algorithms can precisely find and define these lesions, which helps with measuring disease severity and tracking the development of the disease. To forecast the progression of DR, deep learning algorithms can examine longitudinal retinal pictures and clinical data. These models can forecast the probability of illness worsening and help with individualized therapy planning and management by learning patterns and features from sequential photos. Deep learning algorithms are capable of evaluating the quality of retinal images acquired during screening or diagnostic procedures. These algorithms contribute to the accuracy of the analysis and increase the overall efficacy of DR screening programmes by automatically detecting photos with poor quality or artefacts. Deep learning can be used to evaluate the treatment response in patients with DR. These algorithms can evaluate treatment efficacy and identify changes in lesion features by examining subsequent retinal images. This information is crucial for optimizing treatment plans. Deep learning models can be integrated into decision support systems for diabetic retinopathy (DR) management. Based on the analysis of retinal pictures and clinical data, these systems can help healthcare practitioners by offering automated risk assessment, treatment suggestions, and personalized patient care plans. Deep learning has a number of benefits for diabetic retinopathy, including increased accuracy, scalability, automation, and significant cost savings [19]. However, in order for these methods to be used more widely in clinical practise, issues including the requirement for sizable annotated datasets, the interpretability of deep learning models, and regulatory constraints must be resolved. Overall, deep learning has the potential to revolutionize the identification, assessment, and treatment of diabetic retinopathy, improving patient outcomes and enabling quick responses to stop diabetics from losing their eyesight.

9.7   SELECTION OF RETINAL IMAGE DATASETS

For creating and assessing deep-learning models for diabetic retinopathy, it is essential to choose the right retinal imaging datasets. Here are some factors to take into account while choosing retinal image datasets:

Annotated Ground Truth: Look for datasets that accurately annotate or label the lesions associated with diabetic retinopathy. The existence and severity of various lesions, such as microaneurysms, haemorrhages, exudates, and neovascularization, should be included in these annotations. Effective training and evaluation of deep learning models require high-quality annotations [20].

Large and Diverse: Pick datasets that are sizable enough to adequately represent the complexity and heterogeneity of diabetic retinopathy. A larger dataset enables the generated models to be more robust and generally applicable. To ensure the model's applicability to a variety of groups, also take into account datasets that cover various ages, disease stages, and ethnicities.

Representative of Clinical Practice: It is beneficial to select datasets that reflect real-world clinical scenarios. The images should resemble those captured during routine screening or diagnostic examinations. This ensures that the deep learning models are trained on data that closely matches the data they will encounter in clinical settings.

Multiple Modalities: Diabetic retinopathy can be assessed using various imaging modalities, such as colour fundus photography, optical coherence tomography (OCT), and fluorescein angiography. Consider datasets that include multiple modalities to develop models that can handle different types of retinal images and provide a comprehensive analysis of the disease.

Longitudinal Data: Longitudinal datasets that contain follow-up pictures of patients throughout time are useful for examining the development of disease and evaluating the efficacy of treatments. With the aid of such datasets, deep learning models may be created that analyze consecutive photos and reveal the temporal changes related to diabetic retinopathy.

Quality Control: Verify that stringent quality control procedures have been applied to the datasets you've chosen. High-resolution photos that are devoid of artefacts or distortions are necessary to ensure that the analysis is done accurately. Procedures for quality control aid in preserving the dataset's consistency and dependability.

Compliance With Ethical Norms: Take patient privacy laws and ethical norms into account while choosing datasets. Verify that the datasets were acquired and disseminated in accordance with applicable ethical standards and legal requirements, and that the patient information in them was de-identified.

The EyePACS dataset, the Kaggle Diabetic Retinopathy Detection dataset, the Messidor dataset, and the publicly accessible data from the Diabetic Retinopathy Challenge are some examples of regularly used retinal imaging datasets for diabetic retinopathy research. These datasets have seen extensive usage and can act as a foundation for the creation of deep learning models in this area. When using publicly accessible datasets, keep in mind to properly credit and acknowledge the dataset creators and abide by any licencing or usage limitations related to the datasets.

9.8   IMAGE ENHANCEMENT AND NOISE REMOVAL IN DIABETIC RETINOPATHY

The reliability and quality of retinal images utilized for diabetic retinopathy analysis are greatly enhanced by image enhancement and noise reduction procedures. Here are several methods that are frequently used in this situation. By enhancing the contrast between various structures, contrast enhancement techniques seek to increase the visibility of minute details in retinal images. Popular techniques for improving the contrast of retinal pictures include histogram equalization, adaptive histogram equalization, and contrast-limited adaptive histogram equalization (CLAHE) [21]. Different factors, such as the imaging procedure, lighting conditions, or camera sensor noise, can cause noise in retinal images. In order to lessen the noise and increase the quality of retinal pictures, denoising techniques are used. Common methods include wavelet, median, and Gaussian filters. Image registration methods align several retinal images that were taken over time from the same patient or using various imaging modalities [22]. In order to align images for proper comparison and analysis, registration helps to correct for motion artefacts. The images are often aligned using transformations including scaling, rotation, and translation.

9.8.1   ILLUMINATION CORRECTION

The quality and interpretation of retinal pictures might be affected by uneven illumination or non-uniform lighting conditions. The goal of illumination correction techniques is to eliminate any undesirable differences in lighting and normalize image intensity across the field of view [23]. For lighting correction, methods like top-hat transform and morphological processes are frequently used.

9.8.2   SUPER-RESOLUTION

With the use of super-resolution techniques, retinal pictures can have greater resolution and level of detail. These techniques use cutting-edge algorithms to transform low-resolution inputs into high-resolution outputs. When working with photographs taken using inexpensive photographic equipment or when zooming in on certain areas of interest, super-resolution can be especially helpful. Diagnosing diabetic retinopathy involves identifying blood vessels in retinal pictures. In order to analyze vessel features and spot anomalies, vessel segmentation techniques are used to separate the vessel structure from the background. For vessel segmentation, a number of techniques can be used, including as thresholding, morphological procedures, and methods based on machine learning.

9.9 CONVOLUTIONAL NEURAL NETWORKS (CNNs)

CNNs have become a potent deep learning technique for the identification and diagnosis of diabetic retinopathy. Due to their capacity to automatically learn hierarchical representations of visual data, CNNs are especially adept at analyzing images. CNNs can be trained to categorize retinal pictures into various severity categories for diabetic retinopathy or to find particular lesions linked to the condition [24].

The following are some essential elements of CNN use for diabetic retinopathy:

First, architecture convolutional, pooling, and fully linked layers are among the many layers that make up CNNs. By applying convolving filters to the input image, convolutional layers extract local characteristics and identify patterns at various sizes. Down sampling layers reduces the spatial dimensionality of feature maps. Fully interconnected layers carry out sophisticated decision-making and reasoning. In order to get retinal pictures ready for CNN-based analysis, preprocessing is essential. Resizing the photos to a constant input size, normalizing the pixel values, and enhancing the dataset with tricks like rotation, flipping, or introducing noise to increase generalization are typical preprocessing procedures. CNN-based diabetic retinopathy detection frequently makes use of transfer learning. Utilizing pre-trained CNN models that were initially trained on huge picture datasets (like ImageNet) is how it works [25]. The CNN model can profit from the mastered low-level visual features by utilizing transfer learning, which enables effective training even with sparse diabetic retinopathy data. To train CNN models for diabetic retinopathy detection, retinal image datasets that have been annotated are necessary. These datasets are made up of photos that have been classified according to the disease's severity. For training CNN models in this field, large-scale datasets like the EyePACS dataset and the Kaggle Diabetic Retinopathy Detection Challenge dataset have been extensively employed.

Model Interpretability: Understanding the choices made by CNN models is essential for learning about the process of diagnosing diabetic retinopathy. Clinicians can better comprehend and validate the model's predictions by using techniques like Grad-CAM (gradient-weighted class activation mapping), which makes it possible to visualize the areas of the image that contribute most to the classification decision. Metrics including accuracy, sensitivity, specificity, and area under the receiver operating characteristic curve (AUC-ROC) are frequently used to assess how well CNN models perform at detecting diabetic retinopathy [26]. For evaluating the generalizability of the models, cross-validation and external validation on separate datasets are crucial. Trained CNN models can be implemented for diabetic retinopathy detection in a variety of contexts. In order to provide automated screening and triage, they can be linked into medical imaging systems, aiding ophthalmologists in their decision-making. CNN models can be used by telemedicine platforms and mobile applications to diagnose and track diabetic retinopathy from a distance. In general, CNNs have demonstrated considerable potential in the identification of diabetic retinopathy, allowing precise and effective processing of retinal images. Improved early identification and management of diabetic retinopathy could result from continued research and development in this field, which would ultimately benefit patients.

9.10 CUTTING-EDGE CNN ARCHITECTURES FOR DIABETIC RETINAL DISEASE

The performance of CNN architectures for the diagnosis of diabetic retinopathy has significantly improved. Here are several significant CNN architectures that are frequently employed in studies on diabetic retinopathy:

1. **AlexNet:** After triumphing in the 2012 ImageNet Large-Scale Visual Recognition Challenge, AlexNet emerged as one of the pioneering CNN architectures. Its architecture, which consists of numerous convolutional and fully linked layers, has been modified for diabetic retinopathy detection tasks even though it was initially intended for generic object recognition [27].
2. **VGGNet:** Known for its intricate architecture and tiny (3 x 3) convolutional filters, the Visual Geometry Group (VGG) network was developed. There are other variations of VGGNet with different depths, such as VGG16 and VGG19 [28]. These networks have been used for the identification of diabetic retinopathy detection, achieving competitive performance.
3. **GoogLeNet/Inception:** GoogLeNet, also known as Inception, popularized the idea of "Inception modules" that carry out convolutions at various sizes and combine the resulting feature maps [29]. The architecture seeks to strike a compromise between computational effectiveness and model complexity. Research on diabetic retinopathy has made use of updated versions such as InceptionV3 and InceptionV4.
4. **ResNet:** ResNets, or residual networks, introduced skip connections that let the network pick up residual mappings. By addressing the vanishing gradient issue, this architecture enables the training of extremely deep networks (such as ResNet50, ResNet101, and ResNet152) [30]. State-of-the-art performance has been achieved using ResNets in the detection of diabetic retinopathy tasks, achieving state-of-the-art performance.
5. **DenseNet:** Using dense connections, DenseNet connects every layer to every other layer in a feed-forward manner. This architecture increases gradient flow and promotes feature reuse, allowing for effective parameter use. DenseNet has been used in numerous research projects and has demonstrated good results in the diagnosis of diabetic retinopathy [31].
6. **EfficientNet:** To improve performance and efficiency, the EfficientNet family of CNN topologies progressively scales the network's width, depth, and resolution. It balances these dimensions by using a compound scaling technique. Competent performance has been shown by EfficientNet models on tasks involving the identification of diabetic retinopathy, such as EfficientNet-B0 and EfficientNet-B7 [32].

Using transfer learning, these CNN architectures have been modified and improved to identify diabetic retinopathy. These architectures are capable of extracting pertinent characteristics from retinal images and achieving high accuracy in diabetic retinopathy classification by utilizing large-scale datasets or pre-training on general image datasets like ImageNet. It's crucial to remember that the decision regarding the CNN architecture is influenced by a number of variables, such as the computational resources available, the amount and variety of the dataset, and the intended trade-off between model complexity and performance. To further advance the state-of-the-art, researchers keep investigating and creating cutting-edge CNN architectures that are specifically designed for diabetic retinopathy detection [33].

9.11   USING TRANSFER LEARNING

Transfer learning is a potent deep learning technique that uses models that have already been trained on massive datasets and adapts them to new tasks using smaller datasets. Transfer learning has been frequently employed to enhance the performance of deep learning models in the context of the identification of diabetic retinopathy [34]. Here are a few typical transfer learning techniques used in studies on diabetic retinopathy:

Pre-Trained Models: Pre-trained models that were trained on extensive datasets like ImageNet are frequently used in research. These models, including VGGNet, ResNet, InceptionNet, and EfficientNet, can extract significant characteristics from retinal images and have developed rich representations from a variety of images. The pre-trained models can be improved on diabetic retinopathy datasets by deleting the final fully connected layer(s) and replacing them with new layers.

Feature Extraction: Using pre-trained models as feature extractors is another transfer learning strategy. The pre-trained network is frozen, and the output from one of the intermediate layers is used as input to a new classifier instead of fine-tuning the entire model. A different classifier, such as a support vector machine (SVM) or a fully connected layer, which is trained particularly for diabetic retinopathy diagnosis, receives the features retrieved by the pre-trained model as input. When the dataset is small or there aren't enough processing resources, this strategy is helpful.

Domain Adaptation: The datasets for diabetic retinopathy may be different from the datasets used to build pre-trained models. In these situations, domain adaptation techniques can be used to fill the gap between the source domain (the dataset for the pre-trained model) and the target domain (the dataset for diabetic retinopathy). In order to enhance the model's performance on the target domain, domain adaptation approaches seek to align the feature distributions between the two domains. In order to solve domain shift and boost generalization, methods like as self-ensembling and domain adversarial neural networks (DANN) have been applied to diabetic retinopathy detection.

Improved performance, quicker convergence, and shorter training times are just a few benefits of using transfer learning algorithms to identify diabetic retinopathy. Transfer learning makes it possible to learn well with little labelled data, as is frequently the case in medical imaging, by utilizing the knowledge gathered by pre-trained models.

9.12 ENSEMBLE METHODS AND MODEL FUSION

The performance and resilience of deep learning models are frequently enhanced in diabetic retinopathy diagnosis using ensemble approaches and model fusion techniques. These methods combine predictions from various separate models to provide a final forecast [35]. Some ensemble approaches and model fusion strategies applied in diabetic retinopathy research are listed next:

Bagging: Bagging, also known as bootstrap aggregating, is a strategy that entails separately training various models on various subsets of the training data. Each model makes a prediction, and the overall prediction is created by averaging or voting all of the model projections. Bagging aids in lowering variance and enhancing the ensemble's overall accuracy.

Boosting: Boosting is another ensemble strategy that trains models successively while concentrating on the examples that the prior models misclassified. To create an ensemble of models with better performance, diabetic retinopathy detection methods like AdaBoost and gradient boosting have been used.

Stacking: Also referred to as a layered generalization, stacking entails training several models and feeding the output of those models' predictions into a meta-model that generates the final prediction. Individual models can be trained using various deep learning architectures or variants in the context of diabetic retinopathy. In order to train a meta-model, such as a fully connected neural network or a support vector machine, which produces the final prediction, the predictions of various models are then integrated as features.

Model Fusion: At the decision level, model fusion strategies try to merge the outputs of many models. By averaging the probabilities or results projected by each model, this can be accomplished. More sophisticated fusion methods can also be used, such as weighted averaging, where models are given varying weights based on how well they perform, or majority voting, where the class with the most votes is chosen.

In order to diagnose diabetic retinopathy, ensemble approaches and model fusion techniques have shown promising results by enhancing precision, decreasing overfitting, and enhancing the generalizability of the model. These strategies can capture various patterns and capitalize on the advantages of different models by integrating their predictions, resulting in enhanced performance and resilience in the detection of diabetic retinopathy.

9.13 TRAINING STRATEGIES

9.13.1 Optimization Algorithms

In order to build deep learning models to identify diabetic retinopathy, optimization strategies are essential. These algorithms are in charge of changing the model's parameters in order to reduce the loss function and enhance performance [36]. Several frequently employed deep learning optimization algorithms are listed:

Stochastic Gradient Descent (SGD): SGD is a well-liked deep learning optimization approach. By computing the gradients of the loss function pertaining to the parameters based on a randomly chosen mini-batch of training data, it updates the model's parameters [37]. To reduce the loss, the parameters are then updated in the opposite direction of the gradients.

Adam: Adam (adaptive moment estimation) is an extension of SGD that adapts the learning rate for each parameter based on the estimates of the first and second moments of the gradients. It combines the benefits of both momentum and RMSprop algorithms and is widely used due to its efficiency and fast convergence [38].

RMSprop: RMSprop (root mean square propagation) is an optimization algorithm that adjusts the learning rate for each parameter based on the average of the squared gradients. It reduces the learning rate for parameters with large gradients and increases it for parameters with small gradients, allowing for faster convergence.

AdaGrad: AdaGrad (adaptive gradient) is an optimization algorithm that adapts the learning rate for each parameter based on the historical sum of squared gradients. It gives more weight to less frequently updated parameters and less weight to too frequently updated parameters, enabling effective learning rates for different parameters.

AdaDelta: AdaDelta is an extension of AdaGrad that addresses the problem of the learning rate continuously decreasing during training. It replaces the historical sum of squared gradients with an exponentially decaying average, allowing for a more stable and effective learning rate throughout training.

AdamW: AdamW is a variation of the Adam optimizer that incorporates weight decay regularization. Weight decay helps prevent overfitting by penalizing large parameter values. AdamW has been shown to improve generalization and stability in training deep learning models.

For deep learning models to perform better in the identification of diabetic retinopathy, these optimization algorithms are crucial for determining the ideal set of parameters that minimize the loss function. The size of the dataset, the complexity of the model, and the available computer resources are only a few of the variables that affect the optimization algorithm selection.

9.13.2 REGULARIZATION TECHNIQUES

In order to avoid overfitting and enhance the models' capacity for generalization in the diagnosis of diabetic retinopathy, regularization techniques are used in deep learning optimization [39]. Here are a few regularization methods that are frequently used:

L1 and L2 Regularisation: Also referred to as weight decay, L1 and L2 regularization adds a regularization component to the loss function that penalizes high parameter values. By adding the absolute values of the parameters to the loss function, L1 regularization promotes sparsity while L2 regularization adds the squared values [40]. The regularization term encourages a more evenly distributed distribution of weights and discourages the model from relying excessively on a small number of features, which helps prevent overfitting.

Dropout: During training, a portion of the neurons are randomly removed using the regularization approach dropout. This method avoids individual neurons from becoming overly dependent on particular input properties and forces the network to learn redundant representations. Dropout enhances generalization and lessens overfitting by adding noise to the network.

Batch Normalization: Using a small batch of training examples, batch normalization normalizes the activations of each layer. By minimizing internal covariate shift – a change in the distribution of layer inputs during training – it aids in stabilizing the learning process. Higher learning rates are made possible by batch normalization, which enhances gradient flow and speeds convergence and generalization.

Early Stopping: This strategy checks the model's performance on a validation set while it is being trained and halts training when the performance begins to decline. By determining the ideal balance between model complexity and generalization, it helps prevent overfitting. The model is saved before it reaches the point where it performs optimally on the validation set.

Data Augmentation: By performing numerous modifications to the original images, such as rotations, translations, flips, and brightness adjustments, data augmentation is a technique that artificially expands the training dataset. Data augmentation lessens overfitting while improving the generalizability of the model by enhancing the diversity of the training data.

Dropout regularization [41], where a portion of the weights are set to zero during training, can also be applied to the weights inside a layer. This method promotes robustness by preventing the network from depending too much on certain connections. These regularization methods are combined with optimization algorithms to boost the effectiveness and generalizability of deep learning models for the identification of diabetic retinopathy. The precise needs of the problem and the features of the dataset determine the regularization approaches to be used and how they should be combined.

9.13.3 HYPERPARAMETER TUNING

Hyperparameter tuning is an essential step in optimizing the performance of deep-learning models for diabetic retinopathy detection [42]. Here are some commonly used techniques for hyperparameter tuning:

Grid Search: Grid search involves manually specifying a list of hyperparameter values to explore and then training and evaluating the model for each combination of hyperparameters. It exhaustively searches the entire parameter space, making it time consuming but comprehensive. Grid search helps in finding the optimal hyperparameters but can be computationally expensive, especially when dealing with a large number of hyperparameters.

Random Search: Random search involves randomly sampling hyperparameter values from a predefined range or distribution. Unlike grid search, it does not exhaustively search the entire parameter space but instead randomly explores different combinations. Random search can be more efficient than grid search when the hyperparameter space is large and only a few hyperparameters significantly affect the model's performance.

Bayesian Optimization: Bayesian optimization is an iterative method that builds a probabilistic model of the objective function and uses it to make informed decisions about which hyperparameters to explore next. It balances exploration and exploitation by selecting hyperparameters based on their expected improvement in performance. Bayesian optimization is particularly useful when the evaluation of the objective function is time consuming or expensive.

Genetic Algorithms: Genetic algorithms are inspired by natural evolution processes. They maintain a population of candidate solutions (representing sets of hyperparameters) and iteratively evolve the population to find the optimal solution. Genetic algorithms use selection, crossover, and mutation operations to generate new candidate solutions. They can efficiently explore the hyperparameter space and have been successful in hyperparameter optimization.

Automated Hyperparameter Tuning Libraries: There are several libraries and frameworks available that provide automated hyperparameter tuning capabilities. Examples include Optuna, Hyperopt, and SciKit Learn's GridSearchCV and RandomizedSearchCV. These libraries typically offer more advanced algorithms and techniques for hyperparameter optimization, such as tree-structured Parzen estimators (TPE), population-based training (PBT), and sequential model-based optimization (SMBO) [43].

Relevant factors such learning rate, batch size, number of layers, number of neurons per layer, dropout rate, regularization strength, and optimization technique should be taken into account when tuning hyperparameters for diabetic retinopathy diagnosis. The deep learning architecture that is used as well as the features of the dataset may influence the precise hyperparameters that need to be tuned. Cross-validation is frequently used to obtain more accurate estimates of model performance when hyperparameter tuning. Cross-validation evaluates the model's generalizability and enables a fair comparison of various hyperparameter settings by dividing the dataset into training and validation sets. Hyperparameter tuning, as a whole, is an iterative process that includes experimenting with various combinations of hyperparameters, training and assessing models, and choosing the configuration that produces the best performance on a validation set. Consideration of the trade-offs between computing resources and model performance, together with thorough experimentation, are necessary.

9.13.4 CROSS-VALIDATION AND DATA-SPLITTING STRATEGIES

Cross-validation and data-splitting strategies are crucial in assessing the performance of deep-learning models for diabetic retinopathy and ensuring their generalizability. Here are some commonly used approaches:

Holdout Validation: The dataset is split into two sets for holdout validation: a training set and a validation set. The training set is used to develop the model, while the validation set is used to assess it. A typical split is 70% training and 30% validation, chosen at random. The split ratio, however, can change based on the size of the dataset and the particular specifications of the problem.

K-Fold Cross-Validation: In K-fold cross-validation, the dataset is divided into K folds of equal size. Each fold serves as the validation set once and the remaining folds as the training set as the model is trained and evaluated K times. The total performance estimate is then calculated by averaging the performance characteristics from each fold. In comparison to holdout validation, K-fold cross-validation offers a more reliable estimate of model performance, particularly when the dataset is small.

Stratified Sampling: Stratified sampling is advised when working with datasets that are unbalanced and have underrepresented classes. The class distribution is preserved in both the training and validation sets thanks to stratified sampling. Given that the prevalence of the condition can differ across the sample, this is particularly crucial for the diagnosis of diabetic retinopathy.

Leave-One-Out Cross-Validation (LOOCV): When working with datasets that are uneven and include underrepresented classes, stratified sampling is recommended. Because of stratified sampling, the class distribution is kept constant in both the training and validation sets. This is critical for the diagnosis of diabetic retinopathy because the prevalence of the disorder can vary depending on the sample.

Time-Based Splitting: Consider time-based splitting algorithms if the dataset comprises sequential data, such as retinal pictures gathered across time. This method divides the dataset into training and validation sets while maintaining the data's temporal order. This makes sure that the model is assessed using hypothetical data and realistic scenarios.

While executing it is essential to make sure that the splits used for cross-validation or data splitting are impartial and representative. It is frequently advised to randomly shuffle the dataset before separating it to avoid any ordering bias. Furthermore, it is crucial to assess the model's performance on a different test set, which ought to be totally distinct from the training and validation sets. The test set offers a fair assessment of the model's performance with unknown data. Cross-validation and data-splitting techniques enable a thorough assessment of the model's performance, assist in spotting potential problems like overfitting or underfitting, and shed light on the model's capacity for generalization.

9.14   METRICS FOR PERFORMANCE EVALUATION

9.14.1   SENSITIVITY, SPECIFICITY, AND ACCURACY

Accuracy, sensitivity, and specificity are commonly used performance metrics in evaluating the performance of models for diabetic retinopathy detection [44]. Let's define these metrics:

1. Sensitivity (True Positive Rate): Sensitivity, also known as the true positive rate or recall, measures the model's ability to correctly identify positive cases (diabetic retinopathy) out of all actual positive cases. It indicates how well the model detects diabetic retinopathy.

   Sensitivity = (Number of true positive samples)/(Number of true positive samples + Number of false negative samples)

   Sensitivity is particularly important in the context of diabetic retinopathy detection, as missing positive cases can have severe consequences for patients.

2. Specificity (True Negative Rate): Specificity measures the model's ability to correctly identify negative cases (non-diabetic retinopathy) out of all actual negative cases. It indicates how well the model distinguishes non-diabetic retinopathy cases.

   Specificity = (Number of true negative samples)/(Number of true negative samples + Number of false positive samples)

   Specificity is important to ensure that the model does not misclassify non-diabetic retinopathy cases, which can lead to unnecessary interventions or treatments.

   In the context of diabetic retinopathy, a high sensitivity is desirable to ensure the detection of positive cases, while a high specificity is crucial to minimize false positives. It is important to strike a balance between these metrics based on the specific requirements of the application. For instance, in a screening scenario, a high sensitivity might be prioritized to avoid missing any cases, even if it results in more false positives. On the other hand, in a diagnostic setting, a high specificity might be more important to minimize unnecessary interventions.

   It's worth noting that these metrics provide a binary evaluation (positive or negative) and may not capture the full spectrum of disease severity in diabetic retinopathy. Additional metrics such as the area under the receiver operating characteristic curve (AUC-ROC) or the F1 score can be used to assess the overall performance of the model, taking into account both sensitivity and specificity.

3. Accuracy: Accuracy measures the overall correctness of the model's predictions and is calculated as the ratio of correctly classified samples to the total number of samples. In the context of diabetic retinopathy, accuracy represents the percentage of correctly classified images (both positive and negative) out of the total number of images.

   Accuracy = (Number of correctly classified samples)/(Total number of samples)

While accuracy provides a general measure of the model's performance, it can be misleading when the dataset is imbalanced, meaning one class (e.g., diabetic retinopathy) is much more prevalent than the other class (e.g., non-diabetic retinopathy).

9.14.2 Confusion Matrix Analysis

Confusion matrix analysis is a method for assessing a classification model's performance, including in the case of diabetic retinopathy. By classifying the model's predictions into four groups – true positives (TP), true negatives (TN), false positives (FP), and false negatives (FN) – it offers a more thorough evaluation of them [45].

In the case of diabetic retinopathy, a confusion matrix can be constructed as follows:

Predicted Negative and Predicted Positive
Actual Negative TN (True Negative) FP (False Positive)
Actual Positive FN (False Negative) TP (True Positive)

The confusion matrix allows us to calculate various performance metrics:

1. Accuracy: It measures the overall correctness of the model's predictions and is calculated as (TP + TN)/(TP + TN + FP + FN).
2. Sensitivity (Recall or True Positive Rate): It measures the proportion of actual positive cases correctly identified by the model and is calculated as TP/(TP + FN). In the context of diabetic retinopathy, it represents the ability of the model to correctly identify patients with the disease.
3. Specificity: It measures the proportion of actual negative cases correctly identified by the model and is calculated as TN/(TN + FP). In the context of diabetic retinopathy, it represents the ability of the model to correctly identify individuals without the disease.
4. Precision: It measures the proportion of correctly predicted positive cases out of all positive predictions made by the model and is calculated as TP/(TP + FP). Precision is useful when the focus is on minimizing false positives.
5. F1 Score: It is the harmonic mean of precision and sensitivity and provides a balanced measure of the model's performance. It is calculated as 2 * (Precision * Sensitivity)/(Precision + Sensitivity).

Analyzing the confusion matrix and these metrics can provide insights into the model's strengths and weaknesses in classifying diabetic retinopathy cases. For example, a high number of false negatives (FN) would indicate that the model is missing a significant number of positive cases, while a high number of false positives (FP) would suggest that the model is incorrectly classifying individuals without the disease as positive. By considering the confusion matrix and related metrics, researchers and clinicians can evaluate the model's performance, understand its limitations, and make informed decisions about its use in diabetic retinopathy detection and diagnosis.

9.15 CONCLUSION

In conclusion, deep learning has become a potent diagnostic and screening tool for diabetic retinopathy. It has demonstrated promising results in increasing the precision and effectiveness of diabetic retinopathy screening thanks to its capacity to automatically learn complicated patterns and features from retinal pictures. Deep learning algorithms have the ability to identify early indicators of diabetic retinopathy, enabling prompt intervention and therapy. In order to manage the disease's course and prevent vision loss, early detection is essential. When it comes to diagnosing diabetic retinopathy, deep learning models have shown remarkable accuracy that is frequently on par with or even better than that of human specialists.

This can lower diagnostic blunders and provide dependable, repeatable outcomes. Deep learning makes it possible to automatically screen huge volumes of retinal pictures for diabetic retinopathy, improving accessibility and efficiency. This is especially helpful where there is little access to ophthalmologists or where the condition is prevalent. Deep learning models can reduce the strain of ophthalmologists and other medical specialists by automating the screening process, allowing them to concentrate on other important activities and enhancing overall healthcare efficiency. Deep learning models can be applied to a variety of populations and environments since they can generalize well to new, unobserved data. The versatility of deep learning models is further enhanced by transfer learning approaches, which enable effective retraining on fresh datasets using limited labelled samples [46].

Deep learning models frequently lack interpretability, which makes it difficult to grasp the precise variables influencing their predictions despite their great performance. To get insight into model decision-making processes, interpretability techniques are currently being developed. Collaboration with healthcare providers is necessary for deep learning to be effective in detecting diabetic retinopathy. Deep learning algorithms can be used in conjunction with the knowledge of ophthalmologists and other medical specialists to improve the accuracy of diagnoses and the efficiency of patient treatment. Overall, by offering precise and effective detection methods, deep learning has the potential to revolutionize diabetic retinopathy screening and care. Deep learning models are anticipated to continue to advance with continuous research and developments, improving the outcomes for people with diabetic retinopathy.

REFERENCES

[1] Wilkinson CP, Ferris III FL, Klein RE, Lee PP, Agardh CD, Davis M, Dills D, Kampik A, Pararajasegaram R, Verdaguer JT, Global Diabetic Retinopathy Project Group. Proposed international clinical diabetic retinopathy and diabetic macular edema disease severity scales. Ophthalmology. 2003 Sep 1;110(9):1677–1682.

[2] Ting DS, Cheung GC, Wong TY. Diabetic retinopathy: global prevalence, major risk factors, screening practices and public health challenges: a review. Clinical & Experimental Ophthalmology. 2016 May;44(4):260–277.

[3] Gardner TW, Antonetti DA, Barber AJ, LaNoue KF, Levison SW, Penn State Retina Research Group. Diabetic retinopathy: more than meets the eye. Survey of Ophthalmology. 2002 Dec 1;47:S253–S262.

[4] An D, Chandrasekera E, Yu DY, Balaratnasingam C. Non-proliferative diabetic retinopathy is characterized by nonuniform alterations of peripapillary capillary networks. Investigative Ophthalmology & Visual Science. 2020 Apr 9;61(4):39.

[5] Danis RP, Davis MD. Proliferative diabetic retinopathy. Diabetic Retinopathy. 2008:29–65.

[6] Gadekallu TR, Khare N, Bhattacharya S, Singh S, Maddikunta PK, Ra IH, Alazab M. Early detection of diabetic retinopathy using PCA-firefly based deep learning model. Electronics. 2020 Feb 5;9(2):274.

[7] Vujosevic S, Aldington SJ, Silva P, Hernández C, Scanlon P, Peto T, Simó R. Screening for diabetic retinopathy: new perspectives and challenges. The Lancet Diabetes & Endocrinology. 2020 Apr 1;8(4):337–347.

[8] Bansal M, Goyal A, Choudhary A. A comparative analysis of K-nearest neighbour, genetic, support vector machine, decision tree, and long short term memory algorithms in machine learning. Decision Analytics Journal. 2022 May 27:100071.

[9] Naithani S, Bharadwaj S, Kumar D. Automated detection of diabetic retinopathy using deep learning. International Research Journal of Engineering and Technology. 2019 Apr;6(4):2945–2947.

[10] Gundluru N, Rajput DS, Lakshmanna K, Kaluri R, Shorfuzzaman M, Uddin M, Rahman Khan MA. Enhancement of detection of diabetic retinopathy using Harris hawks optimization with deep learning model. Computational Intelligence and Neuroscience. 2022 May 26;2022.

[11] Muchuchuti S, Viriri S. Retinal disease detection using deep learning techniques: a comprehensive review. Journal of Imaging. 2023 Apr 18;9(4):84.

[12] Gulshan V, Peng L, Coram M, Stumpe MC, Wu D, Narayanaswamy A, Venugopalan S, Widner K, Madams T, Cuadros J, Kim R. Development and validation of a deep learning algorithm for detection of diabetic retinopathy in retinal fundus photographs. Jama. 2016 Dec 13;316(22):2402–2410.

[13] Alzubaidi L, Zhang J, Humaidi AJ, Al-Dujaili A, Duan Y, Al-Shamma O, Santamaría J, Fadhel MA, Al-Amidie M, Farhan L. Review of deep learning: concepts, CNN architectures, challenges, applications, future directions. Journal of Big Data. 2021 Dec;8:1–74.

[14] Schlagenhauf T, Lin Y, Noack B. Discriminative feature learning through feature distance loss. Machine Vision and Applications. 2023 Mar;34(2):25.

[15] Kawaguchi K. On optimization and scalability in deep learning (Doctoral dissertation, Massachusetts Institute of Technology).

[16] Kirk R, Zhang A, Grefenstette E, Rocktäschel T. A survey of zero-shot generalisation in deep reinforcement learning. Journal of Artificial Intelligence Research. 2023 Jan 9;76:201–264.

[17] Franke JK, Köhler G, Biedenkapp A, Hutter F. Sample-efficient automated deep reinforcement learning. 2020 Sep 3. arXiv preprint arXiv:2009.01555.

[18] Dai L, Wu L, Li H, Cai C, Wu Q, Kong H, Liu R, Wang X, Hou X, Liu Y, Long X. A deep learning system for detecting diabetic retinopathy across the disease spectrum. Nature Communications. 2021 May 28;12(1):3242.

[19] Nadeem MW, Goh HG, Hussain M, Liew SY, Andonovic I, Khan MA. Deep learning for diabetic retinopathy analysis: a review, research challenges, and future directions. Sensors. 2022 Sep 8;22(18):6780.

[20] Huang X, Wang H, She C, Feng J, Liu X, Hu X, Chen L, Tao Y. Artificial intelligence promotes the diagnosis and screening of diabetic retinopathy. Frontiers in Endocrinology. 2022 Sep 29;13:946915.

[21] Ningsih DR. Improving retinal image quality using the contrast stretching, histogram equalization, and CLAHE methods with median filters. International Journal of Image, Graphics and Signal Processing. 2020 Apr 1;10(2):30.

[22] Deng K, Tian J, Zheng J, Zhang X, Dai X, Xu M. Retinal fundus image registration via vascular structure graph matching. Journal of Biomedical Imaging. 2010 Jan 1;2010:1–3.

[23] Laliberté F, Gagnon L, Sheng Y. Registration and fusion of retinal images-an evaluation study. IEEE Transactions on Medical Imaging. 2003 May;22(5):661–673.

[24] Yamashita R, Nishio M, Do RK, Togashi K. Convolutional neural networks: an overview and application in radiology. Insights into Imaging. 2018 Aug;9:611–629.

[25] Mohammadian S, Karsaz A, Roshan YM. Comparative study of fine-tuning of pre-trained convolutional neural networks for diabetic retinopathy screening. In 2017 24th National and 2nd International Iranian Conference on Biomedical Engineering (ICBME) 2017 Nov 30 (pp. 1–6). IEEE.

[26] Dunnmon JA, Yi D, Langlotz CP, Ré C, Rubin DL, Lungren MP. Assessment of convolutional neural networks for automated classification of chest radiographs. Radiology. 2019 Feb;290(2):537–544.

[27] Kandel I, Castelli M. Transfer learning with convolutional neural networks for diabetic retinopathy image classification. A review. Applied Sciences. 2020 Mar 16;10(6):2021.

[28] Sushma L, Lakshmi KP. An analysis of convolution neural network for image classification using different models. International Journal of Engineering Research & Technology. 2020 Oct;9(10).

[29] Heta Desai. Biomedical data classification with improvised deep learning architectures (Dissertation, Georgia State University), 2020. https://doi.org/10.57709/18808634

[30] He K, Zhang X, Ren S, Sun J. Deep residual learning for image recognition. In Proceedings of the IEEE Conference on Computer Vision and Pattern Recognition 2016 (pp. 770–778).

[31] Jégou S, Drozdzal M, Vazquez D, Romero A, Bengio Y. The one hundred layers tiramisu: fully convolutional densenets for semantic segmentation. In Proceedings of the IEEE Conference on Computer Vision and Pattern Recognition Workshops 2017 (pp. 11–19).

[32] Tan M, Le Q. Efficientnet: rethinking model scaling for convolutional neural networks. In International Conference on Machine Learning 2019 May 24 (pp. 6105–6114). PMLR.

[33] Jabbar MK, Yan J, Xu H, Ur Rehman Z, Jabbar A. Transfer learning-based model for diabetic retinopathy diagnosis using retinal images. Brain Sciences. 2022 Apr 22;12(5):535.

[34] Gangwar AK, Ravi V. Diabetic retinopathy detection using transfer learning and deep learning. In *Evolution in Computational Intelligence: Frontiers in Intelligent Computing: Theory and Applications (FICTA 2020)*, Volume 1, 2021 (pp. 679–689). Springer.

[35] Das D, Biswas SK, Bandyopadhyay S. A critical review on diagnosis of diabetic retinopathy using machine learning and deep learning. Multimedia Tools and Applications. 2022 Jul;81(18):25613–25655.

[36] Mehboob A, Akram MU, Alghamdi NS, Abdul Salam A. A deep learning based approach for grading of diabetic retinopathy using large fundus image dataset. Diagnostics. 2022 Dec 7;12(12):3084.

[37] Naddaf-Sh MM, Naddaf-Sh S, Zargarzadeh H, Zahiri SM, Dalton M, Elpers G, Kashani AR. Defect detection and classification in welding using deep learning and digital radiography. In *Fault Diagnosis and Prognosis Techniques for Complex Engineering Systems*, 2021 Jan 1 (pp. 327–352). Academic Press.

[38] Jais IK, Ismail AR, Nisa SQ. Adam optimization algorithm for wide and deep neural network. Knowledge Engineering and Data Science. 2019 Jun 23;2(1):41–46.

[39] Das D, Biswas SK, Bandyopadhyay S. A critical review on diagnosis of diabetic retinopathy using machine learning and deep learning. Multimedia Tools and Applications. 2022 Jul;81(18):25613–25655.

[40] Rahangdale A, Raut S. Deep neural network regularization for feature selection in learning-to-rank. IEEE Access. 2019 Apr 26;7:53988–54006.

[41] Xie X, Xie M, Moshayedi AJ, Noori Skandari MH. A hybrid improved neural networks algorithm based on L2 and dropout regularization. Mathematical Problems in Engineering. 2022 Nov 3;2022.

[42] Parthiban K, Kamarasan M. Diabetic retinopathy detection and grading of retinal fundus images using coyote optimization algorithm with deep learning. Multimedia Tools and Applications. 2023 May;82(12):18947–18966.

[43] Ting DS, Pasquale LR, Peng L, Campbell JP, Lee AY, Raman R, Tan GS, Schmetterer L, Keane PA, Wong TY. Artificial intelligence and deep learning in ophthalmology. British Journal of Ophthalmology. 2019 Feb 1;103(2):167–175.

[44] Hemanth DJ, Deperlioglu O, Kose U. An enhanced diabetic retinopathy detection and classification approach using deep convolutional neural network. Neural Computing and Applications. 2020 Feb;32:707–721.

[45] Kalyani G, Janakiramaiah B, Karuna A, Prasad LN. Diabetic retinopathy detection and classification using capsule networks. Complex & Intelligent Systems. 2021 Mar 17:1–4.

[46] Indrakumari R, Poongodi T, Khaitan S, Sagar S, Balamurugan B. A review on plant diseases recognition through deep learning. Handbook of Deep Learning in Biomedical Engineering. 2021 Jan 1:219–244.

10 Enhancing Cardiovascular Health Diagnosis through Predictive Analysis of Electronic Health Records

Vijayaprabakaran K and Ilavendhan Anandaraj

10.1 INTRODUCTION

In the healthcare industry, disease diagnosis is the most crucial healthcare function. Early diagnosis of any disease can reduce the severity of the disease and help to plan suitable treatment or medication that can save people's lives. In disease diagnosis, the individual experience and knowledge lead to bias in diagnosis and diagnostic error. To address these challenges several methods have been proposed to automate the diagnosis with the knowledge of the previous medical history of the patient. Traditional methods such as rule-based expert systems with a knowledge base are used to diagnose the disease. In the medical expert system, the construction of a knowledge base requires a large source of information that is very expensive. The potential of machine learning techniques shows the remarkable achievements in the complex task of various fields. Artificial intelligence in the medical field introduced machine learning techniques to learn the complex pattern of the medical data and help the physicians in diagnosing diseases. The classification technique of machine learning supports medical experts by providing reliable and fast disease diagnosis. Cardiovascular disorders have risen to prominence as a significant contributor to global mortality. According to the World Health Organization, heart-related ailments account for a substantial 17.7 million fatalities annually, constituting 31% of worldwide deaths. This trend is evident in India as well, where heart-related conditions have ascended to the forefront as the primary cause of mortality [1]. According to the 2016 Global Burden of Disease Report, in India, heart diseases killed 1.7 million Indians in 2016. Heart-related diseases increase the cost of healthcare expenses and became a hindrance to the productivity of an individual [2]. The expenses associated with heart disease treatment are notably high, rendering it unaffordable for

DOI: 10.1201/9781003343172-10

a wide spectrum of individuals. Consequently, many people exhibit hesitation in pursuing appropriate medical care during the initial phases of the ailment. Thus, feasible and accurate prediction of heart-related diseases is very important. By leveraging advanced algorithms and computational power, machine learning techniques are employed to analyze complex medical data, extract meaningful insights, and enhance decision-making processes. These applications encompass a wide range of areas, including disease diagnosis, treatment optimization, patient monitoring, drug discovery, personalized medicine, and predictive analytics. The integration of machine learning in healthcare holds the potential to revolutionize medical practices, improve patient outcomes, and drive advancements in medical research.

The early detection of heart disease can save the life of the person. To accomplish this goal of predicting heart disease several methods have been proposed in the literature. In the past decade, several traditional methods like statistical and mathematical models obtained better diagnostic results with a high accuracy rate. Machine learning methods within the healthcare sector assume a pivotal role across diverse domains within the medical field. Employed for the analysis of medical data, these techniques facilitate physicians in disease diagnosis and forecasting future health outcomes [3].

The motivation behind this research is to explore the potential of the deep learning network models to predict heart disease at an earlier stage based on medical history. The main objective of this work is to design a deep learning-based framework for diagnosing heart disease from the electronic health record that consists of the medical history of the patient. The key contributions of this framework are

- Data preprocessing for improving the quality of the data to reduce the false prediction
- Developing an LSTM model for predicting the heart disease
- A genetic algorithm is applied to tune the hyperparameter of the LSTM model to improve the prediction accuracy

The proposed heart disease diagnosis framework is evaluated with the benchmark datasets and results are compared with the existing models. The results show that the proposed framework provides a better prediction accuracy of percentage.

The rest of the chapter is organized as follows: Section 10.2 describes the various methods and research contributions toward the heart disease diagnosis, Section 10.3 elaborates the key components of the proposed framework for predicting heart disease. The detailed summary of the analysis of the proposed framework is discussed with experiments are present in Section 10.4. In Section 10.5, the authors conclude the paper by highlighting the performance of the proposed method and future scope to work in this direction.

10.2 LITERATURE SURVEY

In the healthcare industry, machine learning techniques have applied to the various problems and achieved a better result [4, 5]. The authors, K. Polara and D. Durga Prasad [6] have proposed a prediction model for diagnosing heart disease using several algorithms and verified that the multiple linear regression model has gained a better prediction accuracy in the diagnosis of heart disease. The experimental study and analysis on raw clinical dataset contain 1000 test samples and 10 various characteristics. In the experimental study the aforementioned clinical data is two sets of data of 70 percent and 30 percent for training and testing respectively. The experimental results show that the regression algorithms performed quite well when compared to other algorithms.

The author Sultana [7] has proposed a ML-based framework to predict heart diseases from patients' health data using three different machine learning techniques, namely naïve Bayes, J48, sequential minimal optimization, and multilayer perception. In an experimental study of these machine learning techniques, the multilayer perceptron and J48 based prediction models using K-fold cross-validation achieve better performance than KStar. The accuracy achieved by these machine learning algorithms are not satisfactorily good. Therefore, the authors enhanced the efficiency of the accuracy to make the right step toward diagnosis. The authors Deepika and Seema in [8] mainly focused on machine learning techniques including naïve Bayes, support vector machine (SVM), decision tree, and ANN to find chronic disease from the medical data stored in previous health records. The authors performed a comparative analysis on the aforementioned classifiers to find the appropriate output at a specific scale. This experiment has achieved the highest precision rate of SVM while naïve Bayes performs to help maximum accuracy in results.

P. Sai Chandrasekhar Reddy et al. [9] proposed an ANN-based data mining method for the prediction of heart disease. Due to the escalating diagnostic expenses in health care, there arose a necessity for the development of novel technology capable of cost-effectively predicting heart diseases. Subsequent to estimation, a prediction model is employed to assess the patient's condition using diverse parameters such as pulse rate, blood pressure, cholesterol levels, and more.

The utilization of non-linear classification algorithms for heart disease prediction is discussed by the authors Sharmila and Chellama in [8]. They propose the incorporation of big data tools like HDFS and MapReduce along with SVM for an optimized selection of attributes to predict heart disease. This study also investigates the application of different data mining techniques for detecting heart disease. The recommendation involves employing HDFS for the storage of extensive data across multiple nodes and the simultaneous implementation of the SVM prediction algorithm across these nodes. This approach yields improved processing efficiency compared to conventional methods. Mahajan and Kaur [10] introduced the genetic algorithm to optimize the topology of the neural network. They used binary encoding to represent the existence of connections between the neurons. Similarly, Nicolas et al. [11] proposed a genetic algorithm to tune the hyperparameters of the LSTM model to improve the performance of the model for NLP tasks.

10.3 PROPOSED METHOD

This section describes the deep learning-based heart disease prediction framework. In the area of disease diagnosis, several approaches were proposed and achieved significant results. In this work, the deep learning model of the LSTM network is

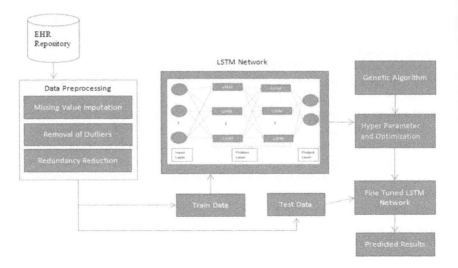

FIGURE 10.1 System diagram of the proposed framework for heart disease diagnosis

used to build the heart disease prediction framework using the patient's medical history from the EHR data. The architecture of the proposed framework is shown in Figure 10.1. The proposed heart disease prediction framework consists of the following phases:

- Data preprocessing
- Developing the LSTM model
- Hyperparameter tuning
- Validating the model.

10.3.1 DATA PREPROCESSING

The health data present in the EHR repository is a large volume and needs to be pre-processed for further analysis because these EHR data were collected from various sources and the following issues persist in the EHR data, namely missing values, outliers, and redundancy of data. To address these issues 1) Bayesian principal component analysis is applied to impute the missing values present in the EHR data; 2) Cook's D method is used to detect the outliers; and 3) Pearson correlation analysis is performed to remove the redundancy of the data present in the EHR.

BPCA Based Missing Value Imputation: Absent values within electronic health records (EHR) arise from mishandled samples, low signal-to-noise ratio (SNR), measurement inaccuracies, non-responses, or the removal of anomalous data points. The method of Bayesian principal component analysis (BPCA), grounded in probabilistic Bayesian theory, is utilized for imputing these missing values [12]. BPCA employs observed values to compute the missing ones, disregarding the presence of missing data. By employing Bayes theorem, PCA is determined, and Bayesian estimation is employed to calculate the absent values.

Removal of Outliers: The outliers of the health data lead to inaccurate prediction. Multiple linear regression is applied to predicted outliers. Compare Cook's D [13] with the cut-off value (three times the mean value of the outlier) and remove the outliers present in the dataset.

Removal of Redundancy: Redundancy of data present in health care lead to inaccurate results in medical data analysis on EHR. It can be determined by performing a correlation analysis among the attributes of the dataset. Pearson correlation [14] measures the strength of the association between two given attributes. If the correlation is greater than the threshold, discard the redundant feature.

$$r = \frac{n\left(\sum xy\right) - \left(\sum x\right)\left(\sum y\right)}{\sqrt{\left[n\sum x^2 - \left(\sum x\right)^2\right]\left[n\sum y^2 - \left(\sum y\right)^2\right]}} \qquad (10.1)$$

where r is the correlation coefficient, x and y are the two independent attributes in the dataset.

10.3.2 LONG-SHORT-TERM MEMORY (LSTM)

LSTM, a well-known neural network model, is part of the recurrent neural network family [15]. This LSTM network finds extensive application across various domains and has achieved significant advancements in the analysis of time series data. Unlike traditional RNNs, LSTMs are capable of addressing the vanishing gradient problem, making them well-suited for tasks involving sequences with long-range dependencies. LSTMs' capability to capture long-term dependencies and adapt to varying patterns makes them suitable for medical data analysis, where patient data often involves complex temporal relationships and contextual information. In medical data analysis, LSTM can analyze medical time series data such as patient vital signs, electrocardiograms (ECGs), and blood glucose levels. It can capture patterns and fluctuations over time, aiding in early detection of anomalies or predicting future values. LSTMs can predict the likelihood of specific medical conditions based on patient history, lab results, and other relevant data. This aids in timely intervention and personalized patient care.

Each basic unit of the LSTM network consists of three gates (input gate, output gate, and forget gate) and one memory unit to store the output of the previous state. The structure of the LSTM block is shown in Figure 10.2 [16].

The LSTM architecture consists of three key components:

1. Memory Cell: The core memory unit that maintains information over time and is controlled by three gates.
2. Input Gate: Determines how much new information is added to the cell state.
3. Forget Gate: Determines what information from the cell state should be discarded.
4. Output Gate: Controls the output of the cell state based on the input and internal state.

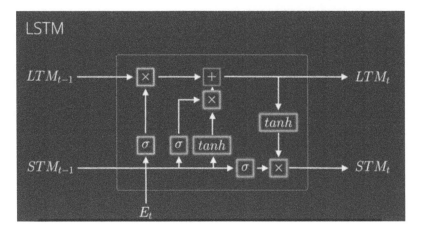

FIGURE 10.2   Architecture of a LSTM cell

The memory cell in the LSTM stores the previous state of the output given as the feedback to the current state along with the input data. The equations of the input, forget, and output gates are given here:

$$f_t = \sigma(W_f[h_{t-1}, x_t] + b_f) \tag{10.2}$$

$$i_t = \sigma(W_i[h_{t-1}, x_t] + b_i) \tag{10.3}$$

$$O_t = \sigma([W_{t-1}, x_t] + b_o) \tag{10.4}$$

The output of the forget gate at time step "t," represented by "f_t," is derived using the activation function σ. Similarly, "i_t" and "o_t" represent the outputs of the input gate and output gate, respectively. "x_t" stands for the input, while "h_{t-1}" signifies the previous hidden state. The weight matrices W_f, W_i, W_o, along with the bias terms b_f, b_i, and b_o, constitute the learnable parameters in this context.

10.3.3   HYPERPARAMETER TUNING

The neural network has various hyperparameters that are responsible for network performance. Some of the hyperparameters are activation function, number of layers, optimizer, loss function, learning rate, etc. In this work, we concentrate on the activation function optimizer and learning rate for tuning the performance of the LSTM model. There are several methods used for hyperparameter optimization in the literature, among them evolutionary algorithms are popular in selecting the optimal value of the hyperparameters. In this work, we proposed a genetic algorithm-based hyperparameter tuning of the LSTM network to improve the prediction accuracy of heart disease prediction task. The genetic algorithm for tuning the hyperparameters of the LSTM is given in Algorithm 1.

Algorithm 1: Genetic Algorithm for Hyperparameter optimization of LSTM

1: population ← [list of n combination of hyperparameters]
2: generation ← 0
3: while (generation < l) do:
4: train and evaluate the LSTM(population)
5: new_gen ← retrain them fittest individuals
6: new_gen ← append random individuals to promote diversity
7: mutate (new_gen)
8: new_gen ← append offspring through crossover until k
9: population ← new_gen
10: generation ← generation + 1
11: output the hyperparameter of the fittest in population

In the hyperparameter optimization, the genetic algorithm takes the hyperparameter values as follows: sigmoid, ReLU, and tanh as activation functions; SGD, AdaGrad, and Adam as optimizers; and $10^{-1}, 10^{-2}, 10^{-3}$ as the learning rates. The genetic algorithm takes these values as the search space for finding the optimal combination of hyperparameter for improving the prediction accuracy. First, the GA initializes the population from the search space and selects the values for the hyperparameters randomly. Second, it validates the fitness of the model with two objective functions, namely accuracy and loss. In the genetic algorithm, while training the model, the hyperparameters with the highest accuracy are transferred for the new generation as parents. Subsequently, proceed with the processes of crossover and mutation. In the context of the initial algorithm variation, mutation is exclusively implemented on the survivor individuals. As per the second variation, mutation is introduced across an entirely new generation once the crossover phase concludes. The crossover procedure involves the random selection of hyperparameters from each parent with equal probabilities. Parent selection is also executed with equiprobable chances among the survivor pool. Following the formation of the new generation, the cycle recommences from the second step, iteratively persisting until the specified termination condition is met. The output gives the LSTM model with optimal hyperparameter values for activation function, optimizer, and learning rate. The optimized LSTM model achieves high prediction accuracy in heart disease prediction.

10.4 EXPERIMENTAL RESULTS AND DISCUSSION

In the view of validating the proposed model, several experiments were conducted to analyze the performance of the framework in two different heart disease benchmark datasets.

10.4.1 EXPERIMENTAL SETUP

All the experiments were done on Ubuntu 16.4 using the Anaconda Navigator with Python 3.6. The Keras [17] version 3 is used for the deployment of deep neural networks, and TensorFlow [18] is used as the backend to process the data.

10.4.2 DATASET

This study takes the Cleveland heart dataset [19] from the University of California Irvine Machine Learning Repository that is widely used as the standard dataset to train the machine learning model to predict heart disease. This heart dataset is provided by Dr. David Aha, and it consists of 303 individual clinical records in which 164 did not have any disease. This dataset was created from three hospitals, and the data was collected from 303 volunteers of which 97 are female and 206 are male. In this dataset, there are 139 (25 female and 114 male) records identified with heart disease. The dataset contains 76 attributes about the patients, but only 14 attributes are taken for this study of predicting heart disease. The details of the attributes are given in Table 10.1.

10.4.3 DATA PREPROCESSING

The dataset is allowed to perform the data preprocessing to impute the missing values in the dataset. The BPCA computes the missing values using Bayesian estimation.

TABLE 10.1
Attributes of Heart Disease Dataset

Sl. No	Attribute Name	Value
1	Age	Age in years
2	Sex	1 = male; 0 = female
3	Chest pain	Chest pain typer
4	Trestbps	Resting blood pressure (in mm Hg)
5	chol	Serum cholesterol in mg/dl
6	Fbs (fasting blood sugar >120mg/dl	1 = True; 0 = False
7	restecg	Value 0 = normal
		Value 1 = abnormal in ST waves
		Value 2 = showing probable
8	Thalach	Maximum heart rate achieved
9	Xang (exercise include angina)	1 = yes
		0 = no
10	Old peak	ST depression induced by exercise relative to rest
11	slope	1 = upsloping
		2 = flat
		3 = downsloping
12	ca	number of major vessels (0–3)
13	Thal	3 = normal
		6 = fixed defect
		7 = reversable defect
14	num	0 = < 50% diameter narrowing
		1 = > 50% diameter narrowing

The Cook's D method and Pearson correlation methods are applied to remove the outliers and redundancy of data present in the given dataset.

10.4.4 TRAINING THE **LSTM** MODEL

The LSTM model consists of an input layer, three LSTM data layers, and one output layer. The weights are initialized with a random initializer and trained with pre-processed data to predict heart disease. The hyperparameters of the LSTM model needs to be set. The proposed LSTM model is trained and validated using a 10-fold cross-validation method. The hyperparameters are optimized using a genetic algorithm. The GA takes the given set of hyperparameter values to fine tune the LSTM model. The best hyperparameters values were selected based on the two objective functions, namely prediction accuracy and loss.

For each combination of the hyperparameter from the GA, the LSTM model gets trained and validated with the objective functions. During the process of hyperparameter optimization, the value of activation function, optimizer function, and learning rate get optimized. Then, the LSTM model with the hyperparameters ReLU activation function, Adam optimizer with learning rate 10^{-2} performs well when compared to LSTM model with other combinations of hyperparameter.

This chapter selected the ANN [20], decision tree [21], and traditional LSTM [22] without hyperparameter tuning as the benchmarks for the comparison with the proposed fine-tuned LSTM model in heart disease prediction task. Figure 10.3 shows a comparison of the prediction accuracy of proposed LSTM and benchmarks on

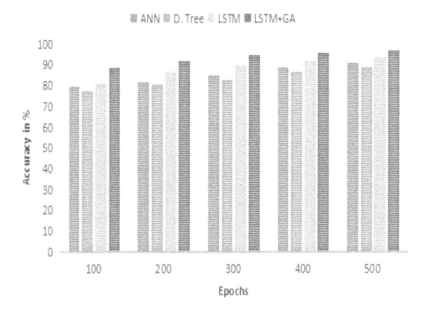

FIGURE 10.3 Comparison of the accuracy of proposed LSTM+GA model with benchmark methods (ANN, decision tree, and traditional LSTM)

TABLE 10.2

Top Three Combination of the Hyperparameter Values and Its Accuracy

Sl. No	Activation Function	Optimizer	Learning Rate	Accuracy
1	ReLU	Adam	10^{-2}	97%
2	tanh	AdaGrad	10^{-2}	96%
3	ReLU	SGD	10^{-3}	94%

TABLE 10.3

Comparison of Proposed LSTM Model with State-of-the-Art Model in Heart Disease Prediction

Sl. No	Methods/Models	Accuracy
1	ANN [23]	91%
2	CNN [24]	93%
3	Decision tree [25]	89%
4	LSTM [26]	94%
5	SVM [27]	87%
6	LSTM+GA	97%

the UCI heart disease dataset. The accuracy of the proposed LSTM model with GA-based hyperparameter method achieved a better accuracy of 97% than other benchmark methods considered for this study.

The experiment results of the LSTM model with the top 3 combinations of the hyperparameter are tabulated in Table 10.2.

The proposed model achieved better accuracy than state-of-the-art models presented in the literature. The comparison of the LSTM+GA with other existing models are given in Table 10.3.

10.5   CONCLUSION

In this chapter, a deep learning-based framework is developed to predict heart disease from the EHR records of patients' medical history. The proposed framework is validated with UCI Heart disease data. The preprocessing methods are applied to address the missing values, presence of outliers, and redundancy of data [28]. LSTM network is built to predict heart disease and to improve the performance of the LSTM network hyperparameter tuning is performed. The genetic algorithm is applied to find the optimal values for the hyperparameters of the LSTM model. The experimental results show that the proposed DL base heart disease prediction framework performs better than the other existing state-of-the-art methods and achieved an accuracy of 97%. While comparing the results with the benchmark methods on the heart disease dataset the proposed LSTM model with genetic algorithm-based hyperparameter optimization achieved significant accuracy. In future work, we apply the data validation methods to improve the quality of the EHR data and improve the prediction framework with cloud computing to achieve scalability in processing the high volume of health data.

REFERENCES

[1] Ramadoss, A., et al. "Responding to the threat of chronic diseases in India". Lancet. 366 (2005): 1744–1749. https://doi.org/10.1016/S0140-6736(05)67343-6.

[2] Ramalingam, V. V., Ayantan Dandapath, and M. Karthik Raja. "Heart disease prediction using machine learning techniques: a survey." International Journal of Engineering & Technology 7.2.8 (2018): 684–687.

[3] Lakshmanarao, A., Y. Swathi, and P. Sri Sai Sundareswar. "Machine learning techniques for heart disease prediction." Forest 95.99 (2019): 97.

[4] Diwakar, M., A. Tripathi, K. Joshi, M. Memoria, and P. Singh. "Latest trends on heart disease prediction using machine learning and image fusion." Materials Today: Proceedings 37 (2021): 3213–3218.

[5] Adhikari, N. C. D., A. Alka, and R. Garg. "Hpps: Heart problem prediction system using machine learning." International Conference on Heart Problem Prediction System using Machine Learning (HPPS) (pp. 23– 37). 2017. https://doi.org/10.5121/csit.2017.71803.

[6] Polaraju, K., and D. D. Prasad. "Prediction of heart disease using multiple linear regression model." International Journal of Engineering Development and Research Development 5.4 (2017): 1419–1425.

[7] Sultana, M., and A. Haider. "Heart disease prediction using WEKA tool and 10-Fold cross-validation." The Institute of Electrical and Electronics Engineers 9.4 (2017): 6766–6773.

[8] Deepika, K., and S. Seema. "Predictive analytics to prevent and control chronic diseases." 2016 2nd International Conference on Applied and Theoretical Computing and Communication Technology (iCATccT) (pp. 381–386). IEEE, 2016.

[9] Mr. Sai Chandrasekhar Reddy, P., Mr. Puneet Palagi, and S. Jaya. "Heart disease prediction using ANN algorithm in data mining." International Journal of Computer Science and Mobile Computing (March 2017): 168–172. "Heart disease prediction using machine learning and data mining technique".

[10] Mahajan, R., and G. Kaur. "Neural networks using genetic algorithms". International Journal of Computer Applications 77.14 (2013): 6–11.

[11] Gorgolis, Nikolaos, et al. "Hyperparameter optimization of LSTM network models through genetic algorithm." 2019 10th International Conference on Information, Intelligence, Systems and Applications (IISA). IEEE, 2019.

[12] Lai, Wai Yan, and K. K. Kuok. "A study on Bayesian principal component analysis for addressing missing rainfall data." Water Resources Management 33.8 (2019): 2615–2628.

[13] Xie, Ling, et al. "GMDH-based outlier detection model in classification problems." Journal of Systems Science and Complexity (2020): 1–17.

[14] Sabilla, Shoffi Izza, Riyanarto Sarno, and Kuwat Triyana. "Optimizing threshold using pearson correlation for selecting features of electronic nose signals." International Journal of Intelligent Engineering and Systems 12.6 (2019): 81–90.

[15] Kim, Tae-Young, and Sung-Bae Cho. "Predicting residential energy consumption using CNN-LSTM neural networks." Energy 182 (2019): 72–81.

[16] Vijayaprabakaran, K., and K. Sathiyamurthy. "Towards activation function search for long short-term model network: A differential evolution based approach." Journal of King Saud University-Computer and Information Sciences 34.6 (2022): 2637–2650.

[17] https://keras.io/

[18] www.tensorflow.org/

[19] https://archive.ics.uci.edu/ml/datasets/heart+disease

[20] Deshmukh, Jyoti, et al. "Heart disorder prognosis employing KNN, ANN, ID3 and SVM." International Conference on Advanced Machine Learning Technologies and Applications. Springer, Singapore, 2020.

[21] Maji, Srabanti, and Srishti Arora. "Decision tree algorithms for prediction of heart disease." In *Information and Communication Technology for Competitive Strategies* (pp. 447–454). Springer, 2019.

[22] Djerioui, Mohamed, et al. "Heart disease prediction using MLP and LSTM models." 2020 International Conference on Electrical Engineering (ICEE). IEEE, 2020.

[23] Akgül, Miray, Özlen Erkal Sönmez, and Tuncay Özcan. "Diagnosis of heart disease using an intelligent method: a hybrid ANN – GA approach." International Conference on Intelligent and Fuzzy Systems. Springer, Cham, 2019.

[24] Dutta, Aniruddha, et al. "An efficient convolutional neural network for coronary heart disease prediction." Expert Systems with Applications (2020): 113408.

[25] Mohan, Senthilkumar, Chandrasegar Thirumalai, and Gautam Srivastava. "Effective heart disease prediction using hybrid machine learning techniques." IEEE Access 7 (2019): 81542–81554.

[26] Sun, Le, et al. "A stacked LSTM for atrial fibrillation prediction based on multivariate ECGs." Health Information Science and Systems 8 (2020): 1–7.

[27] Keerthika, T., and K. Premalatha. "An effective feature selection for heart disease prediction with aid of hybrid kernel SVM." International Journal of Business Intelligence and Data Mining 15.3 (2019): 306–326.

[28] Indrakumari, R., P. Shukla, and A. Sehgal. "Heart disease prediction using Tableau." In *Exploratory Data Analytics for Healthcare* (pp. 125–141). CRC Press, 2021 December.

Index

For Product Safety Concerns and Information please contact our EU
representative GPSR@taylorandfrancis.com
Taylor & Francis Verlag GmbH, Kaufingerstraße 24, 80331 München, Germany

www.ingramcontent.com/pod-product-compliance
Ingram Content Group UK Ltd.
Pitfield, Milton Keynes, MK11 3LW, UK
UKHW021121180425
457613UK00005B/179